PRAYER COURSE FOR HEALING LIFE'S HURTS

PRAYER COURSE FOR HEALING LIFE'S HURTS

MATTHEW LINN
DENNIS LINN &
SHEILA FABRICANT

 Paulist Press • New York/Ramsey

ISBN: 0-8091-2522-6

Published by *Paulist Press,* 545 Island Road, Ramsey, N.J. 07446

Printed and bound in the United States of America

Contents

Dedicated to

_____

Leonard and Agnes May Linn
in gratitude for the life
they have given to the three of us

Introduction
PRAYER IS BECOMING A FRIEND

Twenty years ago when I asked my novice master what I should do in order to pray better, he paused and then said, "Prayer is not doing something but being with Someone." Although this book suggests over one hundred ways to pray, prayer happens not when we find the right words or method but the right friend. The methods are simply ways to become receptive to our friend Jesus through focusing our posture, attention and desires so that the Spirit can take over and lead us into a deeper friendship with him.

The gift of friendship and of prayer may happen overnight, but usually it comes in stages. When I meet a stranger, I often talk at first about the world outside me — sports, the weather, how well he looks, the news, and what *he* thinks or is doing. As I begin to like the stranger and to feel his care for me, I begin to trust him with my world — what I think and feel. And, in the deepest friendships, I can share what is hardest to share of my world — my fears, fragile dreams, mistakes, frustrations, times I was hurt, and even my guilt that says, "I'm sorry; forgive me." But ultimately even words are not enough, and so with a close friend I can watch the sun set without saying a word because just being together speaks beyond words.

The deepest prayer and friendships move even beyond just being together with someone to becoming that person. After fifty years of a close marriage, my grandfather died leaving my grandmother alone with only memories and tears. But my grandfather lived on in her because their years together had made them think, feel and even speak as one. She knew his mind and heart intimately and knew exactly to whom he would give his watch or what he wanted to say to each of his grandchildren and friends. When she spoke it was as if my grandfather were speaking and he

was still with us when she said, with his business-like voice, "Wipe your feet." Although my grandmother could only become like my grandfather, in prayer we can not only become like Jesus but even be Jesus.

Although I agree with my novice master that prayer is being with Someone, deep prayer goes beyond being with Jesus to even being Jesus. As I pray over the Gospels, rest with Jesus, or receive him in the Eucharist, I gradually become him with his mind, heart, and reactions. So, whether I am saying the Lord's Prayer or bouncing a child on my knee, I find myself saying the phrases or stroking the child not as I did before but as Jesus within me now wants to do. Prayer becomes not only talking to Jesus outside myself, but letting Jesus within me more and more talk to the Father. Prayer immerses me in the mind and heart of Jesus until I discover that he is my deepest identity. As St. Paul said, "It is no longer I who live but Christ lives within me" (Galatians 2:20). Prayer is letting the same spirit of Jesus that is within me cry out, "Abba" (Romans 8:15), and knowing that the Father is looking at me and crying out, "Jesus." Prayer is not doing something but being with Someone until I become him — until I become Jesus.

COURSE PURPOSE AND FORMAT

Today the average family moves every four years and in one out of three cases moves permanently apart in a shattering divorce. In this age of rootlessness there is a longing to return to roots and rooted relationships, where friends really know and love each other so much that the wounds of fractured relationships are healed. This course of spiritual exercises helps friends to share their growth and need for healing, and then in

1

prayer to walk together down the road to Emmaus with another friend who can ignite and heal hearts.

Thus, there are two main purposes to making these spiritual exercises. The first purpose is to deepen one's prayer life in order to meet Jesus, whose unconditional love can heal all hurts. Jesus' freedom brings not an insulating peace but a new freedom to seek God's will at any cost. The second purpose, for those making these exercises with another, is to build a friendship deep enough to mutually share joys and hurts while praying with each other for healing. When friends walk with Jesus the road leads to Emmaus and the building of community.

We have taught this course in parishes, schools, retreat houses and hospitals, to laity, religious, married couples and those who are in the healing professions. The course is for anyone who wants to grow in giving and receiving love with Jesus and others.

The format of the twenty-four weekly sessions is as follows: welcome and prayer, a half-hour presentation in either audio or videotape form, companion sharing and companion prayer, as well as other optional experiences. The session, lasting from one to two hours depending on how many options are included, can conclude with an open-ended snack time to deepen friendships through informal sharing. Although there are twenty-four lessons offered here, a group may choose to take only a part of the course using whatever lessons they wish. Between group meetings, each participant is encouraged to pray daily for ten minutes and then to sum up the prayer and the day's experiences with five minutes of journaling. Each group is encouraged to tailor the course to meet their needs. The emphasis is not on a rigid format but on walking with Jesus wherever he goes.

Each of the book's twenty-four lessons begins with an introduction briefly summarizing the content of the taped lesson. Thus it is possible to take this course using only the book's written introductory summary to each lesson. But ideally, the lesson should be used with the more complete taped introductory teaching.

EXPECTATIONS FOR MAKING THE EXERCISES

This book contains twenty-four spiritual exercises for healing the whole person. There are as many options for making these exercises as there are ways of healing. What follows is one suggested format which you may wish to use. Each exercise invites you to receive a particular grace of healing. Following is a description of home and group experiences which may be used to increase your receptivity to the particular grace of healing that each exercise is designed to offer.

I. Group Experience *(By "group" is meant two or more people.)*

A. Common Prayer (5 minutes). At the beginning of each exercise, your group may wish to begin with prayer or song to thank the Father for all that he has done and to ask him to help you to be receptive to how the Spirit wishes to heal you.

B. Audio or Videotape (approximately 30 minutes). A tape is presented which describes some aspect of healing and usually ends with a prayer to receive that gift of healing.

C. Silent Reflection (3 minutes). Each person remains quiet in order to get in touch with what part of this day's tape was most moving.

D. Guided Journaling (Optional — 10 minutes). Many people are unsure whether they are journaling correctly or not. It is often helpful to have a group experience of journaling in which many different kinds of responses can be shared and affirmed.

E. Companion Sharing (5 minutes minimum for each person to share). Companions share with one another their responses to the following questions:

1. Share with your companion as much as you wish of what is in your heart after seeing this week's tape. Perhaps you will want to share what you have just written during the guided journaling.
2. Share with your companion how you have experienced the Lord's presence in your life during the previous week. You may wish to share the journal response from last week that touched you the most.
3. What are you most grateful for now and how do you need Jesus' help?

F. Companion Prayer (5 to 10 minutes of prayer for each person). Companions pray for one another according to the suggestions for each lesson. The prayer usually has two parts:

1. Giving thanks and asking for any way in which you need Jesus' help.
2. Praying with one another to receive the healing grace of the present lesson.

G. Group Sharing (Optional — 15 minutes minimum). As people pray and journal at home, they experience both blocks and breakthroughs. The purpose of this group sharing time is to help people know they are not alone in their struggles and to gain encouragement by hearing of the growth and breakthroughs from others.

1. Take two minutes of silence for all to ask themselves what has been most helpful and what has been most difficult in prayer and journaling during the past week. Those who wish to may share their reflections with the whole group.
2. After those who wish to have shared themselves and responded to one another, close with a prayer thanking the Lord for the breakthroughs and for discovering the blocks where the Lord is already bringing forth further growth.

H. Closing Snack and Celebration (Optional). An open-ended time to enjoy one another and to continue sharing.

II. Home Experiences

(Although we suggest that you do these each day, it may be more life-giving for you to be with the Lord in another way from time to time.)

A. Daily Healing Prayer (10 minutes). Each exercise suggests several options for daily prayer. Each prayer focuses on the healing asked for in that exercise. Some of the healing prayers are called "Contemplation in Action Prayers." These prayers focus on activities (visiting the sick, writing a letter, etc.) which invite you to put into action the grace asked for in that particular exercise. Choose a prayer that seems helpful. Feel free to repeat that same prayer the following day and for as many days as you wish, or to choose a different one.

B. Daily Journal (5 minutes). The journal writing is done immediately after the healing prayer. Before writing, take a moment to share with Jesus where you found gratitude for growth or longing for healing during the prayer or during the day. You may wish to focus especially on receiving the healing grace of that exercise. Then write how Jesus responds (what he says or does) to what you have just told him. If you can't get in touch with how Jesus responds, write what most moves you as you speak to him or what are the most

loving words you want him to say to you. (See Appendix A, "Journaling: Writing a Love Letter," for instructions.)

OPTIONAL HOME EXPERIENCES

C. Personal Reflection Questions. These questions focus on how your life experience relates to the healing grace of a given exercise.

D. Scripture Readings.

E. Additional Readings. Readings from *Healing Life's Hurts* and other books help to put the healing desired into a broader context.

As previously mentioned, there are as many options for making these exercises as there are ways of healing. Thus, you may wish to make them alone, listening only to the tape and having the home experiences. But ideally these exercises should be made with one or more companions. For adaptations for married couples wishing to make this course together, see Appendix F, "Prayer Course Adaptations for Couples." The best companion would be the person you are most comfortable sharing with. It is not necessary that you have prayed with this person before, as these exercises will help you learn to pray together. Besides sharing the group experiences, companions (especially married couples) may also decide to do some of the home experiences together.

Perhaps you and your companion(s) may wish to make these exercises with a larger group. Ideally, larger groups should be broken into smaller groups for companion sharing and companion prayer. A group of two promotes intimacy and allows more time for each person to share, while a group of three may sacrifice some depth of sharing but increase its variety. If you don't know your companion well, you may feel more comfortable in a group of three. We suggest that the final choice of a companion for companion sharing and prayer be made at the third session. Unless difficulties arise, we suggest that you remain with this companion throughout the whole course.

Not only can there be variations regarding with whom the exercises are made, but also regarding the timing. The times suggested are minimal. Thus, a person or group may wish to spend more time with each part of a lesson (e.g., Companion Sharing, Companion Prayer), as well as more time for the entire lesson (perhaps meeting every two or three weeks instead of weekly). Perhaps you may wish to skip a meeting —often a vacation is helpful after the eighth and sixteenth sessions in order to rest and integrate the experience of the course. There may also be variations regarding what is shared. For example, a group may wish to add more time for discussion or for sharing the Personal Reflection Questions. In considering all the options, what is most important is that you meet the Lord and allow him to be with you in the most loving way.

Prayer is always healing if we are simply grateful for whatever was given and even for the struggle which teaches us that without Jesus we can do nothing. Prayer is a gift, and sometimes all our effort can do is to quiet us so we can open our heart as Teresa of Avila says, "Not to think much but to love much." These one hundred and one prayers merely offer possible ways to meet Jesus, but each of us must follow our heart rather than the instructions. The instructions are like directions in a cookbook, mere guidelines that every good cook may choose to ignore because she likes a little less salt or more sugar. Feel free to ignore any instructions which get in the way of "loving much."

(For other considerations and options, such as what a group leader does, suggestions for journaling, Scripture prayer helps, gratitude session, final sessions, possible retreat schedule and additional variations in format, see the Appendix.)

COMMITMENT TO JESUS
AND TO COMPANION(S)

Because I want to give my life entirely to the Lord Jesus Christ, I commit myself to full involvement in this prayer course. This means that I will cooperate with Jesus in trying to be as faithful as possible to the following:

1. I will strive to attend each meeting.

2. During the meetings, I will share as honestly as I can with my companion(s).

3. I will prepare for each meeting by praying for a minimum of 10 minutes each day and keeping a daily journal of my prayer experience.

4. I will pray every day for my companion(s).

5. Out of reverence for my companion(s), I will keep anything that is shared in confidence.

6. I agree to be a companion (not a teacher or savior), being vulnerable in sharing my own experience to the extent that I can and reverently taking to heart the sharing of another in a deep love that affirms all the good that is hidden within that person. I cannot take away problems or pain, but I will empathetically listen and pray with my group so that we can grow in commitment to the healer. I agree to be a companion with Jesus Christ so that I might grow in the process of giving and receiving his love with those he loves.

7. If I find myself struggling with the course in a way that I am unable to work through myself, I will share my struggle with the group leader or someone else who can help me.

Lesson One
SIMPLE WAYS TO PRAY

INTRODUCTION

About two thousand years ago three men, whom Jesus had healed of blindness, met at the pool of Siloam to write a book on how to cure the blind. The first said, "I called this meeting at Siloam because here when Jesus prayed for me, he showed how we should always pray for the blind. We are to make mud out of spittle, smear the blind eyes with it, and then wash it off." But the second interrupted him, "No, that's not the way you do it. You were blind and didn't know what Jesus was doing. He does use spittle but not mud. He also lays hands on you and asks 'Can you see anything?' You just see men like trees, so he prays again and the second time the healing is complete." But Bartimaeus rose and objected, "No, Jesus doesn't need spittle or laying on of hands. I just said, 'Rabboni, I want to see' and Jesus said, 'Be on your way for your faith has healed you.' All you need is faith." But the first man argued, "No, at Siloam I didn't even ask for healing nor did I have faith, for I didn't even know who cured me." So they argued on and never wrote their book because they were focusing on finding the right method for healing rather than on finding the Healer. There are as many ways of healing as there are ways of receiving and giving the Healer's love (John 9; Mark 8:22-26; 10:46-52).

As we pray for healing, many people ask the questions the three blind men were asking at Siloam. How do I begin to be healed? How continue the healing that is started? How should I pray with others? Rather than tell them how to pray lovingly, we show a film, "Simple Ways To Pray," that shows healing love given in eight different ways to eight different people we had never met previously. We prayed with these people for only five to ten minutes because we wanted to show how much the Lord can do when we have only five minutes to pray, rather than the ideal hour or more. We chose the simplest of prayers (summarized in this lesson's prayer exercises) that anyone can do — repeating a word, watching an image, or praying with a gesture. Despite the brief time limit, each person experienced Jesus' love and so experienced the beginning of a deep healing described in Lesson Two. The film "Simple Ways To Pray" is therefore offered in this lesson as an overview of the course by showing how varied, simple, and deep prayer for healing can be, if done lovingly. Hopefully, "How should I pray for healing?" will become "I can pray for healing in as many ways as I can give and receive Jesus' love, and I know now one way to start."

Many times in the film, we did not pray with the person but chose just ordinary people, like housewives, to pray for healing with another. (The last time I mistakenly told housewives they were "ordinary," I was lectured on how no housewife is ordinary. So perhaps I should say we chose extraordinary housewives who had seldom or never prayed for healing.) Although everyone who can love can also pray for healing, we have found that there are three people who can best pray for healing. For example, if a person has a back problem as did Judy whom we filmed, we will ask three people to pray with her: her best friend, someone who, in prayer, has been healed of a back problem, and someone now suffering like her from a back problem.

These three people often pray a deeper prayer because they have a deeper love which makes more present God who is love (1 John 4:16). They don't have to convince God to love but simply offer him a channel to pour out his love. A friend is one of the deepest channels God can find. Besides a friend, God can readily use the compassionate love that persons have because they are suffering in the same manner as when a person in back pain compassionately prays for another in back pain. Finally, the third group, persons who have suffered and been healed through prayer, pray not only with compassionate love but with expectation that what has happened to them in prayer will happen to another. The more we love, the more healing occurs in us and in others with whom we pray.

The way healing occurred with Judy's back can also teach us how healing might occur in this course. As a waitress, Judy had injured her back when lifting hard to reach a tray full of dishes. Although she began the prayer in pain and was unable to straighten up, with just ten minutes of prayer her back was totally healed. Likewise, when the man with back pain prayed for Judy, he was ninety percent healed from a painful disk that for years had imprisoned him in constant pain. Judy felt so well that after several days of pain-free waiting on tables, she risked raising a hand to reach a tray and again her back vibrated in agony. The doctor told her to rest in bed and take muscle relaxants for two weeks.

Shortly after Judy began to rest, Joan called, saying, "I hear your back was healed. Mine has been killing me for about twenty years. Do you mind if I come for prayer?" Judy knew that if a man in pain could be used by God to heal her back a week before, perhaps her painful prayer could help another. As Judy prayed, Joan's back was healed and to her surprise Judy's own back was healed in the act of reaching out and praying. Both have remained healed.

I asked Judy why she thought her back required two healings. She said that she always believed she could be healed with prayer but never believed that her prayer could help another. When her own back was hurting so much she knew how Joan was suffering and thus compassion overcame her fear of praying.

> I think the Lord wanted to show me that now he will heal me not just as I keep asking for prayer but also as I step out and pray. He has healed not just my back but even more importantly my heart of deep resentments. Because so much was happening through prayer, I quit my job as a waitress to work at less pay in a nursing home where I could pray with the most discouraged. I liked

the work so much that now I am going to school to be a nurse.

In this course, too, the process of healing will happen not just as we receive the healer's love but also as we give it. The method is unimportant; the healer is.

Note: 1. Each lesson introduction, such as the one you just read, will summarize briefly the content of the taped lessons. Although it is possible to do the lessons using only the content summaries, ideally the lessons should be used with the fully taped teaching. (See Appendix for information on ordering audio or video tapes.) 2. Since Lesson One, and only Lesson One, depends heavily upon visual impact, we suggest that you rent the film or videotape "Simple Ways To Pray" if you are using audio tapes. (See page 169 for information on ordering films and videotapes.)

I. Group Experience

A. **Common Opening Prayer** (5 minutes)

B. **Introductions.** Take time for all present to introduce themselves and to share why they came to the course. If the group is small, they might also share what gives them life (e.g., their family, a new baby, a hobby, etc.) The group leader might begin and then go around in a circle.

C. **Explanation of the Course.** The group leader might want to summarize the reasons that people have shared for coming to the course and how these fit into the purpose of the course, which is to teach people how to pray in a simple, healing way alone or with others. Then the leader might discuss the expectations for the course, as described previously and outlined below.

1. Attendance at regularly scheduled group meetings. Format:
   a. 30 minute video (or audio) presentation.
   b. 30 minutes for Companion Sharing and Companion Prayer.
   c. Optional experiences include Guided Journaling, Group Sharing and Closing Snack and Celebration.

2. Home Experiences
   a. 10 minutes of daily prayer, using any one of the suggested Daily Healing

Prayers, e.g., those outlined later in this lesson.

b. 5 minutes of daily journal writing. (Be ready next week to share from your journal what moved you the most when doing the daily prayers for this week. See Appendix A, "Journaling," for complete instructions on how to journal.)

c. Optional Home Experience include Personal Reflection Questions, Scripture Readings and Additional Readings.

You need not make the final choice of a companion until the third week. After discussing the expectations for the course, the group leader should allow some time for questions. (Some questions will be answered by the presentation "Simple Ways To Pray" which follows.)

D. Video or Audio Tape: "Simple Ways To Pray" (30 minutes) (Summary of video tape and film; audio tape includes #1 and #2 only.)

The power to heal is the power to love. There are as many ways of praying as there are ways of loving.

1. Praying through our breathing, emptying our darkness as we exhale and inhaling Jesus' love until we are able to breathe out his love to the Father (e.g., woman filled with fear).

2. Silent prayer by three people: one who is suffering in the same way, one who has been healed of that illness, and the one who loves the person the most (e.g., woman with back pain).

3. Becoming another and letting ourselves be loved by the Father as that person (e.g., Leo and his father, Frank).

4. Recalling a painful memory and inviting Jesus into it: the prayer of creative imagination (e.g., Tommy and her son, Scott).

5. Filling another with the Lord's love and letting tears be a prayer (e.g., woman praying for her father).

6. Writing how we feel and listening for Jesus' response (e.g., man who wrote out his hurt and anger).

7. Praying for someone we love by re-leasing that person into the Father's hands (e.g., woman praying for her husband, Denny).

8. Praying for others by looking at their photos, seeing them through Jesus' eyes and praying Jesus' prayer for them (e.g., woman praying for her son, Bill).

E. Silent Reflection (3 minutes). Quiet time to get in touch with what part of today's tape moved your heart most deeply.

F. Guided Journaling (10 minutes)

1. Write down what is in your heart. Write as if you were writing a love letter to your best friend—Jesus—sharing what you feel most deeply. Don't worry about having the "right" words, but only try to share your heart.

2. Now get in touch with Jesus' response to you, as he is already speaking to you within. You might do this by asking what are the most loving words that you want him to say to you in response, or perhaps by imagining that what you have just written is a note to you from the person you love most, and you want to respond to that person in the most loving possible words.

3. Write Jesus' response. Perhaps it will be just one word or one sentence. You can be sure that anything you write which helps you to know more clearly that you are loved is not just your own thoughts or imagination but is really what Jesus wants to say to you.

4. One or two people in the group might want to share what they have written with the whole group.

G. Closing Sharing and Discussion

1. Anyone who wishes to may share reflections on today's tape.

2. Discuss any remaining questions about the format of the course. (The next session, "Simple Ways To Pray [Follow-Up]" is optional. The group leader should have previewed it and be ready to answer any questions about the people shown in today's tape, or, if it will be included in the course, announce that it will be the next unit.)

H. Closing Snack and Celebration. An open-ended time to enjoy one another and continue sharing.

II. Home Experiences

A. Daily Healing Prayer (10 minutes). You may wish to develop a habit of daily prayer gradually by praying two or three times during this first week. Each day choose one of the following healing or contemplation in action prayers and pray it for at least 10 minutes. These prayers are only *suggestions*. Perhaps you will find yourself drawn to pray what is in your heart using varied breathing, a symbol, a repeated word, a melody, a gesture, a drawing, or a piece of clay which you can mold. Although there are many prayers suggested, it would be best to pray only a few of them, parts of them, or to repeat for as long as you wish the prayer that most moved your heart. Use whatever way you can best give your heart to Jesus and enter into his heart. Perhaps your prayer will be as simple as looking at a beautiful flower and taking in God's love for you. You may wish to begin your prayer by centering yourself, using the breath prayer which follows.

1. *Breath Prayer*
   a. Sit erect, feet flat on the floor, hands on your lap, palms up without touching each other. Become aware of the openness of your hands and the air at your fingertips, between your fingers, on your palms.
   b. Take a deep breath, as if you were breathing through your toes, and let that breath be carried up through your legs, abdominal muscles, lungs-your entire body. As you breathe in, say silently, "Lord Jesus Christ," while taking in whatever you need from him: his peace, joy, risen sexuality, wisdom etc. You may want to visualize him standing before you or see him looking into your eyes. See his body of light and experience that light coming into your own body as you inhale his presence.
   c. Check your body for any tension. Release the tension by tensing up a given muscle and then relaxing it or

by rotating your jaw or other joint. As you exhale, smile and breathe out whatever may have been behind that tension. With each exhalation, surrender more deeply until you hunger for Jesus as much as you hunger for air. (See *Healing Life's Hurts*, page 97.)

2. *Becoming Another*
   a. Prayerfully read Hebrews 2:14: Surely he did not come to help angels, but rather the children of Abraham: therefore he had to become like us in every way, that he might be a merciful and faithful intercessor before God on their behalf."
   b. Ask Jesus what one person he would like you to intercede for. Then ask him for the grace to intercede by becoming like that person in every way but sin.
   c. Let your body be molded into the body of the person for whom you hear Jesus asking you to pray. Ask Jesus to help you to experience what he wishes you to experience. Perhaps he will help you to feel the person's problems until your heart beats as anxiously or as lethargically as that person's heart. Let these problems mold your forehead, face, jaws, shoulders, back, hands and feet. Let your entire body resemble that person's body. Note how your body expresses that person's fears, anger, guilt, loneliness, discouragement, etc.
   d. When you are in touch with how that person needs healing, pray the prayer which Jesus within that person prays to the Father for healing. (Perhaps this prayer is only one or two sentences.)
   e. As that person, let the Father lay his hand on and begin to heal you until you have no more burdens to breathe out to him, but instead find yourself breathing out his healing love.
   f. Close by praying the Lord's Prayer in the way that Jesus within you now prays.

3. *Prayer of Creative Imagination*
   a. Do the Breath Prayer.
   b. Ask Jesus to bring you back to a time in your life when you were hurt.

c. Ask Jesus to help you to enter the scene until you can smell what was in the air, feel what was beneath your feet, see the faces of each person who was present and hear what each was saying. Continue this until you experience with Jesus some of the pain and destruction from this hurt.

d. When you have felt some of the hurt, look into the compassionate eyes of Jesus and breathe out to him the pain and destruction you wish to hand over to him. Watch what he says and does to heal you and the others in the scene. Pray Jesus' prayer for those people and for yourself.

e. Ask Jesus to help you live out his response. (See *Healing Life's Hurts,* page 205.)

4. *Writing Prayer*
   a. Write a note to Jesus asking him for what you would like to have changed in your life.
   b. Do the Breath Prayer.
   c. Ask Jesus when he or another person in the Gospels felt this way. Write down how he responds to you.
   d. Ask Jesus to help you to live out his response.

5. *Release Prayer*
   a. Do the Breath Prayer
   b. Cup your hands and place in them a person you are concerned about.
   c. Tell the Father or Jesus about all that you long to have happen for that person. With each request, squeeze your hands more tightly as if you were squeezing into that person all that you long to give.
   d. When you have said it all, open your hands and release the person into the hands of the Father or Jesus.
   e. Watch what the Father says or does for the person. Be ready for surprises.

6. *Picture Prayer*
   a. Do the Breath Prayer
   b. Hold against your heart a photo of a person for whom you want to pray.
   c. Ask Jesus to help you to love this person as he does and to have his prayer for the person in your heart.
   d. When you love this person with Jesus'

heart, hold the photo up to the Father and pray Jesus' prayer to the Father.

CONTEMPLATION IN ACTION PRAYERS

Take a minute and ask for the grace to pray simply. Then go and do one of the following:

7. *Relaxing Visit*
   a. Pray by enjoying the presence of Jesus as you enjoy a close friend. Visit a close friend or recall a previous visit with someone you felt especially close to.
   b. Then ask Jesus to be even closer to you than your friend, and just spend a few minutes relaxing and enjoying Jesus' presence.

8. *Breathing In and Out All*
   a. During the day, pray simple by the way you breathe. Perhaps you might want to take deep breaths which say that you want all of God's life that surrounds you.
   b. Perhaps you might want to exhale deeply, emptying and surrendering everything to the Lord of all who loves you the most.

B. **Daily Journal** (5 minutes). You may wish to develop a habit of daily journaling gradually, by writing in your journal two or three times during this first week. See Appendix A for suggestions on how to keep a journal.

The grace you are asking for this week is to pray simply. By asking "What moved you most during prayer?" we hope to help you to cut through the extras and get to the heart of prayer.

1. Share with Jesus what moved you the most during this prayer (the moment of greatest surrender, peace or struggle).
2. Write in your journal how Jesus responds (what he seems to do or say in response to what you have told him). If you can't get in touch with Jesus' response, write what moves you as you speak to him or what are the most loving words you want him to say to you.

OPTIONAL HOME EXPERIENCES

C. Personal Reflection Questions

1. Which way of praying in the tape "Simple Ways To Pray" seemed a way that you would want to use? Would not want to use? Why?
2. When has your prayer been most healing and how did you pray?
3. Has the way you pray changed as you change?
4. What you have suffered through gives you compassion. In what way have you suffered that makes you want to reach out compassionately and pray with another?
5. Whom in the film do you feel drawn to be with in the midst of their pain? Whose suffering scares you or makes you wish someone else could be with them?
6. When have you experienced tears to be healing?

D. Scripture Readings

James 5:14-16: Pray with the sick to help them find forgiveness and healing.
Mark 11:20-26: Prayer requires belief and forgiveness.
Matthew 6:5-15: The Lord's Prayer.
Luke 18:9-14: The prayer of the Pharisee and the tax collector.
John 17:9-26: Jesus' prayer for his followers.
Romans 8:26-27: The Spirit will teach us how to pray.
Luke 1:46-55: The Magnificat, a model prayer.
Psalm 51: 103-104: Model prayers of petition, praise, thanksgiving, pardon.

E. Additional Readings

Healing Life's Hurts, by Dennis Linn, S.J. and Matthew Linn, S.J. (New York: Paulist Press, 1978).

Chapter 6, "With a Loving God I Can Share All My Feelings." If we are afraid to share our real feelings with Jesus, our relationship with him will remain superficial, just as with any person before whom we wear a mask. Our conversations with Jesus can be as transforming for us as they were for the Emmaus disciples every time we offer him our deepest feelings and then absorb his loving and healing view of us.

Chapter 16, "Getting Started: Praying Alone and with Others." We can learn to pray for healing by beginning with whatever way it is easiest for us to experience God's love. We can receive healing alone as we share our hurts with Jesus in prayer, but often it is helpful to pray with a friend who can mediate Jesus' love and acceptance for us and draw us out to love in return.

Sadhana: A Way to God, by Anthony de Mello, S.J. Available from Institute of Jesuit Sources, 3700 W. Pine Blvd., St. Louis, Mo. 63108. Price: $3.00. This book describes forty-seven different ways of praying.

The Breath of Life: A Simple Way to Pray, by Ron DelBene (Minneapolis: Winston Press, 1981). Teaches how to discover and pray our own special "prayer without ceasing."

How To Pray for Spiritual Growth: A Practical Handbook of Inner Healing, by Theodore Dobson (New York: Paulist Press, 1982.

Lesson Two
SIMPLE WAYS TO PRAY (FOLLOW-UP)

INTRODUCTION

What do you do when your prayer isn't answered? Although everyone speaks about the immediate answers to prayer, it is a well-kept secret that most prayer for healing is not immediately and totally answered but becomes only the first step of a lengthy healing process. For example, over a three-year period we interviewed the eight people with whom we prayed in the film, "Simple Ways To Pray." We found that only two had an immediate and total healing while the other six experienced their healing over a period of time ranging from a few hours to two years. We will try to illuminate that process by focusing on two of those who struggled the most: Chuck and Gail.

Chuck tried the writing prayer.[1] The first step was to write a note to Jesus that described four struggles Chuck wanted changed in his family and job. Then he paused, looked at a picture of Jesus, listened, and wrote what he thought Jesus was saying: "Chuck, I know the hurts you feel. Men have hurt me too. Trust in me and have faith and I will help you."

These words so moved Chuck that he began to cry. He was the only person whose tears were so copious that we decided to assign his friend simply to love him and let him cry for the next half hour.

Chuck was moved to tears because although he always believed God could talk to others, this time God had spoken to him. He didn't hear a voice or see a vision, but his heart was overwhelmed by God's personal love for him. Did Chuck hear God or only his imagination projecting what Chuck wanted to hear? The test for hearing God is simple. Does what we hear open us more to giving and receiving love with God, others, and ourselves? To

answer that we have to know what happened to Chuck.

To Chuck's surprise, although not much changed in the four situations he gave to Jesus in prayer, much changed in him. When I interviewed Chuck four months later, he was delighted because the work and family situations no longer filled him with so much stress. This occurred because in sharing the pain with Jesus, Chuck no longer felt alone. He felt closer to those at work and to his family even if they didn't change. One couple saw such a loving change in Chuck's reactions toward his daughter that they finally asked him, in the event of an emergency, to be the legal guardian of their children. They felt that if they were to die, Chuck would be the most loving father their children could have.

Besides being able to love others more, Chuck also could love himself, and he finally took treatment for his alcohol addiction. Chuck says that the one part of his prayer that was answered is that he is no longer addicted to alcohol. Though it was a long road, part of the impetus to start treatment came when Chuck heard God speak to him. After that he noticed that each time he drank, the closeness that he felt during that prayer would leave. Finally, he decided to no longer keep fighting God and to get help. It is fairly certain that Chuck really did hear the Lord because the words Chuck heard helped him grow in giving and receiving love with God, others and himself. Prayer is measured not by how others change but by how the person praying grows in love even when others don't change. The answer to prayer is often more struggle but with the power to give and receive love in the midst of the struggle.

Like Chuck, Gail also discovered that the answer to prayer came over time amid struggles

1. For the writing prayer steps, cf. page 11, #4.

13

and doubts. Gail was the focus of the simplest prayer in the film, "Simple Ways To Pray." In total silence three people laid hands on Gail and for five minutes tried to love her as Jesus loved her. Gail had been unable to share with them how she needed prayer, but she needed deep prayer because she was recalling years ago when she was nineteen and couldn't get along with her father. The relationship became so tense that Gail planned to run away and elope. On the very day she was going to elope, her father had a heart attack and died. Gail believed she had literally stopped her father's heart and so was filled with guilt. From that time on she disliked herself and could not relate to men.

While all were praying silently, Gail shared her heart with Jesus. She asked Jesus to tell her father, "I understand why he was the way he was. I want to know that he is with me and he loves me. But most of all I want him to know I love him. I never told him that, Lord." As Gail shared her heart with Jesus, for the first time she really knew that her father loved her, forgave her, and knew how much she loved him. She then began to cry and years of guilt and self-hatred dissolved. But about an hour after the prayer, Gail began to doubt her experience. She thought that she had psyched herself into feeling love and forgiveness because she was in front of a movie camera. When she shared her doubts with a priest, he said, "Gail, you were praying from your heart and your tears came from really being healed. The Lord isn't going to let you throw away your healing. In the next three months he will send you some sign to show that you were healed."

Three months later a friend called on her and said, "Gail, I had a dream about you that I don't understand." He then described in detail a man standing in a bay window with God the Father. Both were looking at Gail and God the Father was saying, "Gail, this man knows that you love him and forgive him. He loves you and forgives you. But I love you even more. Come and follow me." These were the very words Gail heard three months earlier during the healing prayer but had begun to doubt. Although her friend knew neither Gail's father nor her childhood home, in describing his dream to Gail he described each in detail. He described exactly the clothes her father wore on the day he died, down to the checkered shirt that hung out over his baggy pants. Gail cried again, for here was the sign she was told would come within three months — a stranger telling her exactly what the Lord had told her three months ago. The new part was "I love you even more.

Come and follow me." For the first time Gail felt a close relationship to the Father who had healed all the hurts with her father.

From that moment on Gail's life changed dramatically. Although this was her first experience with inner healing, it was so real for her that she joined a prayer group so that she could continue to rest in the Father's love. She says, "Before, I couldn't get close to people. When they hugged me, I felt cold and wanted to run away. Now I want to hug them because I feel real warmth and kindness. I am more trusting and open, especially toward men, and it all began when I forgave my father and let him forgive me." Her self-confidence has grown to where she has successfully taken on a tough challenge, teaching language arts to junior high school students. She also reaches out now and helps other women who can't relate to men. She knows that what the Lord did for her, he can do for another.

Sometimes, as in the cases of Chuck and Gail, our prayers do not seem to be immediately answered. It may be because others don't change, as in Chuck's case; it may be because we doubt what the Lord has changed in us, as in Gail's case. Jesus, like Chuck, prayed for people who didn't change. Some of the people Jesus prayed for refused his love and crucified him. Jesus, like Gail, doubted whether his Father was with him in the midst of his darkest hour. Prayer is not a short-cut to instant answers but is letting Jesus take us where he has already walked. If we, like Chuck and Gail, persist in walking with Jesus, we will find what they found—a Father who loves us even when others can't or when we can't love ourselves. We have a Father who loves us so much that he speaks through Jesus to everyone, even to those like Chuck who don't believe that God would speak to them. He pursues, even through dreams, those like Gail who have heard him but can't believe. When we think the Father is doing nothing, he is doing infinitely more than we ask for or imagine (Ephesians 3:20-21). The Father says to us what he said to Chuck, "Trust in me and have faith, and I will help you."

I. Group Experience

A. **Common Opening Prayer** (5 minutes)

B. **Video or Audio Tape:** "Simple Ways To Pray (Follow-up)" (30 min.) (Summary of video tape and film; audio tape includes #5 and #6 only.)

What has happened to the eight people prayed for in "Simple Ways To Pray" during the three years since the program was made?

1. Woman with cancer did die — but peacefully.
2. Judy, whose back was healed — her pain returned, but was healed again when she began to reach out to others.
3. Leo, whose father was senile and seemed not to know Jesus, learned how much God loves his father, and his father was healed of his senility.
4. Tommy was able to release her son who had died many years earlier. Many things in Tommy's personality were healed after this experience of releasing another.
5. Gail, who felt responsible for her father's death, came to know how much her father loved her.
6. Chuck learned that God would speak to *him* through the writing prayer. He became a man who could trust God. We know a word is from the Lord if it leads us to trust God and others more.
7. Jan had prayed a release prayer for her husband Denny — a former alcoholic. Their marriage relationship deepened as a result of ways in which she was able to be less protective of Denny (e.g., allowing him to go to an A.A. meeting).
8. Laurie prayed for her son by looking at his photo. Her son eventually changed when she learned to love him just as he was.

Closing Prayer: releasing someone we love into God's care, trusting him to work in their life.

C. **Silent Reflection** (3 minutes). Quiet time to get in touch with what part of today's tape moved your heart most deeply.

D. **Guided Journaling** (10 minutes)

1. Write down what is in your heart. Write as if you were writing a love letter to your best friend — Jesus — sharing what you feel most deeply. Don't worry about having the "right" words, but only try to share your heart.
2. Now get in touch with Jesus' response to you, as he is already speaking to you within. You might do this by asking what are the most loving words that you want him to say to you in response, or perhaps by imagining that what you have just written is a note to you from the person you love most and you want to respond to that person in the most loving possible words.
3. Write Jesus' response. Perhaps it will be just one word or one sentence. You can be sure that anything you write which helps you to know more that you are loved is not just your own thoughts or imagination but is really what Jesus wants to say to you.
4. One or two people in the group might want to share what they have written with the whole group. During the companion sharing time which follows, companions may wish to share what they have written with each other.

E. **Companion Sharing** (5 minutes minimum for each person to share his or her reaction to today's tape and to the past week).

Choose one or two people whom you would be comfortable sharing with today. The final choice of a companion need not be made until next week.

1. Share with your companion as much as you wish of what is in your heart after seeing this week's tape. Perhaps you will want to share what you have just written during the guided journaling.
2. Share with your companion how you have experienced the Lord's presence in your life during the previous week. You may wish to share the journal response from last week that touched you the most.
3. What are you most grateful for now and how do you need Jesus' help?

F. **Companion Prayer** (Optional this week —5 minutes of prayer for each person). Pray for your companion for about 5 minutes, either silently or aloud in your own words. Give thanks for what your companion is most grateful for and ask for whatever your companion most needs. Close your prayer by asking that your companion receive the grace of this lesson: *to become grateful for how Jesus acts in his or her life.* After you have prayed for your companion for 5 minutes, let your companion pray for you.

G. Group Sharing (15 minutes minimum). Take two minutes of silence to ask what has been most difficult and what has been most helpful in your prayer and journaling this past week. Share your reflections with the larger group. Close with a prayer thanking the Lord for how he is working within each person.

H. Closing Snack and Celebration (Optional). An open-ended time to enjoy one another and to continue sharing.

II. Home Experiences

A. Daily Healing Prayer (10 minutes). Each day for 10 minutes, pray any of the prayers from the previous lesson, "Simple Ways To Pray."

B. Daily Journal (5 minutes).

1. Share with Jesus when during this prayer or during the day your heart was deeply moved — perhaps a moment of being grateful for or of longing for healing in *seeing how Jesus is acting in your life.*
2. Write in your journal how Jesus responds (what he seems to do or say in response to what you have told him). If you can't get in touch with Jesus' response, write what most moves you as you speak to him or what are the most loving words you want to hear.

OPTIONAL HOME EXPERIENCES

Same as in previous lesson, *"Simple Ways To Pray."*

Lesson Three
HEALING POWER OF GRATITUDE

INTRODUCTION

Sometimes we can try and try to solve a problem . . . and there is a time for that. But sometimes just letting ourselves be loved can solve so many problems. When we let go and just soak up love from the Lord and others who care for us, we have a whole new power to go on again. When we get burned out, it isn't usually because we're doing too many things but because we're not letting ourselves be loved.

One psychiatrist surprised us with the importance he gave to the healing power of love. Therapists know that the first visit is very important for getting a history and building rapport with the patient. We asked this doctor, "What do you do that is crucial on that first visit?" He said, "The first thing I do when patients come in for an hour visit and are expecting fifty minutes is to give them an hour and a half. They usually start by telling me all the things that are wrong in their lives. I let them go on for a few minutes. Then I stop them and I say, 'Now, what I want to hear for the rest of the time is what's going *well* in your life. When were you most alive? When have you received love?' For the rest of the appointment, whenever they get off that topic I keep bringing them back to it. If they are focused not just on the problem but on how the Lord is loving them in the midst of the problem, they begin to grow."

Remembering moments of receiving love brings power to grow not only to clients in therapy but to families too. We know a couple whose marital problems several years ago brought them close to divorce. The husband, who is a therapist, told us all the different counseling techniques they had tried with each other. But, he said, none of this helped. He told us, "The turning point in our marriage was one day when my wife came home from the doctor's. The doctor had told her that she probably had cancer. When my wife told me that, the first thing we did was cry together. And then my wife told me two things. She said, 'You've been such a good husband to me. When I die, I want you to promise me that you will marry someone else and give her the same happiness. And you've been so good to my family. I want you to promise that when you get married again you won't move far away from my family.' " Our friend told us that this was the breakthrough in his marriage, when he and his wife could begin to talk to each other about how they are gifts for each other and how much they mean to each other. Healing happens not just when we look at the problem but when we get in touch with the love we have received.

Sometimes the memory of receiving love that can heal us is a memory of God loving us directly rather than through another person. Although St. Teresa of Avila worked and worked for ten years on her inordinate appetite for food, she just grew more frustrated. Finally, a Jesuit came along who suggested what St. Ignatius tells us to do with those who are struggling. He advises us to lead them back to whenever they've had "consolation," which means whenever they've felt most loved, most alive, most deeply at peace. St. Teresa told the Jesuit that she felt most alive when she was praying the Passion. He replied: "Pray the Passion." She did, and it took care of her whole problem with food. She started to identify with how much Jesus really gave himself on that cross to her and to everyone. And she wanted to be that way too. The power to change came from within because she felt Jesus' love for her, and she wanted to be like this person who loved her. 1 John 4:19 tells us that we have power to love because

God has first loved us. This means that God loved us before we were born and brought us into being and baptized us, but it means far more than that. It means that we don't have any power to love unless we have first been loved, by God and by those through whom he sends his love. So often we try to get rid of this or that problem, and Jesus just wants us to look at how we're being loved and where real growth is coming from right now.

We can do this each night before we go to sleep. We can ask ourselves a question which focuses how we are being loved: "What am I grateful for during this day?" Once we're in touch with the good things that are happening to us and where we're growing, then we can look at the things that we're not so grateful for and give those to him rather than swallowing them and letting them work inside of us while we sleep. Whatever we go to sleep with gets buried in the subconscious at night. If we go to sleep angry at someone, that gets buried. If we go to sleep saying, "Thank you, Father" and feeling loved and grateful, that gets buried and the love and gratitude are working on us all through the night, touching other areas and bringing them to life.

Gratitude for how we've been loved gives us life. When I (Matt) am really struggling, I go back to a memory of how I've been loved. For example, about three years ago I hurt my back trying to get into a small car. When I went to see the doctor, he took some bone scans because I have some extra bony growths. The tests indicated that the growths might be cancerous, and he said that I needed to go into the hospital right away. That first night in the hospital I felt really bad. First I blamed everyone else. Then I blamed myself for not going to the doctor sooner. I was angry at the Lord too. I thought, "How come I can pray for so many others with cancer, and they get well? Now it's my turn and people are praying for me, but the tests haven't changed." I felt a great gulf, as if something had come between God and me that wasn't allowing his power to touch me. I looked at a cross on the wall and said, "Lord, I don't understand all this. Where are you in it?"

Then I began to see that Jesus on that cross was going through the same kind of thing and crying out, "My God, my God, why have you forsaken me?" And yet, at that moment when he felt the furthest from his Father, he was closer to God than ever before. Then I began to know that God wasn't going to abandon me. What made his faithfulness so real to me was the love of those around me. I knew that Denny, my parents, and the Jesuits would do anything for me. A real peace came over me, as well as a different way of feeling loved than I had ever known before. Usually when I had experienced God's love it was because I had done something for him. For example, if I prayed for someone who got well, then I knew how much God loved me too because I had seen him love this person and I had seen him use me. But this time there wasn't anything I could do for the Lord. All I could give him was being there in a hospital bed and having needs. I experienced God loving me just because I was Matt Linn, just as my family loved me.

That moment was one of my basic experiences of really being loved. If someone has hurt me and I need to feel loved, I go back and lie in that hospital bed again and get in touch with how the Lord loves me even when I can't do anything right. And if I'm feeling burned out, I just go back to that scene again, and I sit and let myself be loved and know that I don't have to do everything. And if I have a decision to make, I recall that hospital scene and the deep "yes" that I said to the Lord then. I remember telling him, "Lord, whatever is ahead, I'm ready to go through it with you even if it's cancer and death." That's the deepest "yes" I've ever had to say in my life, because that's the deepest time of being loved. The two usually go together, and if I have a "yes" to say in the present I just go back to that time and get in touch with my deepest self wanting to give everything to the Lord.

They did the surgery the morning after I surrendered to the Lord and felt so much peace. They took out the bones that the tests had shown might be cancerous, and there was no evidence of cancer. I still go back each year for a bone scan and the results are always normal. I believe I was healed that night when I just said "yes" to the Lord and let myself be loved for who I was rather than for what I could do. Gratitude for how I was loved gave me life.

One time some people asked St. Ignatius, "What is the greatest sin?" And St. Ignatius told them, "The greatest sin is ingratitude." The grace we are praying for in this lesson is Dag Hammarskjold's motto, "For all that has been, 'thanks.' For all that will be, 'yes.'"

I. Group Experience

A. Common Opening Prayer (5 minutes)

B. Video or Audio Tape: "Healing Power of Gratitude" (30 minutes)

The healing power that comes from letting ourselves be loved.

1. Healing happens when we get in touch with when we have given and received love and are grateful for these gifts (e.g., counselor, married couple).
2. We have power to love only when we have received love. Receiving love enables us to change and become more loving (e.g., St. Teresa).
3. Focusing on what we are grateful for and how much the Lord has loved us helps us to invite the Lord into areas where we need healing (e.g., Matt's experience in the hospital).
4. Recalling our deepest "Yes" in the past helps us to say "Yes" in the present moment.
5. How much the Lord has loved us and how much we have to be grateful for if we only knew it (e.g., mother giving birth to a child she has waited for and labored for).
6. Problems and hard work don't wear us out so much as not taking the time to give and receive love.

Closing Prayer: asking Jesus to help us receive the ways that he has loved us by becoming more grateful for our lives.

C. **Silent Reflection** (3 minutes). Quiet time to get in touch with what part of today's tape moved your heart most deeply.

D. **Guided Journaling** (Optional — 10 minutes).

1. Write down what is in your heart. Write as if you were writing a love letter to your best friend — Jesus — sharing what you feel most deeply. Don't worry about having the "right" words, but only try to share your heart.
2. Now get in touch with Jesus' response to you, as he is already speaking to you within. You might do this by asking what are the most loving words that you want him to say to you in response, or perhaps by imagining that what you have just written is a note to you from the person you love most and you want to respond to that person in the most loving possible words.
3. Write Jesus' response. Perhaps it will be just one word or one sentence. You can be

sure that anything you write which helps you to know more that you are loved is not just your own thoughts or imagination but is really what Jesus wants to say to you.
4. One or two people in the group might want to share what they have writtten with the whole group. During the companion sharing time which follows, companions may wish to share what they have written with each other.

E. **Companion Sharing** (5 minutes minimum for each person to share his or her reaction to today's tape and to the past week).

1. Share with your companion as much as you wish of what is in your heart after seeing this week's tape. Perhaps you will want to share what you have just written during the guided journaling.
2. Share with your companion how you have experienced the Lord's presence in your life during the previous week. You may wish to share the journal response from last week that touched you the most.
3. What are you most grateful for now and how do you need Jesus' help?

F. **Companion Prayer** (5 minutes of prayer for each person). Now that you have shared with your companion, for what do you most want to thank Jesus? Pray aloud in your own words, expressing your gratitude to Jesus. Finish your prayer by asking that you receive the grace of this lesson: *the ability to receive love.* Your companion may also wish to say a prayer of thanks for you, or a prayer asking that you receive the grace of this lesson.

G. **Group Sharing** (Optional — 15 minutes minimum). Take two minutes of silence to ask what has been most difficult and what has been most helpful in your prayer and journaling this past week. Share your reflections with the larger group. Close with a prayer thanking the Lord for the breakthroughs and for discovering the blocks where the Lord is already bringing forth further growth.

H. Closing Snack and Celebration (Optional). An open-ended time to enjoy one another and to continue sharing.

II. Home Experience

A. Daily Healing Prayer (10 minutes). Each day choose one of the following healing or contemplation in action prayers and pray it for at least 10 minutes. These prayers are only *suggestions*. Perhaps you will find yourself drawn to pray what is in your heart using varied breathing, a symbol, a repeated word, a melody, a gesture, a drawing, or a piece of clay which you can mold. Although there are many prayers suggested, it would be best to pray only a few of them, parts of them, or to repeat from this or any other chapter the prayer that most moved your heart. Use whatever way you can best give your heart to Jesus and enter into his heart. Perhaps your prayer will be as simple as looking at a beautiful flower and taking in God's love for you. You may wish to begin your prayer by centering yourself, perhaps using the Breath Prayer (see Lesson 1).

1. *Healing Through Receiving God's Love* (Tape Prayer).
   a. Prayerfully read Isaiah 49:14-17. "I will never forget you, my people. I have carved you in the palm of my hand. I will not leave you orphaned. I will never forget my own."
   b. Place your left hand in the palm of your right hand.
   c. Be attentive to any tenseness in your right hand or left arm. Move your hand or arm until your left hand is resting in the palm of your right hand. Readjust your right hand until it holds the left hand securely.
   d. Let your right hand be the hand of the Father who will never forget you. Feel the strength and sureness of that Father's hand and enjoy how good it feels to rest in the palm of his hand.
   e. Then take a deep breath and ask the Father to bring to mind one moment when you felt especially loved by him, especially held in the palm of his hand. Perhaps it was a moment when you received physical or emotional

healing, or a moment of solitude or forgiveness when you felt loved by him. Perhaps it was the time of your marriage, first child or other joyful event.
   f. Enjoy that moment with him and once again give thanks as you rest in his love.

2. *Embrace Prayer*
   See Jesus standing before you, or seated in a rocking chair. See him open his arms and invite you to him. Go to him, letting him hold you and perhaps rock you in the chair. Feel his arms around you and let yourself be loved as if you were a small child in its father's arms. (You may want to pray in a similar way with the Father, or with Mary as your mother.)

3. *Prayer for Receiving the Grace of This Lesson*
   Ask Jesus to give you his ability to receive love from the Father. Breathe it in with every breath and breathe out all the blocks in yourself to letting the Father love you. (You may wish to pray this prayer with Mary instead of Jesus.)

4. *Period Prayer*
   Recall a specific period of your life (in childhood, adolescence, or adulthood) or a period of life when you felt least loved.
   a. Within the circle on page 170, **write the names of ten people through whom God loved you and called you to grow during this period. Draw a small circle around each of these names.**
   b. Within the circle, write ten events through which God loved you and called you to grow during this period. Draw a small rectangle around each of these events.
   c. Spend time in prayer thanking God for each way he loved you during this time.

5. *Sun Prayer*
   Jesus is the light of the world. Soak yourself in the sun, letting it fill you with Jesus' love. Breathe in Jesus' love and breathe out your thanks.

6. *Body Gratitude Prayer*
   a. Focus your attention on each part of your body, beginning with your forehead and gradually moving down to your toes. As you focus on each part, be aware of how the surface of that part feels, perhaps even tensing it and then relaxing it.
   b. When you have become fully aware of a given part, thank God for it.
   c. In gratitude for the ways in which it serves you, make the sign of the cross on each part of your body as a way of consecrating it to serve God.

7. *Hand Prayer*
   a. Take the hand of another person, or imagine yourself holding another's hand.
   b. Now let the hand you are holding become the hand of the person who has loved you the most, the person with whom you have had the most good times.
   c. Thank Jesus for all that this person has been for you.
   d. This person's hand is the hand that has been most like Jesus' hand in your life. Because Jesus was with your friend, your friend was able to forgive you, to heal you, to perhaps even be willing to lay down his or her life for you. Let that hand gradually become the hand of Jesus.
   e. Thank Jesus for all that he has been for you through your friend.

8. *Sleep Prayer*
   a. Skim over the events of the day and give thanks for the events that you are most grateful for.
   b. Breathe out into Jesus' healing hands the event for which you are least grateful.
   c. When the event for which you are least grateful is in Jesus' hands, fall asleep saying, "Thank you, Jesus."

9. Recall a moment when you felt deeply loved. Recall the beauty that you felt within yourself and the sense of your own goodness. Re-experience that moment, thanking God for revealing to you then the wonderful person that he sees when he looks at you.

10. Prayerfully read Psalm 139:13-16. Imagine that you are with the Father just after he has created you and is about to send you forth to be born into this world. Imagine that he tells you the special kind of person that he has made you to be, and all that he wants you to do in this world. Hear him say your name over and over with the greatest love. Thank him for the miracle of yourself.

11. Find a created object which you especially love, and which speaks to you of God's goodness and the beauty of his creation (e.g., a plant, tree, cloud, lake, shell, etc.). Let it speak to you of his goodness and give thanks to him for all that you hear.

CONTEMPLATION IN ACTION PRAYERS

Take a minute and ask for the grace to be able to receive love. Then go and do one of the following:

12. Take a walk of thanksgiving in which you just thank God for the ways you see his love. You might thank him through words, by the way you take deep breaths of his care, or just by the way you rejoice in seeing and touching his creation. Maybe you will want to stop in one spot and thank him for all you can hear, smell, touch and see. Let him smile at you and smile back.

13. A favorite prayer of St. Teresa was to work with an awareness of Jesus being at her side. Invite Jesus to be with you as you work during part of the day. You might speak to him about what you are doing, or ask for help. How does he look at you and rejoice in what you are doing? For what is Jesus most grateful? Least grateful? How does he see your day?

14. Recall a moment in your life when someone helped you. Or perhaps there is a person in your life who is always there for you. Toward whom do you have unexpressed gratitude in your heart? Find a way to express your gratitude to this person, or perhaps, if that

person is far away, to someone else instead—call, write a note, make cookies, help another in a similar way, etc.

B. Daily Journal (5 minutes).

1. Share with Jesus when during this prayer or during the day your heart was deeply moved — perhaps a moment of being grateful for or of longing for healing in *receiving love.*
2. Write in your journal how Jesus responds (what he seems to do or say in response to what you have told him). If you can't get in touch with Jesus' response, write what most moves you as you speak to him or what are the most loving words you want to hear.

OPTIONAL HOME EXPERIENCES

C. Personal Reflection Questions

1. Graph your life with its peaks and valleys of growth. Let the horizontal line on the graph reflect your age, and let the vertical line represent the extent of the peak or valley of growth in receiving love at a given age. For example, the graph below would represent a person 35 years of age, whose most growthful period was between the ages of 17 and 22, and whose least growthful time was between the ages of 31 and 33. When was your period of most growth and of least growth in receiving love?

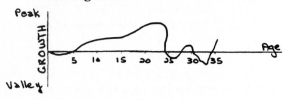

2. The person easiest for me to receive love from is . . . .
   The person hardest for me to receive love from is . . . .
3. The time when I felt most loved in my childhood (adolescence, adulthood) was . . . .

4. My earliest memory of being loved is . . . .
5. The time when I felt most loved by God was . . . .

D. Scripture Readings

1 John 4:17-21: God is love.
Romans 5:7-11: Christ died for us while we were sinners.
Luke 12:22-32: Trust as do the lilies of the field.
1 Corinthians 13:1: Love is . . .
Psalm 23: The Lord is my shepherd.
Psalm 103: God is love.
Psalm 104: The love of the Creator.
Ephesians 3:14-21: The fullness of God's love.
Psalm 139: God has loved us at every moment of our lives.
Luke 1:46-55: Mary's gratitude.
Luke 1:67-79: Zechariah's gratitude.

E. Additional Readings

Healing Life's Hurts, Chapter 5, "First Predisposition: God Loves Me Unconditionally." Before we can grow or even begin to face our painful memories, we need to know the truth about God and about ourselves. We need to know that God is unconditional love itself and that our true self-image is that we are loved infinitely and totally. When we know these two things, we are transformed ourselves and we have the creative power to give life to others.

Born Only Once by Conrad Baars (Chicago: Franciscan Herald Press, 1975). Those who have never received unconditional love have not experienced a second or "psychic birth"—the birth of their true identity as persons. We all need to receive affirmation in order to be born as our true selves.

As Bread That Is Broken, by Peter van Breemen (Denville, N.J.: Dimension Books, 1974).

Lesson Four
HEALING THROUGH BEATITUDES

INTRODUCTION

The most challenging part of Scripture is the Beatitudes (Matthew 5:3-12). How can it be that when we're poor, when we're mourning, when everyone else is arguing and we have to be peacemakers — that those are the times when we're to be happiest? ("Blessed," *makarios*, means happy.) The challenge of the Beatitudes is to know that we're loved and can be happy at the darkest moments of our lives because no matter what has happened those moments are gifted times, times that are going to end in celebration for those who love God (Romans 8:28).

When we worked as therapists at Wohl Psychiatric Clinic in St. Louis, we saw how darkest moments can become gifted times of new life. Many of the people who came to us were depressed. We'd ask them when it all began and they'd tell us about the death of a spouse, a difficult job, or some other painful crisis situation. On weekends we'd give retreats and we'd ask people, "When did it all begin? When did you start to know that God loves you and to have his deep happiness?" These happy people cited the same crises as did the depressed patients at Wohl. One woman on a retreat told us, "It was when my husband died. I had to take care of the children myself and make all the decisions. I had to really depend on God, and that's when he became real for me." We found that it wasn't the crisis that made one person go into a depression and led another into a deep religious experience that helped them come alive. The crisis might be the same; what made the difference was how people reacted to it. The psychiatric patients in the first group were characterized by resentment. They went over and over what had happened to them, speaking only of the pain and unable to get past wishing that things were different. The retreatants in the second group were able to forgive the people who had hurt them. The group that could forgive and find a loving God in a difficult time experienced it as a time of life, growth and blessing.

I (Matt) want to share a time where a difficult experience became a blessing for me. When I was seven years old and Dennis was five, we had a younger brother named John. That winter John came down with bronchitis and he died in the ambulance on his way to the hospital. I remember getting angry at ambulance drivers, at doctors and at God. But finally it came back on myself. Although I didn't reason it out, I thought that I must have done something to hurt John or God wouldn't have taken him away. I began to dislike myself, to make mistakes in school, to feel inferior to other children. In high school I tried working hard and winning honors but I still disliked myself.

I continued to dislike myself until, soon after joining the Jesuits, I made a thirty-day retreat that included a general confession. I wrote out twelve single-spaced pages full of all the things I disliked in myself and gave them to the novice master. He asked me to share just what I was most sorry for, and as I began to speak I heard myself say, "I just feel that I'm somehow responsible for my brother's death." I began to cry, unable to go on. The part of me that I really disliked had finally come out, after years of covering it over with grades and activities. The novice master put his arms around me and said, "The Lord loves you and I really love you too." A shell that I had built up around myself began to come off as I felt loved in the worst moment of my life.

From then on I began to see how the Lord had

gifted me in that painful moment. For example, my close relationship with Dennis began when John died, and I knew that if ever Dennis were taken from me I didn't want there to be any hurt between us. After John died our family adopted my sister, Mary Ellen, because we had so much extra love to give. The gifts that I value most in my ministry have also grown out of the experience of John's death. For example, I like to hear confessions because for twelve years I carried a burden of guilt all alone and I was released through confession. In the confessional I can feel the pain of others and I don't want them to leave with the same pain — together we can hate the sin but love the sinner. I like to work in hospitals with parents who have just lost a child because I've been there. I know what it's like and I know that the Lord can bring gifts out of it because he's done that for me. I like to give healing workshops because I know that the Lord can take any hurt in a person's life, and the deeper it is the more he can do with it. I know that if we forgive ourselves and forgive others and let the Lord love us, any hurt can be turned into good the way John's death was turned into good for me. As a result of that deep hurt, I've been able to give and receive a lot of love and happiness, and that's the promise of the Beatitudes.

The promise of the Beatitudes was focused most for me (Dennis) when we went to the Holy Land. The first few days were really frustrating. We were staying in overcrowded rooms in the YMCA instead of the first-class hotel we'd been promised. We went out to walk along the Via Dolorosa, but while hoping to have a deep experience of the Way of the Cross we were deluged by noisy children selling flutes and postcards. Toward evening, hoping finally to have a few hours to pray, we went up to the Mountain of the Transfiguration. However, after arriving at the mountain top, we were told that our buses had to be all the way back down the hill in a half-hour. Being in the Holy Land was a frustrating experience for me until we got to the Mount of the Beatitudes. There each person in the group was asked to pick up a rock that symbolized the sufferings and hardships the Beatitudes described. All I could think about were those days since we'd arrived, with all their discomfort and inconvenience. During the liturgy I saw clearly the choice I had. I could go to Jerusalem and do it my way, which meant seeing all the places where the Lord had been. But the Lord was inviting me not to see his places but to be with him and live as he lived — to have no place to lay my head, to have

the money changers in the temple, to never have enough time to pray. I wanted just to see his places, and he wanted me to be with him.

The choice we have when a hurt comes is to stay hurt or to choose to let Jesus draw us closer to himself because he went through hurts and he's going through our hurts with us right now. The times when we have to make this choice can be the most gifted times because they are the beginning of finding Jesus' love at all times in our life. "Rejoice always, never cease praying, render constant thanks: such is God's will for you in Christ Jesus" (1 Thessalonians 5:16-18).

Note: You may wish to take two sessions for "Healing Through Beatitudes." Optional session 4B suggests a format for the second session.

I. Group Exerience

A. **Common Opening Prayer** (5 minutes)

B. **Video or Audio Tape:** "Healing through Beatitudes" (30 minutes)

How can hurts become blessings?
1. The Beatitudes are the most challenging part of Scripture, calling us to know that we are loved during the darkest moments of our lives. The promise of the Beatitudes is that such moments are gifted times which can become occasions for celebration (e.g., patients at Wohl Clinic vs. others who experienced similar hurts but reacted differently).
2. When we can forgive those who hurt us and find a loving God in an experience of suffering, that experience becomes a blessing. The deeper the hurt, the more the Lord can do with it (e.g., John's death).
3. When we are hurt, the choice is to remain in our hurt or to let the Lord use it to draw us closer to him. He invites us to share his life rather than just observe it (e.g., trip to the Holy Land).

Closing Prayer: receiving the gift of the Beatitudes, seeing how even hurtful situations can become gifts.

C. **Silent Reflection** (3 minutes). Quiet time to get in touch with what part of today's tape moved your heart most deeply.

D. Guided Journaling (Optional—10 minutes). See Lesson 3.

E. Companion Sharing (5 minutes minimum for each person to share his or her reaction to today's tape and to the past week).

1. Share with your companion as much as you wish of what is in your heart after seeing this week's tape. Perhaps you will want to share what you have just written during the guided journaling.

2. Share with your companion how you have experienced the Lord's presence in your life during the previous week. You may wish to share the journal response from last week that touched you the most.

3. What are you most grateful for now and how do you need Jesus' help?

F. Companion Prayer (5 minutes of prayer for each person). Pray for your companion for about 5 minutes, either silently or aloud in your own words. Give thanks for what your companion is most grateful for and ask for whatever your companion most needs. Close your prayer by asking that your companion receive the grace of this lesson: *to find the gift in moments of disappointment or tragedy.* After you have prayed for your companion for 5 minutes, let your companion pray for you.

G. Group Sharing (Optional — 15 minutes minimum). Take two minutes of silence to ask what has been most difficult and what has been most helpful in your prayer and journaling this past week. Share your reflections with the larger group. Close with a prayer thanking the Lord for the breakthroughs and for discovering the blocks where he is already bringing forth further growth.

H. Closing Snack and Celebration (Optional). An open-ended time to enjoy one another and to continue sharing.

II. Home Experiences

A. Daily Healing Prayer (10 minutes). This week during the ten-minute prayer time, let Jesus tell you about the events in your life that have led you to him. It may be tragedies that were turned into blessings (e.g., Matt's experience of John's death), as Jesus promised in the Beatitudes. Or, it may be everyday ways in which you were loved and which you have used to learn how to love others. Use the following exercises in whatever way they might help you to get in touch with your life story of following Jesus. The goal of this week's prayer is to discover the main events in your life that have opened the way to Jesus — i.e., your testimony.

1. *Beatitude Prayer on the Emmaus Road* (Tape Prayer)

   a. Prayerfully read the Beatitudes in Matthew 5:1-12. You may also wish to review the story of the disciples on the road to Emmaus (Luke 24:13-36).

   b. Close your eyes, and as you do so be attentive to the darkness closing in. Like the Emmaus disciples, begin sharing with Jesus the darkest moments of your life — the times when you were hurt the most. If you were to graph your life with its ups and downs, what would be the biggest down? Open your hand and ask Jesus to be with you in that darkness. Tell Jesus how you were hurt and share with him all the pain and destruction that you felt. Let Jesus, who has experienced every hurt (whether it be the death of a loved one, sexual harrassment, or betrayal by a friend), share the hurt with you.

   c. Just as the disciples at Emmaus began to give thanks with Jesus as he explained the Scriptures relating to their hurtful situation, give thanks with Jesus as he explains the Beatitudes relating to your hurtful situation.

   1. "Happy are they that mourn, for they shall be comforted." The neediness of the disciples allowed them to develop a friendship with the stranger (Jesus) as they shared their neediness. Perhaps you wish to give thanks with Jesus for any way your neediness has brought out the gifts of others and deepened friendships as you asked for help.

2. "Blessed are the peacemakers, for they shall be called children of God." After learning from Jesus his interpretation of the Scriptures and after having broken bread with him, the disciples returned to Jerusalem to bring peace to those who had hurt them and to those who were still hurting in the same way. Give thanks with Jesus for any way in which your hurt has given you the desire to learn and develop new skills for serving, and for any way it has given you the compassionate wish to bring peace to those who hurt you or who are still hurting in the same way you were.

3. "Blessed are the pure of heart, for they shall be called children of God." The hurt of feeling deceived by people they had trusted left the empty Emmaus disciples with a thirst for Scripture and a hunger to break bread with an intimate Jesus who could share how he had been hurt in a similar way. Give thanks with Jesus for any way in which the painful situation you experienced helped you to know that you couldn't go on alone, that you needed to receive bread and strength from an intimate God. Also give thanks for any way that being hurt by others has helped you to be Jesus, especially as you begin forgiving more immediately and more unconditionally.

(For a list of the remaining Beatitudes and how each relates to a hurtful situation, see *Healing Life's Hurts,* pages 169-171.)

d. Finish the prayer by letting Jesus lead you slowly from darkness to light as you open your eyes. Give thanks with him for the ways that the Father will bring more light into the situation in the future.

2. *Embrace Prayer* (See Lesson 3, Prayer #2)

3. *Stepping Stones*
Imagine a stream with Jesus on the other side and stepping stones between you and him. Look into his face and ask him to show you the main stepping stones (persons and events in your life) that have allowed you to cross closer to Jesus. Perhaps you even want to take a piece of paper and draw a stream. Then draw in the stones and observe the water (placid or stormy, deep or shallow, slow stream or rushing current) as Jesus shows you where each stone was placed in your life walk.

4. *Spiritual Road Map*
Draw a road map of your journey toward Jesus, from as far back in your life as you want up until the present moment. Use crayons, paints, colored markers, etc. on any kind and size of paper you want. Think about the kinds of things that a road map shows — mountains, valleys, freeways, stop lights, intersections, detours, construction sites, rivers, landmarks, etc. — and include them on your map. (For example, maybe your experience of baptism in the Spirit seems to you as though it should be pictured as a mountain peak . . . or maybe it seems to you more like a construction site.) Include the important people you have known along the way — perhaps you could depict them as landmarks or as roads intersecting the one you are on. (Perhaps you would want to bring your road map to the next session of the course and share it with your companion.)

5. *New Life in Nature*
Consider a moment or an object in nature in which you can see how the Lord brings new life out of darkness and death. For example, watch a rainstorm as it waters the earth and perhaps even leaves a rainbow behind it; look at a plant that you have uprooted in order to transfer it to a larger pot where it will have more room to grow; hold a seed in your hand that has fallen to the earth and lies dormant. Ask the Lord to show you how a painful moment in your life can be compared to the way he brings forth new life in nature.

6. *Matchbook Prayer*
    a. At night, take a matchbook and sit in front of a crucifix. Ask Jesus to reveal to you the time in your life when he was most present to you.
    b. When you are in touch with that time, light a match to symbolize his presence again in the darkness and thank him while the match burns. Rest in his care just as the match rests in your hand.

7. *Candle Prayer*
    At another time in front of the cross, you might ask Jesus to reveal when in your life the most growth came out of a seeming tragedy. Perhaps you could light a candle and thank him for the ways his light pushed back the darkness.

8. *Your Testimony*
    a. Read Acts 26:1-23 where Paul shares his life story, or testimony, of receiving and giving Christ's love, even with all his weakness.
    b. Ask Jesus to show you the events in your own life that have affected you the most and that are your testimony.
    c. Write down the main events and hold up the paper, giving thanks to Jesus.

9. *Prayer of St. Francis*
    Lord, make me an instrument of your peace.
    Where there is hatred, let me sow love;
    Where there is injury, pardon;
    Where there is doubt, faith;
    Where there is despair, hope;
    Where there is darkness, light;
    Where there is sadness, joy.

    O Divine Master, grant that I may not so much seek
    To be consoled as to console;
    To be understood as to understand;
    To be loved as to love;
    For it is in giving that we receive;
    It is in pardoning that we are pardoned;
    It is in dying that we are born to eternal life. Amen.

    a. Pray this prayer very slowly, asking Jesus to reveal to you one phrase at a time how he has already done for you what is in that phrase. For example, when did you have a struggle with sadness, and who helped to bring you joy? Draw a heart, and in the heart write down the main people and events that carried Jesus' love to you. Thank Jesus for these people and events.
    b. Then (or during the following day's prayer time) pray the prayer slowly again, but this time ask Jesus to reveal to you how he has already used you to bring his love to others. For example, when did he most use you to bring pardon or joy to another? Write down and underline in the heart the main persons and events in which Jesus has used you as an instrument of his love. Thank him for these times.

Contemplation in Action Prayers

Take a minute and ask for the grace to be able to find the gift in moments of disappointment or tragedy. Then go and do one of the following:

10. As you become aware of a gift that has grown out of a tragic situation, decide with the Lord how you are to use that gift today. Who most needs it?

11. Help another person or persons discover how they are special and loved by you and the Lord. Perhaps you will do this through simply enjoying them, through giving an honest compliment, through really listening to them because they have so much to say, etc. Ask the Lord to show you how they are special to you and how you can best express this.

12. Let another person know how he or she has been important in your journey or life story.

B. Daily Journal (5 minutes)

1. Record each day a part of your life story or testimony (the events, people, etc. that have helped you to grow and that have deepened your relationship with Jesus).
2. Be prepared to briefly share your life story with your companion at the next meeting. At this meeting, you may want to start with the video or audio tape teaching and then use all of the remain-

ing time to share your life story through your journal entries, spiritual road map, stepping stones drawing or in whatever way you wish.

(Most groups find that they need an extra session for this lesson. A suggested format for this session is in Lesson 4B: Healing through Beatitudes [Optional Session].)

OPTIONAL HOME EXPERIENCES

C. Personal Reflection Questions

1. What tragic event in your life is hardest for you to see as a gift? Easiest? What makes it so?
2. What tragic event in your life has most helped you to develop new skills and to reach out to others who are hurting in the same way?
3. What gift or talent do you believe the Lord has most developed in you? When did that gift begin growing, and what helped it to grow?
4. If you could live your life over, what event would you most want to have happen again?

D. Scripture Readings

Matthew 5:1-12: The Beatitudes.
Acts 26:1-23: Paul's testimony (also 2 Corinthians 11:23-27).
John 9: Testimony of a man born blind.
Romans 8:28: We know that in everything God works for good with those who love him.
Genesis 37-47: Story of Joseph and his brothers.
Ruth: How the Lord brought blessing out of hardship for Ruth and Naomi (and ultimately for all of Israel through Ruth's descendants, David and Jesus).

Job: Classical biblical story of tragedy turned into blessing.

E. Additional Readings

Healing Life's Hurts
Part I, "What Happens in Healing a Memory?" Healing of memories happens when we discover that a painful moment of our past need no longer cripple us but can bless us. In healing a memory, we go through five stages of forgiveness, similar to the five stages a a person goes through in facing death. Chapter 11, "Fifth Stage: Acceptance," pages 167-173. To the degree that we live the Beatitudes (Matthew 5:1-12), we live a life of acceptance in which we focus not on the pain from hurts but on the growth from hurts.

Man's Search for Meaning, by Viktor Frankl (New York: Washington Square Press, 1963). In prison, psychiatrist Viktor Frankl discovered that everything can be taken away from a person except his ability to choose his attitude no matter what the circumstances.

Sealed Orders, by Agnes Sanford (Plainfield, N.J.: Logos International, 1972). Autobiography of the great teacher of faith in God's power to heal through prayer, who learned the ways of prayer through her own experience of overcoming depression.

The Hiding Place, by Corrie ten Boom (Washington Depot, Ct.: Chosen Books, 1971). Personal story of terrible suffering in a concentration camp which was transformed into blessing.

Healing the Hidden Self, by Barbara Shlemon (Notre Dame: Ave Maria, 1982). Discusses the difficulties that can arise at each stage of human development and suggests prayers for healing.

Lesson Four B
HEALING THROUGH BEATITUDES (OPTIONAL SESSION)

Many groups find that they need an extra session for the material in the lesson "Healing Through Beatitudes." Following is a suggested format.

I. Group Experience

A. Common Opening Prayer (5 minutes)

B. (Omit Video or Audio Tape)

C. (Omit Silent Reflection)

D. (Omit Optional Guided Journaling)

E. Companion Sharing (20 minutes)

Share your life story with your companion. What are the main turning points in your life that brought you to Jesus?

F. Companion Prayer (5 minutes of prayer for each person)

Pray in thanksgiving for your companion, for all the ways that God has worked in his or her life.

G. Group Sharing (40 minutes)

1. Briefly share with one another the turning point in your life during which you most experienced the presence of God. How did it feel?
2. Optional Question (10 minutes)
   Today as you have listened to each person share his or her turning point, when did you most sense the presence of God and how did it feel?

II. Home Experiences

Repeat those in Lesson 4, "Healing Through Beatitudes."

Introduction to Lessons on Forgiveness
IS IT GETTING HARD TO PRAY OR JOURNAL?

When I taught this course for the first time, I found that during the first sessions some people acted as if they were in love with the course and on a honeymoon. Not only would they come early to the meetings and stay late, but they were also putting in extra time at home for prayer and journaling. After about the fourth session, however, I found that some of these same people were experiencing great resistance to doing what before had given them so much life. So, I began asking people to identify their difficulty with the course. Their comments were focused mainly on struggles with prayer and journaling.

Some identified their struggle with prayer by saying, "I have trouble trying to do it every day and I feel guilty when I don't." But others who were able to pray every day would say, "I feel I have to do all the prayers and there's just too much for me to do." And finally some who had time to try all the different prayers would describe their struggle by saying, "When I try to pray, nothing happens."

Besides their struggle with prayer, they also struggled with journaling. One woman showed me the blank pages of her journal and said, "I can't write. I don't have words like other people. I'm afraid I'll do it all wrong." But even some who had full pages in their journal were having difficulty. One man said, "I can't tell if it's Jesus speaking or if it's just me. It's hard for me to believe that Jesus would take time to talk with me." Another who did feel able to identify the voice of Jesus explained her struggle by saying, "I'm afraid of what Jesus wants to say to me. I'm afraid that he will ask too much of me."

I could see that it was the goodness of these people that brought on the struggle. They loved God and were struggling only because they wanted to love him more. Their temptation was to feel that they had to do everything and to do it perfectly in order to earn God's love. They felt that something was wrong with them, that they were spiritual failures because they were having difficulties with the course. They would feel guilty, be hesitant to share what was really going on — or even be tempted to give up completely.

I found that good people were tempted to give up not only because of their struggles with prayer and journaling, but also because of the content of the eight chapters that follow. These chapters invite us to bring to the Lord painful memories, times we are not grateful for. Some found this invitation frustrating because they were not aware of any painful memories they wanted the Lord to heal. They thought that the content of their prayer had to be past memories and hurts, not knowing that they could invite Jesus into present struggles — even struggles with prayer, journaling or other aspects of this course.

Breakthroughs happened when people began to identify their present struggle and then use the exercises in the following chapters to invite Jesus into that struggle. Sometimes they would invite Jesus into what they were feeling in the present moment; at other times they found it more helpful to invite Jesus into a past memory that seemed to be at the root of their present struggle. The story of Ann exemplifies both ways of praying.

Ann's honeymoon with the course was cut short during the first session when she learned that she would be expected to write in a journal. She was immediately aware of her lifelong difficulty in expressing herself and afraid that she could not do what would be asked of her. As the group was led through a guided journaling exercise, she wrote, "Why have I no words?" As she listened for Jesus' response, she heard him say to her, "That's why you're here." Because she experienced this response as not only Jesus' loving acceptance of her in her present struggle but also as a personal invitation to let him give her the words, she felt a desire to write down faltering words and phrases about other situations. Slowly the first page of her journal began to take shape.

Gradually Ann was able to share herself with the Lord at deeper and deeper levels through the pages of her journal. As her self-awareness developed, she came to understand that the fear of journaling she experienced during the first session of the course was part of a difficulty with self-expression which had begun when she was two years old and her nine-month-old brother died. Ann's mother was so traumatized by the death that she attempted suicide and Ann was sent off to stay with a grandmother. Ann was never allowed to express her feelings of fear, grief, and anger over the loss of her baby brother. She had felt ever since that all her words were bottled up inside of her. Ann's deeper breakthrough came when she used Scripture prayer to identify with Jesus at the death of the Holy Innocents. Knowing that Jesus had experienced a similar hurt when he was two years old meant for Ann that now she had someone to share her bottled-up feelings with. As she joined Jesus and his mother in their fear, grief and anger, her own buried emotions were released and healed. Her husband, a Freudian psycho-analyst, said that years of therapy would have been required to bring about the change he saw in his wife.

Not only Ann, but many others in the course experienced new freedom as they invited Jesus into root memories which seemed to underlie their present struggle with prayer and journaling.

- Mary was afraid to write and felt unable to journal. She made a breakthrough when she was able to forgive a teacher who had publicly ridiculed her in the classroom for spelling "Spirit" as "sprite."

- Susan was struggling with prayer and journaling because she feared that if she listened to Jesus he would ask too much of her. Susan's father was a demanding doctor who had always expected her to achieve more than she could. She was gradually able to relax and listen to Jesus after several weeks of praying the Embrace Prayer. As she repeated this prayer, the tense body of her over-achieving inner child became more and more relaxed in the Father's arms until she could be content with just resting and not trying to achieve or do anything.

In the following chapters, it is not so important to decide whether to invite Jesus into a painful present struggle or into a painful past situation. The more important question is to ask Jesus how and where he wants to love me now. Sometimes how and where Jesus chooses to love and heal us may surprise us, as in the case of Tom. Tom could never remember his father or other significant people in his life having time to talk with him. Thus he found it difficult to pray or journal because he couldn't believe that Jesus would be interested in taking time to talk with him either. Tom came to trust more in Jesus' desire for conversation with him as he realized how much his companion Ed enjoyed talking with him both during and outside of the companion sharing times. Prayer and journaling then became easy for Tom, as he invited Jesus to companion him and talk with him just as Ed had. The following chapters will be healing to the extent that we view them not so much as a course with many hoops to jump through, but rather as many invitations to receive Jesus as he loves us in prayer or in some simple and surprising way such as a talk with another.

Lesson Five
FORGIVE AND RE-MEMBER

INTRODUCTION

Several years ago researchers at the University of Nebraska tried to diagnose which of fourteen illnesses a person had on the basis of a fifteen-minute psychological interview.[1] The researchers were able to guess which illness a person had with sixty percent accuracy on the first guess and eighty-seven percent accuracy on the second guess. They found the most helpful diagnostic question was this: "What would you do if someone your own size and sex came up to you while you were sitting on a park bench and kicked you in the leg?" Researchers found that three responses related to various diseases. A person who became very angry at being kicked would be liable to have heart disease, degenerative arthritis or a peptic ulcer. A person who wouldn't know how to respond to being kicked would be liable to have asthma, migraine headaches or hyperthyroidism. Finally, a person who would continue reading the newspaper and was hardly aware of being kicked would be liable to have an "itis" disease like neurodermatitis, rheumatoid arthritis, ulcerative colitis, etc. ("Itis" refers to inflammation and may mean that we're keeping what is bothering us inside.)

These researchers were measuring the relationship between various physical illnesses and their subjects' handling of three feelings: fear, anger and guilt. Many doctors are now saying that these three feelings control our whole physiological and emotional system. If I am sitting on a bench and someone comes up to me in a threatening way, my first reaction will be fear. Once I know what I'm fearful about, I'll become either angry or guilty. I'll become angry if what I fear is outside of myself, e.g., "This big guy is

coming at me and I'm afraid of the ways he is going to hurt me." I'll become guilty if what I fear is inside of me, e.g., "I'm afraid that I don't know how to react. I'm afraid I'm too small to defend myself." My first reaction in a threatening situation is often fear, and once I've pinpointed this fear I begin to feel either anger or guilt. How do I deal with anger and guilt? Anger and guilt are good insofar as they help me to hate the evil in a situation so that I will change what should be changed.[2] But anger and guilt can make me sick if they also lead me to hate rather than forgive the evil-doer. If I am angry I need to forgive another, and if I am guilty I need to forgive myself. Forgiveness is the key to physical and emotional health.

This forgiveness, which is the key to physical and emotional health, is expressed in the Lord's Prayer. In forgiving and thus dealing with anger and guilt, we are taking both parts of the Lord's Prayer seriously, "Forgive us (guilt) our trespasses, as we forgive those (anger) who trespass against us." Such forgiveness is also the key to spiritual health. Without it we will have difficulty opening ourselves to Jesus' love and thus have difficulty with prayer. If we are filled with anger toward our neighbor, we cannot receive the way Jesus loves us through that neighbor. Jesus is there in our neighbor (Matthew 24:45), and in turning away from our neighbor we are turning away from Jesus.

Though a person may be unaware of such unforgiveness and of turning away from Jesus, that person will frequently be aware of the symptom: difficulty in prayer. Lack of forgiveness is the main barrier we have found in people who are having difficulty with prayer. Some experience difficulty in prayer because they are tired of

---

1. Floyd Ring, M.D., "Testing the Validity of Personality Profiles in Psychosomatic Illnesses," *Am. J. of Psychiatry,* 113, 1957, 1075-80.

2. Forgiveness does not mean allowing destructive, abusive behavior to continue. For example, a woman whose alcoholic husband beats her when he is drinking must take steps to protect herself from the physical abuse while seeking to love and forgive her husband.

asking and not having their prayer answered. But as Mark 11:24 tells us, all we have to do is ask in prayer with expectation and we will receive. However, in the next sentence Mark adds that we can't stand and ask from our Father if we can't stand in prayer and forgive. Perhaps much of our prayer is not answered because the Lord's loving response is sometimes blocked as he tries to channel his love through our unforgiving heart. Some people have difficulty not just in prayers of petition, but in any kind of prayer. Often on our retreats, people will be experiencing dryness in prayer and will interpret it as the "dark night of the soul," the Lord testing them because they're doing so well in the spiritual life. Sometimes it is the dark night, but usually we find that what's really affecting the person's prayer life is buried fear, anger and guilt. We can start to pray and again receive the Lord's healing love when we can forgive God, others and ourselves.

Forgiveness is the way we can allow not just ourselves but also others to receive the Lord's healing love. At our first healing workshop we had seven people who were in their second marriages. These seven people focused their prayer on trying to forgive their first spouse. When we talked with them a year later, five out of the seven told us that their former spouse had contacted them within a short time after the retreat. These five former spouses, some of whom hadn't been heard from for as long as fifteen years, reached out with gestures of reconciliation — even though our workshop participants hadn't initiated contact on their own. All the participants could do was forgive, since most of them didn't even know where their former spouse was. When we don't forgive others, we bind them — and when we do forgive, we release a whole new power to love.

If forgiveness is so important for our health and the health of those we forgive, how do we do it? Sometimes it's hard even to get in touch with the one we need to forgive.

If I (Matt) ask myself "Whom was I angry at today?" I usually won't get any answers to my question. I have to ask myself another question: "What was I not so grateful for in my day?" and then I can get in touch with what I would like to have changed and why I wish I had acted differently. One day when I asked that question I found that I was not grateful for a woman who had called me that afternoon. She had been calling every afternoon and talking for an hour about all her aches and pains. She was an invalid, alone at home with no one to talk to, and she had arthritis. The more I thought about her, the more I was in touch with my anger at having to listen to her talk about nothing but her pains. She never seemed to hear anything I said in response or to follow my suggestions. Lately I had reached the point of putting the phone down and continuing with my work, picking it up every twenty minutes or so to say "uh-huh," and putting it down again while she kept talking. So I was in touch with my need to forgive her for being self-centered and unable to listen.

What do you do when you're in touch with a need to forgive someone? Luke 6:27-28 gives us three steps of forgiveness: love, do good for the person and pray. First step: love. Love doesn't mean a gushy feeling — it means a decision. This woman was wounded and she didn't need more wounds. She needed the power to change that comes from being loved. Second step: do good. I didn't feel like doing good at all, but I decided to do something for her with Jesus. I decided that I would call her before she called me. Just the action of reaching out by calling her helped me *want* to do something for her. But after about half an hour, I was back to feeling put off by all her talk about her aches and pains. So, I had to take the third step: pray. I tried to get into Jesus' heart by first giving him everything in my heart and then taking on his heart. I began by telling him everything in my heart, how angry and frustrated I was, and how I wished she would call someone else.

After I had unloaded what was in my heart, I asked him to share his heart with me. First I saw how much he loved her and how compassionate he was toward her in her wheelchair. That began to move me away from wishing she would change. Then, as Jesus looked at me, I saw how I was like her — and that's really a key to forgiving. What didn't I like about her? She didn't listen. What was I doing? Saying "uh-huh" and then putting the phone down for twenty minutes. She never seemed to change. Well, I wasn't going to change either. I wasn't going to sit there and try to love her for a whole hour. I was giving her the same self-centered ultimatum she was giving me. I was demanding that she change because I didn't want to change and become a person who could love her as she was. The very things I didn't like in her were also in me, and I couldn't love her because she was so much like me. When I could let the Lord love me in all my selfishness toward her, then I could start to do the same for her and start to pray Jesus' prayer for her. I could even be grateful for her phone calls which healed me as I was called to forgive and love more unselfishly and without return.

When we need to forgive someone, the first step is to decide with Jesus to love. The next step is to do a loving thing with Jesus — and pretty soon we start wanting to do what we didn't want to do before. The third step is to pray, sharing our heart with Jesus and taking on his heart for the person and for us. The more we do this, the more we will be grateful — not for the evil but for the growth that has come or can come from it as we love more unselfishly without return. To the degree we are grateful for a hurt, we are healed.

I. Group Experience

A. Common Opening Prayer (5 minutes)

B. Video or Audio Tapes: "Forgive and Re-Member" (30 minutes)

How does forgiveness heal us and how do we forgive those who have hurt us or whom we don't like? When we don't forgive, we pay a price physically, emotionally and spiritually.

1. We have three basic reactions to threatening situations: fear, anger and guilt. These reactions affect us so deeply that each one may be expressed in specific *physical* illnesses (e.g., what would be my typical reaction to being kicked?)

2. Forgiveness releases us from fear, anger and guilt and their destructive *emotional* effects upon us (e.g., Providence Hospital).

3. *Spiritually*, to forgive is to live out the Our Father. In that prayer, we ask God not to forgive us if we don't forgive others. Likewise, our forgiveness of another invites God's forgiveness.

4. When we can't pray, it may be because we need to forgive (e.g., sister who wanted a family).

5. Forgiveness has the power to heal beyond ourselves. To forgive others is to release them and to pray for them (e.g., divorced and remarried people who forgave their former spouses).

6. How do we forgive?
   a. Finding out whom we need to forgive. (At the end of a day, what am I not grateful for?)
   b. Luke 6:27-28 gives us three steps to forgiveness: decide to love, do good to others, pray for them (e.g., woman who kept calling Matt).
   c. Forgiving others includes discovering how we are like them and forgiving ourselves too.
   d. Forgiveness happens when we get into the heart of Jesus and take the three steps: decide to love, do it, pray for the other (e.g., Italian grandmothers).

Closing Prayer: asking Jesus to help us forgive one person.

C. Silent Reflection (3 minutes). Quiet time to get in touch with what part of today's tape moved your heart most deeply.

D. Guided Journaling (Optional — 10 minutes). See Lesson 3.

Note: If you did not use Lesson 4B, "Healing Through Beatitudes (Optional Session)," you may wish to skip E and F this time and use all of your remaining time to share your life story with your companion.

E. Companion Sharing (5 minutes minimum for each person to share his or her reaction to today's tape and to the past week).

1. Share with your companion as much as you wish of what is in your heart after seeing this week's tape. Perhaps you will want to share what you have just written during the guided journaling.

2. Share with your companion how you have experienced the Lord's presence in your life during the previous week. You may wish to share the journal response from last week that touched you the most.

3. What are you most grateful for now and how do you need Jesus' help?

F. Companion Prayer (5 minutes of prayer for each person). Pray for your companion for about 5 minutes, either silently or aloud in your own words. Give thanks for what your companion is most grateful for and ask for whatever your companion most needs. Close your prayer by asking that your companion receive the grace of this lesson: *to become aware of those we need to forgive, of the people we are not grateful for.* Then let your companion pray for you.

G. Group Sharing (Optional — 15 minutes minimum). Take two minutes of silence to

ask what has been most difficult and what has been most helpful in your prayer and journaling this past week. Share your reflections with the larger group. Close with a prayer thanking the Lord for the break-throughs and for discovering the blocks where he is already bringing forth further growth.

H. **Closing Snack and Celebration** (Optional). An open-ended time to enjoy one another and to continue sharing.

II. Home Experience

A. **Daily Healing Prayer** (10 minutes). Each day choose one of the following healing or contemplation in action prayers and pray it for at least 10 minutes. These prayers are *suggestions*. Perhaps you will find yourself drawn to pray what is in your heart using varied breathing, a symbol, a repeated word, a melody, a gesture, a drawing, or a piece of clay which you can mold. Although there are many prayers suggested, it would be best to pray only a few of them, parts of them, or to repeat from this or any other chapter the prayer that most moved your heart. Use whatever way you can best give your heart to Jesus and enter into his heart. Perhaps your prayer will be as simple as looking at a beautiful flower and taking in God's love for you. You may wish to begin your prayer by centering yourself, perhaps using the Breath Prayer (see Lesson 1). You may wish to continue with the Embrace Prayer (see Lesson 3, Prayer #2), or a similar prayer of simply resting in God's love.

Note: The prayers which follow focus on forgiveness. If you have difficulty knowing whom you need to forgive, you might ask the following questions:
   Whom are you not grateful for?
   Whom would you like to change a little bit?
   Whom would you least like to have as a sharing and prayer companion?

1. *Tape's Closing Prayer*
   a. Prayerfully read Luke 6:27-31: "To you who hear me, I say, love your enemies, do good to those who hate you; bless those who curse you and pray for those who maltreat you. When someone slaps you on the cheek, turn and give him the other; when someone takes your coat, let him have your shirt as well. Give to all who beg from you. When a man takes what is yours, do not demand it back. Do to others what you would have them do to you."
   b. Get in touch with one person that Jesus wants to forgive.
   c. Tell Jesus how this person has hurt you and how you feel about that. After you have expressed your anger, hurt, disappointment, etc. and are ready to begin to forgive, tell Jesus why you want to forgive this person with him.
   d. Ask Jesus what action he wants you to take for this person or for someone like this person. ("When someone takes your coat, let him have your shirt as well . . . do to others what you would have them do to you.") Maybe phone, write, listen, visit?
   e. Listen and pray the prayer in Jesus' heart for that person.

2. *Embrace Prayer* (See Lesson 3, Prayer #2)

   Before we can face our hurts or forgive others, we need to know that we are loved. If what you are most in touch with is your need to experience God's love for you, then pray the Embrace Prayer or a similar prayer that you find helpful, simply resting in his love for as many days as you wish.

3. *Prayer for Receiving the Grace of This Lesson*

   Ask Jesus to give you his willingness to forgive. Breathe it in with every breath and breathe out all the blocks in yourself to being willing to forgive. (You may wish to pray this prayer with Mary instead of Jesus.)

4. *Prayer for Blocks in Prayer and Journaling*

   Note: The most important thing is not to get beyond the block but to know that Jesus loves you just as much with it. This kind of prayer may touch not only difficulties with this course, but may also heal many other times in your life when you felt unloved because you didn't produce enough or do things right.

a. Write down the difficulty you are having.
b. Sit before a candle or other light until you know how much Jesus loves you with the problem, how much he loves you when you cannot pray or write in your journal.
c. Optional: After you are aware of how God loves you with the problem, turn the paper over and write down whatever you think he might be saying to you.

5. *Lord's Prayer*

a. Choose a person you need to forgive.
b. Pray the Lord's Prayer slowly and aloud until you are praying each phrase with the same love and care that Jesus has when he prays the Lord's Prayer for that person.

6. *Prayer for a Heart of Flesh*

a. Read Ezekiel 36:26: "I will put a new heart and a new spirit within you, taking from your bodies your stony hearts and giving you hearts of flesh."
b. Let Jesus reveal to you one person you need to love and forgive.
c. Find a stone that represents the stony heart of the one you are trying to forgive.
d. Let your hands be the hands of Jesus holding and loving the stony heart into a heart of flesh.

7. *Becoming Another* (See Lesson 1, Prayer #2)

Pray this prayer for someone who has hurt you, so that you can understand the suffering in that person's life. You may especially wish to pray this prayer for a teacher, a classmate or anyone else who hurt you during your school days.

8. *Daily Healing of Memories Square*

Slowly and prayerfully look back on your life, at the times when you were hurt.

a. Within the square, on **page 170**, **write** the names of five people who hurt you. (Think of whom you fear, avoid, judge harshly, etc.)
b. Put a circle around those who are not closer to you now. Pick one of these and tell Jesus how you feel. Be honest and expose all.
c. When you can see why that person may have hurt you, put a vertical line through his or her name (to indicate the other pressures that person faced at that time).
d. When you feel that you can say what Jesus would want to say to that person, draw a horizontal line through his or her name.
e. When you can see that you were part of the problem and yet can forgive yourself as Jesus has, make half an "X" through that person's name.
f. When you can see some good coming out of the hurt (at least five ways you grew from it), X out the name. When you can think of some way to build a bridge to that person, draw a triangle around the name. You have begun to forgive that person and yourself, and to allow God to heal the situation.
g. Thank Jesus for this growth and for beginning the healing.

9. *Candle Prayer*
a. Take a look with Jesus at a day, week or year of your life. Light a candle when you discover the event for which you are most grateful.
b. Look at the same time period with Jesus until you see the event for which you are least grateful. Blow out the candle.
c. Ask Jesus who was part of this event that you may need to forgive, so that you can see it as he sees it. When you have some new understanding and light, relight the candle and thank Jesus.

10. *Mirror Prayer*
a. Choose a person you need to forgive.

b. Share with Jesus the attitudes and behaviors that you don't like in this person.

c. Look at Jesus and ask him to reveal to you how any of these same attitudes and behaviors have been or are mirrored in your own life. Perhaps you may wish to stand in front of a mirror and with the eyes of Jesus see yourself with many of these same attitudes and behaviors.

d. Watch Jesus breathe life and forgiveness into both of you.

CONTEMPLATION IN ACTION PRAYERS

Take a minute and ask for the grace to become aware of the people you need to forgive. Then go and do one of the following:

11. Write a letter, telephone, share a meal or in some other way reach out to a person you have forgiven or to another who reminds you of this person.

12. When you have forgiven someone, celebrate this by doing something that you enjoy and that will bring you more life.

B. Daily Journal (5 minutes)

1. Share with Jesus when during this prayer or during the day your heart was deeply moved — perhaps a moment of being grateful for or of longing for healing in *becoming aware of the people you need to forgive, of those you are not grateful for.*

2. Write in your journal how Jesus responds (what he seems to do or say in response to what you have told him). If you can't get in touch with Jesus' response, write what most moves you as you speak to him or what are the most loving words you want to hear.

OPTIONAL HOME EXPERIENCES

C. Personal Reflection Questions

1. Recall a time when you were very angry. What effect did it have on you physically, emotionally and spiritually?

2. Five out of the seven Dallas spouses responded to silent forgiveness offered miles away. Have you ever silently forgiven another and then seen that person change?

3. What helps you most to get in touch with your anger?
Whom do you most want to change? Whom are you least eager to speak to on the phone? Least grateful for?

4. When did you most experience forgiving another?
Did the steps given in Luke 6:27-28 (decide, act lovingly, pray) help? What helped?

5. What kind of person do you find it most difficult to love? Is that person like you in any way?

D. Scripture Readings

Luke 6:27-38: Love your enemies, do good ...

Mark 11:24-25: Forgiving another is necessary if we want to be forgiven and have our prayers answered.

John 20: 22-23: For John, forgiveness is a sign of the Holy Spirit coming.

1 John 4:20: If anyone says that he loves God ...

E. Additional Readings

Healing Life's Hurts
Chapter 1, "What Is Healing a Memory?" Healing a memory is coming to see any hurt in our lives from the Father's viewpoint until we are grateful for the gifts and growth that have come to us through that experience of hurt.

Chapter 2, "Healing a Memory Is Like Dying." A person who is going to die normally goes through five emotional stages: denial, anger, bargaining, depression and acceptance. Healing a hurtful memory is like dying in that we go through the same stages to arrive at forgiveness of ourselves and others that we go through in accepting death.

Chapter 3, "Emotional Healing Through Healing Memories." Many emotional illnesses are caused by unresolved anxiety, fear, anger and guilt. Healing of memories releases and heals these emotions.

Chapter 4, "Physical Healing Through Healing Memory," pages 30-48. The emotions of anxiety, fear, anger and guilt cause physiological changes in our bodies and can lead to physical illnesses ranging from an upset stomach to a heart attack or cancer. As our emotions are healed through healing of memories, our bodies are freed from stress-related physiological changes and we are often physically healed as well. *Feeling and Healing Your Emotions,* by Conrad Baars (Plainfield, N.J.: Logos International, 1979), pages 191ff. Discusses the dangers of premature forgiveness — trying to forgive before we have faced our angry feelings and perhaps tried to correct the situation.

The Healing Light, by Agnes Sanford (Plainfield, N.J.: Logos International, 1976), Chapter 12, "The Healing Power of Forgiveness."

Lesson Six
HEALING ONE MEMORY PRAYER
(THE FIVE STAGES OF FORGIVENESS)

INTRODUCTION

Sometimes we experience hurts that just don't get forgiven right away. If we've been hurt deeply we can decide to forgive and act lovingly, but we may need to pray for a long time as we seek to take on Jesus' heart and his forgiveness.

Corrie ten Boom tells the story of how she and her sister Betsie were in a concentration camp. Betsie died there from all the mistreatment. After Corrie was released, she began traveling and giving talks on forgiveness. Once, as she came out of a church in which she had just spoken, she saw in the line of people coming to greet her a soldier who had been in the camp. He had been part of her sister's mistreatment. Even after all those words on forgiveness, Corrie could feel nothing but anger at how her sister and her whole family had been killed. This man embodied all that pain for Corrie. She stood there shaking, knowing that she had to forgive and feeling powerless to do so. Inside herself she began to say, "Jesus, help me to forgive this person." Suddenly her hand reached out to the soldier and she found Jesus' forgiveness for him in her heart.

But many times I say, "Jesus, help me to forgive this person," and my hand doesn't move at all. Sometimes the Lord moves quickly, because there is real power in prayer. Other times, forgiveness happens more slowly. This lesson is meant to help us with those hurts that take time to heal.

One man who had an experience that took a long time to heal was finally freed as he was led through the Tape Prayer for this lesson. For twenty-three years he had a fear of going to dentists. He didn't know what had caused this phobia. He went to a psychiatrist, who told him that it could take as long as two years to uncover what was behind the fear. He couldn't afford therapy, so he came to one of our workshops. As he was praying for forgiveness in an entirely different situation, what came into his mind was an experience he'd had when he was ten years old. He was at the dentist's, and as he sat in the dental chair the dentist made verbal homosexual advances toward him. Then the dentist tied his hands down and drilled his teeth without any anesthetic. During the prayer this man was able to forgive that dentist. The next day he was able to make a dental appointment and to go without fear to get the treatment he needed (four teeth capped, bridge work, root canals repaired). His healing came from letting the Lord be present and bring to his mind whatever he wished.

We don't always know what the Lord will bring to mind. Sometimes a seemingly insignificant thing may come to mind when we ask Jesus, "Lord, whom do you want me to forgive?" For example, a nun came up to us once at the end of a workshop. She was so excited that we thought something colossal must have happened to her. She told us that she had always disliked other nuns who wore jeans, but now, as she pointed to another nun in jeans, she felt no resentment. Jesus had helped her through the stages of forgiveness until she could forgive the other sister for the way she dressed.

The Tape Prayer for this lesson leads us through the five stages of forgiveness. Elisabeth Kubler-Ross believes that a person who is dying usually goes through these five stages of denial, anger, bargaining, depression and acceptance. Though dying is the deepest hurt we experience, we find that in healing any hurt the Lord often leads us through the five stages. If the Lord touches us at any one stage, we need to feel free to stay there. The deeper the hurt is, the longer it will probably take to forgive and the healing will be much deeper. Progress isn't found in going quickly from stage to stage but in finding the depth of what you feel, giving it all to the Lord, and then taking on his attitudes and feelings. Paul was healed overnight, while it took Peter three years to give his weakness to Jesus. Healing happens to the extent that we give ourselves to Jesus and receive him. We can stay wherever that's happening in our prayer. And if we can't pray, then we can talk to the Lord about the hurt of not being able to pray. Every struggle is a door to healing.

I. Group Experience

A. Common Opening Prayer (5 minutes)

B. Video or Audio Tape: "Healing One Memory Prayer (Five Stages of Forgiveness)" (30 minutes)

Could you forgive the person who murdered your brother or sister?
1. Sometimes deep hurts take a long time to heal (e.g., Corrie ten Boom, man who had a phobia of dentists).
2. In healing a hurt through forgiveness, we go through the same five stages as a person who is dying.
A 20-minute prayer for healing one memory through the five stages of forgiveness (denial, anger, bargaining, depression, acceptance).

C. Silent Reflection (3 minutes). Quiet time to get in touch with what part of today's tape moved your heart most deeply.

D. Guided Journaling (Optional — 10 minutes). See Lesson 3.

E. Companion Sharing (5 minutes minimum for each person to share his or her reaction to today's tape and to the past week).

1. Share with your companion as much as you wish of what is in your heart after seeing this week's tape. Perhaps you will

want to share what you have just written during the guided journaling.
2. Share with your companion how you have experienced the Lord's presence in your life during the previous week. You may wish to share the journal response from last week that touched you the most.
3. What are you most grateful for now and and how do you need Jesus' help?

F. Companion Prayer (5 minutes of prayer for each person). Pray for your companion for about 5 minutes, either silently or aloud in your own words. Give thanks for what your companion is most grateful for and ask for whatever your companion most needs. Close your prayer by asking that your companion receive the grace of this lesson: *to experience in prayer the forgiveness that goes as deep as Jesus' forgiveness.* Then let your companion pray for you.

G. Group Sharing (Optional — 15 minutes minimum). Take two minutes of silence to ask what has been most difficult and what has been most helpful in your prayer and journaling this past week. Share your reflections with the larger group. Close with a prayer thanking the Lord for the breakthroughs and for discovering the blocks where he is already bringing forth further growth.

H. Closing Snack and Celebration (Optional). An open-ended time to enjoy one another and to continue sharing.

II. Home Experience

A. Daily Healing Prayer (10 minutes). Each day choose one of the following healing or contemplation in action prayers and pray it for at least 10 minutes. These prayers are only *suggestions*. Perhaps you will find yourself drawn to pray what is in your heart using varied breathing, a symbol, a repeated word, a melody, a gesture, a drawing, or a piece of clay which you can mold. Although there are many prayers suggested, it would be best to pray only a few of them, parts of them, or to repeat from this or any other chapter the prayer that most moved your heart. Use whatever way you can best give your heart to Jesus and enter into his heart. Perhaps your prayer will be as simple as looking at a beautiful flower and taking in God's love for you. You may wish to begin your prayer by centering yourself, perhaps using the Breath Prayer (see Lesson 1). You may wish to continue with the Embrace Prayer (see Lesson 3, Prayer #2), or a similar prayer of simply resting in God's love.

1. *Healing One Memory* (Tape Prayer)
   Relax and breathe in the Spirit. Find God within.
   a. *Denial:* Lord, let me see what you see in my day. Where did God love me or love through me? Give him thanks, especially for any growth.
   b. *Anger:* Lord, take away my hurt. What am I less thankful for? What do I wish happened differently? Where was I hurt? Whom am I blaming? What am I feeling? When did I most feel like that? Recreate in the imagination all the destructiveness of the situation and share all the feelings with Jesus.
   c. *Bargaining:* Lord, let me forgive like you—unconditionally. Do I want to be healed by thinking and feeling as differently as you? Like Jesus, see the pressures that were upon the one who hurt you; see his or her good side; try to see the whole picture. Say what Jesus said to his close friends, who were sinners. Do what Jesus would do to give the love needed to the one who hurt you. Do this until all conditions for change are gone and you can say and do all that Jesus would like to do through your prayer.
   d. *Depression:* Lord, forgive me. Ask forgiveness for being like that person and for contributing to the problem by over-reacting, closing up, and failing to build bridges. Ask forgiveness for past hurts like this that make it easy to close up. (Another day, you may want to take this and other recent memories through the above steps to heal further roots of hurt within yourself that cause you to close up.) Give thanks for Jesus' forgiveness and unconditional love for both you and the person who hurt you.
   e. *Acceptance:* Lord, thank you. Thank Jesus for the growth and for the possible growth due to the healing (e.g., new openness to God, to others, to your true self).

2. *Prayer for Receiving the Grace of this Lesson*
   Ask Jesus to give you his forgiving heart. Breathe it in with every breath and breathe out all the blocks in yourself to being able to forgive. (You may wish to pray this prayer with Mary instead of Jesus.)

3. *Prayer for Being Raised to Life*
   a. Read Luke 9:41-42, 49-56, the story of Jairus' daughter.
   b. Ask Jesus to show you a part of yourself that has been hurt, perhaps so deeply that you feel as if that part of you has died.
   c. Let Jesus come to you, as he did to Jairus' daughter. Hear him say the words to you, "Child, arise." Hear those words repeated over and over, with all the love and encouragement that Jesus wants to give you.
   d. Be attentive to any stirring of new life in this part of you, perhaps even just the hope that this part of you can rise to new life as Jairus' daughter did. Thank Jesus for any signs of new life.

4. *Nature Prayer*
   Sit quietly in a favorite outdoor spot, or next to a window that looks out on scenery that is beautiful to you. Ask the Lord to show you his love for you through the beauty of nature. Follow wherever your heart leads you—perhaps into the depths of the sky, perhaps to the beauty of a single flower, perhaps the wonder of a bird flying. Rest there for as long as you wish.

5. *Body Prayer*
   a. Picture or recall a person who has hurt you. Let Jesus bring to mind the pain of this situation until you can feel it in your body.
   b. Breathe out your entire self with all that you are feeling. Breathe in, saying silently, "Lord Jesus Christ," until you are filled with Jesus.
   c. Check your body for tension, and if

any remains, feel the breath of Jesus filling that part of your body until it is bursting with his power and becomes relaxed and able to trust in his strength.

6. *Dream Prayer*
Recall a recent dream. Invite Jesus into it and see what he does.

7. *Prayer with a Friend*
   a. Share with a friend a situation in which it is hard for you to forgive.
   b. Pray alone or with your friend for what you and your friend feel you need.

8. *Waterglass Prayer*
   a. Take an empty waterglass and hold it up to Jesus, telling him how a difficult person is empty and in need of healing.
   b. Then ask Jesus how he is praying in you to give that person life. As you join Jesus or express his prayer, fill the glass.
   c. Ask Jesus to help you give life to this person also. When you really want this, receive it and drink the water as a sign of how Jesus' life is now in you, to share with that person.

CONTEMPLATION IN ACTION PRAYERS

Take a minute and ask for the grace to experience the forgiveness that goes as deep as Jesus' forgiveness. Then go and do one of the following:

9. Hug six people today the way that you would like to hug someone you have forgiven. If you would prefer to just greet people, greet 10 people the way that you sense Jesus would greet the person who hurt you.
10. Fast one day for a person who has hurt you and ask for a hunger to forgive as fully as Jesus does.

B. Daily Journal (5 minutes)

1. Share with Jesus when during this prayer or during the day your heart was deeply moved — perhaps a moment of being grateful for or of longing for healing in

experiencing forgiveness that goes as deep as Jesus' forgiveness.

2. Write in your journal how Jesus responds (what he seems to do or say in response to what you have told him). If you can't get in touch with Jesus' response, write what most moves you as you speak to him or what are the most loving words you want to hear.

OPTIONAL HOME EXPERIENCES

C. Personal Reflection Questions

1. When were you hurt the most? (For what time in your life are you least grateful?) What growth came from that hurt? What may still need prayer for healing?
2. What do you fear? What hurt has planted this fear? How does that hurt still need healing?
3. What is your image of your father? Of God as Father? How are they similar or different?
4. How do you handle the hurt of not being able to pray? Are there areas of compromise in your life that keep you from God? Can you be grateful for any way that this struggle builds up in you a hunger to draw closer to God and to love more unselfishly without return?

D. Scripture Readings

Matthew 6:9-15: The Lord's Prayer for forgiveness.
Luke 23:34: Father, forgive them for they know not . . .
Luke 24:39-42: Jesus lovingly and unconditionally forgives the good thief.
1 John 5:14-16: God gives life to sinners when we pray for them.

E. Additional Readings

Healing Life's Hurts. For further help with the Healing One Memory Prayer (Tape Prayer):
Chapter 7, "First Stage: Denial" — If you had trouble pinpointing who hurt you.
Chapter 8, "Second Stage: Anger" — If you had trouble pinpointing how a person destroyed you or another, or if you had trouble dealing with the anger you felt

toward the person causing the destruction.

Chapter 9, "Third Stage: Bargaining" — If you wanted the person to change before you were ready to forgive him or her.

Chapter 10, "Fourth Stage: Depression" — If you had trouble pinpointing how you could have acted differently before, during or after the situation, or if you had difficulty forgiving yourself.

Chapter 11, "Fifth Stage: Acceptance" — If you had trouble pinpointing how the hurt has brought or could bring growth to you or to another.

Lesson Seven
HEALING THROUGH THE FIVE STAGES OF FORGIVENESS

INTRODUCTION

Sometimes things happen that are hard to celebrate. If someone robbed and beat you, would your first words be, "Praise God"? When his persecutors beat him, Jesus said, "My God, my God, why have you forsaken me?" He did not say, "Praise God." Sometimes when you've been emotionally hurt a process of psychological healing needs to take place, just as when you have been cut a physiological process of healing needs to take place. And if you rush the process, if you pick the scab too soon — if you say "Praise God" too soon — you have to start all over. Psychologists have come to recognize that there is also a natural process for healing an emotional hurt. Whether we face the hurt of death, loss of a limb, or a deep hurt from another, we often go through the five stages of dying: denial, anger, bargaining, depression and finally acceptance.[1] If the hurt is deep, then we also go through these stages in forgiving it and in reaching acceptance of its having happened. While working on a Sioux reservation, I (Matt) learned how moving through these five stages of forgiveness could facilitate the process of healing an emotional hurt.

I learned about these stages through an experience in which I had a hard time forgiving. Several years ago I was working on an Indian reservation as a teacher. One day one of the students — a senior named Jack — came charging into the class. He was drunk and he didn't know where he was. Jack was about twice my size. As soon as Jack saw me, a rage came over him. He grabbed me, began pounding me, chased me around the room and threw me to the floor. Jack's girlfriend was in the class, and she knew that he would be thrown out of school if he kept hitting a teacher. The only thing that saved me was that Jack's girlfriend came between him and me and tried to stop him from hitting me. At first Jack didn't even recognize her, and he threw her to the floor too. She got right back up and came between us again. Finally Jack realized who she was, and she was able to lead him out of the classroom.

Even after Jack left the classroom, I was still shaking. I tried to save face in front of my students by pretending that nothing had happened, but I couldn't teach at all that day. I went into a stage of denial, trying to smile and telling myself that I wasn't hurt at all. I can tell when I'm in denial because I only half-listen and I don't want to feel anything. I cover my injured feelings by working harder, and I don't take time to be alone or to pray. I worked and worked all that evening, but finally at the end of the evening I did what helps with denial.

At any one of the stages there are three things we can do: decide we want to forgive, act in a loving way, and pray for the one who has hurt us. When I'm in denial, deciding to forgive begins with recognizing that I need to forgive. The best thing for me to do is to sit down with the Lord and say, "What am I grateful for in this day and what am I not so grateful for?" That's when it came home to me that I was not grateful at all for what had happened with Jack that day. I felt that I had looked like a fool being chased around that classroom. I feared that the students would never respect me again, and I felt ashamed.

But gradually as I became less aware of feeling ashamed and more aware of blaming Jack

1. Elisabeth Kubler-Ross, *On Death and Dying* (New York: Macmillan, 1969).

and wishing that it had never happened, I moved into the second stage of forgiveness: anger. My feelings were all focused outward, against him. I wasn't ready yet to ask whether I had acted immaturely. I began having thoughts such as: "Jack should be thrown out of school!" Usually I don't even catch those angry thoughts, but I am getting better at catching my typical anger-stage behavior. I get "hurry sickness," where I run through yellow lights, eat to finish rather than enjoy a meal, and try to do as much as I can in as little time as possible. I jog fast because anger gets locked into my muscles and releasing physical tension helps me release emotional tension as well. But even while jogging, I compete with those around me because I am full of a floating anger that has to find some kind of a target.

Both talking to a friend and praying to Jesus about the real target of my anger can help me drain some of it out. So I began telling Jesus about all the things that were wrong that day until I felt my anger with Jack. Then I began asking for Jesus' eyes, asking to understand Jack. I asked, "How do you want to change him, Lord?" I had lots of ideas of how Jack should change, but as I got into the prayer I began to see Jack's wounds. Jack's father was a criminal who had spent his life in prison and finally killed himself. I realized that I was the father figure in that classroom. When Jack was drunk in that classroom, all his hurts from his father were directed at me. I can start to forgive people when I become aware of why they're acting as they are. They aren't out to get me but are wounded and need love. So I asked Jesus to help me pray his prayer for Jack.

When I can begin to understand why a person has hurt me by seeing the person with Jesus' eyes and praying his prayer, then I often move into the third stage of forgiveness: bargaining. Bargaining means that I will forgive people if...they do this or that first. I had two bargains. I would forgive Jack if, first, he stopped drinking and, second, if he would apologize and recognize how well I handled the situation. Bargains come from either our strengths or our weaknesses. My first bargain came out of strength, as one of my strengths is that I don't have a drinking problem. If I become proud and think that I'm doing it on my own strength— "If I can do it, he can do it" — then I start to demand the same thing of someone else. I demand of others the very things I'm proud of, not realizing that they are gifts from the Lord. On the other hand, my second bargain, that Jack apologize and recognize how well I handled the situation, came out of my weakness. Through such

an apology and recognition I wanted Jack to cover up the weakness I was ashamed of: the fearful coward running away from Jack as he chased me around the classroom and the volcano of anger that couldn't forgive once he was out the door. Before I would forgive Jack, I wanted him to tell me how much courage I had and how I controlled my anger so well. I wanted this weakness covered so that I would not have to change my volcanic anger and face my shame. Whether I'm bargaining from my strengths or from my weaknesses, I need to get under the cross and say, "Jesus, help me to forgive this person, not because he deserves it but because he needs it." I shared all my bargains with Jesus, telling him all the ways I wanted Jack to change before I would forgive him. Then I asked Jesus for his heart that cancels all bargains and reaches out with unconditional forgiveness.

When I reached the point of beginning to cancel bargains, I moved into the depression stage. In this stage I started asking what was wrong with *me*. Why had I reacted so badly? Why had I been so frightened? Why had I let this hurt affect me for so long? Why didn't I see that Jack was after his father and not me? Why couldn't I forgive him as his girl friend did who forgave him instantly after being thrown to the floor? I realized that I had never spent any time alone with Jack getting to know him, and so, of course, I was just a blank on whom he could project his father. "I should have been a bigger and better person," I thought. When I'm in the depression stage, I say, "I should." When this happens, I have a choice to make. I can keep beating on myself, or I can let the Lord and others love me and forgive me. I had to choose whether I would live for the students' opinions of me, or for Jesus who loved and forgave me and wanted to help me change the things in myself that needed change. The gift of the depression stage is that it can show me ways I really do need to change. As I saw how my attitude of staying distant from people had contributed to Jack's attack, I wanted to change. As a first step I began visiting students in their homes and opened a home for students with alcohol abuse problems.

Since I let the Lord love me and help me change, I could begin to move into the fifth stage of forgiveness: acceptance. Sometimes it is hard to distinguish between acceptance and denial. The difference is that in denial I cannot reach out to another or be grateful, whereas, in acceptance, I can reach out to the very person who has hurt me and grow in gratitude for what before I considered only a hurt. When I asked the Lord to help me grow in gratitude for what Jack had done, I began feeling grateful for three reasons.

The first reason for gratitude was discovering what it was like to be a Sioux. Although I had learned their Lakota language and even lived with a Sioux family one summer, the day I was chased around that classroom taught me the most about what it's like to be a Sioux. Sioux families suffer from seventy percent unemployment and rampant alcoholism. To be an Indian means to have someone out after you, whether it's a white person or another Indian — someone you're afraid of who might come home at night out of control. I had never felt their pain until I experienced in the classroom what the Sioux live with all the time.

The second reason for gratitude was that now I knew how the Sioux could live with resentments and have a hard time forgiving. I saw how long it had taken me to forgive Jack, and I stopped demanding that others forgive and change overnight. I became aware of how I had talked to other teachers about my students, pretending that it was "constructive criticism," but really just trying to make myself look good. I gradually criticized less as I saw how, in ruining a student's reputation, I had been doing to another the very thing I disliked Jack doing to me.

The third reason for gratitude was that my prayer life grew through my experience with Jack. Since I knew that I couldn't forgive Jack on my own, I knew that I needed Jesus. The biggest thing that hurt gave to me was a vision of who I wanted to be and how I needed Jesus' help to become that person. I wanted to be like Jack's girlfriend. I had seen Jesus in her. I had always known that Jesus on the cross could take any abuse and still forgive. But when I saw Jack's girlfriend love him unconditionally and forgive him instantly no matter how much he abused her, I knew that it was possible for human beings to have Jesus' forgiveness if they loved deeply enough. The example of Jack's girlfriend has helped me to ask again and again for the gift of being able to forgive and to give life to others the way she gave it to me by loving Jack so much. In this lesson we're asking for the gift of unconditional forgiveness.

A person usually goes through the five stages described above in dying or in unconditionally forgiving any hurt involving a dying to self. The first stage is denial, when we pretend it didn't happen. The second stage is anger, when we blame the person out there. The third stage is bargaining, when we say, "I'll forgive, *if*...." The fourth stage is depression, when we blame ourselves. And the fifth stage is acceptance, when

we can be grateful not for the evil but for how it has gifted us in many ways, especially in even being able to reach out to the person who has hurt us. Dr. Elisabeth Kubler-Ross first developed these stages from watching the process that dying patients moved through in finally accepting their death. She also saw patients who became stuck at a stage, e.g., remained angry and died that way. Why did some progress to acceptance and others get stuck? The main difference she observed was that all those moving to acceptance had a significant person with whom they could share their feelings and be loved. Having such a person enabled them to move from one stage to the next. The most important thing about these stages, then, is not that we remember them but that we share them with a significant person who loves us. If in prayer we share these stages with Jesus and allow him to be a significant person for us, we'll move automatically through the five stages.

I. Group Experience

A. Common Opening Prayer (5 minutes)

B. Video or Audio Tape: "Healing Through the Five Stages of Forgiveness" (30 min.)

If you were beaten and robbed, would your first words be, "Praise God!"?

1. When we have been deeply hurt, forgiveness is often a process that takes time (e.g., Matt and Indian student).
2. There are five stages that we normally go through in forgiving someone. At each stage, there are three things we can do: decide to deal with the feelings, act in a loving way, pray for the one who has hurt us.
   a. Denial Stage: pretending it didn't happen. (We need to face our hurt.)
   b. Anger Stage: blaming the other person. (We need to see the hurt behind the other person's behavior.)
   c. Bargaining Stage: demanding that other persons change before we will forgive them. (We need to give our conditions to the Lord and ask to be able to forgive not because the other deserves it but because he or she needs it.)
   d. Depression Stage: blaming ourselves and saying, "I *should*." (We need to change what should be changed in

ourselves, and choose to let the Lord love us and help us to grow.)

    e. Acceptance Stage: we're really grateful for what has happened because we see the gift in it, and we're ready to reach out to the person who hurt us and to others.

  3. We can move through these stages if we have a significant person to share our feelings with. In prayer, Jesus can be that person for us.

Closing Prayer: asking Jesus for the ability to forgive unconditionally.

C. Silent Reflection (3 minutes). Quiet time to get in touch with whatever part of today's tape moved your heart most deeply.

D. Guided Journaling (Optional — 10 minutes). See Lesson 3.

E. Companion Sharing (5 minutes minimum for each person to share his or her reaction to today's tape and to the past week).

  1. Share with your companion as much as you wish of what is in your heart after seeing this week's tape. Perhaps you will want to share what you have just written during the guided journaling.

  2. Share with your companion how you have experienced the Lord's presence in your life during the previous week. You may wish to share the journal response from last week that touched you the most.

  3. What are you most grateful for now and how do you need Jesus' help?

F. Companion Prayer (since the purpose of this prayer is healing, you may wish to pray over your companion for about 10 minutes). Lay your hands on your companion and pray as Jesus would for about 10 minutes. Let the words and silences in your prayer be those of Jesus as he is already praying in your heart. Give thanks to Jesus for what your companion is most grateful for and pray for whatever healing your companion most needs. Close your prayer by praying that your companion receive the grace of this lesson: *to forgive one person.* Then let your companion pray over you.

G. Group Sharing (Optional — 15 minutes minimum). Take two minutes of silence to ask what has been most difficult and what has been most helpful in your prayer and journaling this past week. Share your reflections with the larger group. Close with a prayer thanking the Lord for the breakthroughs and for discovering the blocks where he is already bringing forth further growth.

H. Closing Snack and Celebration (Optional). An open-ended time to enjoy one another and to continue sharing.

II. Home Experience

A. Daily Healing Prayer (10 minutes). Each day choose one of the following healing or contemplation in action prayers and pray it for at least 10 minutes. These prayers are only *suggestions*. Perhaps you will find yourself drawn to pray what is in your heart using varied breathing, a symbol, a repeated word, a melody, a gesture, a drawing, or a piece of clay which you can mold. Although there are many prayers suggested, it would be best to pray only a few of them, parts of them, or to repeat from this or any other chapter the prayer that most moved your heart. Use whatever way you can best give your heart to Jesus and enter into his heart. Perhaps your prayer will be as simple as looking at a beautiful flower and taking in God's love for you. You may wish to begin your prayer by centering yourself, perhaps using the Breath Prayer (see Lesson 1). You may wish to continue with the Embrace Prayer (see Lesson 3, Prayer #2), or a similar prayer of simply resting in God's love.

  1. *Bargaining Prayer* (Tape Prayer)

    a. Take a crucifix in your hands.

    b. Ask Jesus on the cross whom he wants you to forgive.

    c. Tell Jesus what changes you want in this person before you would be willing to forgive him or her. What would you want that person to never do again? What would you want him or her to apologize for? What could that person say or do that would make it easier for you to forgive?

    d. Look that person in the face with

Jesus. Repeat with Jesus, "Father, forgive (name of person). He (she) did not know what he (she) was doing." Continue until you are saying these words with the same intensity and sincerity as Jesus.

  e. While saying these words of forgiveness with Jesus, breathe out all the conditions and demands for the other to change and breathe in his power to forgive unconditionally. With Jesus, forgive not because it is earned but because it is needed.

2. *Healing a Memory — Detailed Steps*
Take the most difficult hurt that you are trying to forgive and see if any of the steps of the five stages are helpful. (Cf. *Healing Life's Hurts,* pages 218-229.)

3. *Prayer for Receiving the Grace of This Lesson*
Ask Jesus to give you his forgiveness for one person you need to forgive. Breathe it in with every breath and breathe out all the blocks in yourself to being able to forgive this person. (You may wish to pray this prayer with Mary instead of Jesus.)

4. *Leaving a Hurt with Jesus*
If you get in touch with a hurt that you find too painful to think about, simply ask Jesus to heal that part of you and to fill it with his light. Then leave that part of yourself in Jesus' hands, without pushing yourself to focus on it or think about it any longer. You might want to do this before going to sleep at night, or as you go forward at Eucharist to receive Communion (e.g., as you say the words, "Only say the word, Lord, and I shall be healed," invite Jesus into this part of your life and then leave it in his hands).

Note: Only go as deeply into a hurt as you can while continuing to feel loved. When you feel only the pain and no love, you have gone too far, and it is best to simply leave the hurt in Jesus' hands as suggested above.

5. *Water Prayer*
Find a lake, stream or other body of water that is flowing gently. Let yourself enter into the gentle movement of the water, and let it represent for you Jesus' love, flowing over you and washing away any hurt. Perhaps you might even want to get into the water and float there, carried by Jesus' love.

6. *Door Prayer*
  a. Let Jesus bring you to a door which he will open to reveal a scene or person who needs your forgiveness. Perhaps there is a special word on that door, such as "anger," or "father." Take time to see if you recognize anything about the door before you and Jesus open it.
  b. Let Jesus show you how to deal with whatever is on the other side.

7. *Healing Anger and Depression from Being Abandoned*
  a. With Jesus on the cross, cry out to the Father, "My God, my God why have you abandoned me?" Continue until you are crying out those words with the same volume, intensity and feeling tone as Jesus.
  b. After crying out as Jesus did, find the part of your body that feels most tense and most abandoned. Be present to that part of your body and to any memories or situations that trigger the feeling of abandonment. Breathe out into the Father's hands anything that might be behind the tension and the feeling of being abandoned. Continue to do this until that part of the body becomes relaxed.
  c. Ask the Father what is the next simple step in dealing with the feeling of being abandoned, so that more and more every cell of your relaxed body might pray, "Into your hands I commend my spirit."

8. *Eucharist for Another*
At Eucharist, forgive one person by praying for him or her throughout the liturgy and receiving Communion for that person. (Cf. *Healing Life's Hurts,* Chapter 12.)

9. *Rosary Prayer*
Say the whole rosary, or just a decade of the rosary, for a person who has hurt you.

CONTEMPLATION IN ACTION PRAYERS

Take a minute and ask for the grace to forgive one person. Then do one of the following:

10. Spend 10 minutes cleaning an area just as if you were doing it lovingly for a person who has hurt you.
11. Write a letter to a person whom you need to forgive, saying how you are hurt and angry, and how hard you find it to forgive that person. Give the letter to Jesus by burning it, and write how you think he would respond to you.

B. Daily Journal (5 minutes)

1. Spend each day of this lesson forgiving one person thoroughly. You may need to spend more than one day on a person, and perhaps even the entire week. Recall with Jesus when during the prayer or the day you grew most or struggled most in forgiving this person.
2. Write in your journal how Jesus responds (what he seems to do or say in response to what you have told him). If you can't get in touch with Jesus' response, write what most moves you as you speak to him, or what are the most loving words you want to hear.
3. If there is no more struggle to forgive, you may wish to give thanks and choose another person for the remainder of the lesson.

OPTIONAL HOME EXPERIENCES

C. Personal Reflection Questions

1. Recall a time when you struggled to forgive.
   What were your symptoms of denial, anger, bargaining, depression, acceptance?
   What stage are you most likely to get stuck in? Why? What helps?
   What stage is easiest to work through? Why?
2. Are you grateful for where you are struggling to forgive? Why or why not?
3. When did you most experience being forgiven?

D. Scripture Readings

2 Samuel 12:1-24: David's five-stage struggle to forgive and be forgiven.

Luke 15:11-32: The process of forgiving the prodigal son.

Luke 24:13-35: Jesus taking the Emmaus disciples through the process of forgiveness.

1 Corinthians 13: Love is . . .

Romans 5:7-11: God's unconditional love for us.

E. Additional Readings

Healing Life's Hurts, by Dennis Linn, S.J. and Matthew Linn, S.J. (New York: Paulist Press, 1978).

Healing of Memories, by Dennis Linn, S.J. and Matthew Linn, S.J. (New York: Paulist Press, 1974).

Inner Healing: God's Great Assurance, by Theodore Dobson (New York: Paulist Press, 1978).

Inner Healing, by Michael Scanlan (New York: Paulist Press, 1974).

The Gift of Inner Healing, by Ruth Stapleton (Waco: Word Books, 1976).

Inner Healing Through Healing of Memories, by Betty Tapscott (Houston: Betty and Ed Tapscott, 1975).

May I Hate God? by Pierre Wolff (New York: Paulist Press, 1979). Learning to forgive God, and discovering that he shares our anger at suffering and injustice.

FIVE STAGES IN THE COURSE

As you go through this course, you may experience the five stages of forgiveness as painful memories surface. For example, as you get in touch with your difficulties in school it may become harder to do the prayers and journaling because they will resemble assigned school exercises and are even called a "course." Or, if you are working through a memory of being rejected by your mother, you may find yourself feeling rejection from your companion where there is none, or feeling distant from the group leader who reminds you of your mother. When you have more anger or fear than the present situation deserves, the extra anger or fear is probably being displaced from a past painful memory that is slowly being healed as you love and forgive those who irritate you in the present. Following are examples of how the various stages might affect you in the course.

Denial:
: Becoming too busy to journal and pray, or doing these superficially.
: Being unable to really listen and empathize with another.

Anger:
: Becoming critical — of the course, the leader, your companion, another's sharing, those who talk too much or too little, the videotapes, etc.
: Trying to solve other's problems rather than walk with them and love them with Jesus.

Bargaining:
: I would get more out of this course if only . . .
: I could listen better if he or she would . . .

Depression:
: I wish I were doing as well as he or she is doing. I have nothing to share that's worth listening to.

Acceptance:
: Being more grateful for everything and accepting times of struggle as opportunities for growth.
: Being grateful for those in the course who are hard to love and reaching out to them.

If in the chapters ahead you can pinpoint any difficulty you may have and see how it is only a passing stage of growth, you will be able to grow through the struggles.

Lesson Eight
HEALING THROUGH HONEST LOVE

INTRODUCTION

When we have a hard message to say, it can be really difficult to speak to a person honestly and with love. At one time I lived with a friend whose therapist was teaching him to be assertive. So my friend began telling everyone in the house just what he thought. He would criticize others for not washing their dishes, not taking the garbage out often enough, etc., until no one in the house wanted to be around him. One night he came into my room and told me that the car in the garage needed some work. I found myself saying, "I'll try to get to that car this weekend. But I have to tell you something first. The way you're going around this house criticizing everything is really bothering people. You can't do that, and the reason you can't do that is because you don't love those people."

My friend and I had a really good talk that night, and later, when I tried to get in touch with why I had been able to be so honest with him, a couple of things struck me. First, my friend and I really loved each other. The second thing that helped me talk to him was that about a week earlier I had shared with him a communications problem I was having with one of my teachers. He had listened to me and helped me with my problem. So I could say to him, "You have a communications problem with the people in this house just as I have one with one of my teachers." We can confront a person with honesty when we have died to ourselves, and the key to dying to ourselves is knowing how much we're like that person. The more I hate the sin and *love* the sinner in myself and in the other, the more I am ready to confront.

The five stages of forgiveness can help us reach the point where we know our weakness too and are ready to confront another with honest love. In the story of the prodigal son, the father goes through the five stages of forgiveness before he can confront his elder son. At the beginning of the story, the younger son comes to his father and tells him that he wants his inheritance then and there. This is a very deep hurt for the father, because his son is treating him as if he had already died. But the father does not confront the situation; he simple gives his son the money. This is the stage of denial, where the father wants peace at any price and acts as if nothing had happened. The father will be very different at the end of the story, when he goes to his elder son and confronts him.

By the end of the story the father is ready to confront because he has worked through denial and the other four stages of forgiveness. In the second stage, the father is angry. He is angry because he is disappointed that his younger son whom he loves is gone. The elder brother gets angry too, but his anger causes him to turn inward and to refuse to speak to his brother. The father, however, works through anger and turns it into a creative force for change. The father uses the energy of his anger to develop the gifts — the communications skills — that he needs to remedy the situation. Thus when the father goes to his elder son at the end of the story, he is angry too — angry at the potential loss of unity in his family. But the father has seen the good that came when he finally did communicate with the prodigal, and he's willing to begin the whole process of communication again with the elder son.

When the father goes to his elder son, he has worked through the third stage of bargaining. The father goes without any bargains. He says to his son, "Everything I have is yours." The father is telling his elder son, "I am going to be faithful to you whether you change or not." We can confront if we are willing to love that person unconditionally.

The fourth stage that the father moves through is that of depression. When the prodigal son comes home, the father runs out and places his hands on his son's shoulders. In the Middle East, this was a gesture of reconciliation that took place after two people had been in a public argument. Such a gesture said, "We're both at fault; we've both made mistakes; we both have a communications problem." Later, when the father goes to the elder son, he can be one with his son because he knows what it's like to have a communications problem. We can confront people with honest love when we know how we are like them and so we can with empathy hate the sin and love the sinner in them and in us.

Only after the father has gone through the first four stages of forgiveness and reached the stage of acceptance is he ready to confront his elder son. It isn't always the right time to confront with honest love because a person may not be ready to receive it and we may not be ready to give it. At the beginning of the story the father just gives his money away without confronting his son. But at the end of the story there has been enough healing in the family for the father to think that it is time to confront. The father does three important things when he confronts his elder son. First, the father listens undefensively and tries to understand his elder son's world with all its pain. Second, the father tells his elder son that he is loved unconditionally. "*My* son, all that I have is yours." In saying this, the father reminds his son that he belongs to the family, and the father also shows his willingness to do anything for his son that would help strengthen that bond. When we confront someone, it's not the toughness of our love that helps that person to change; rather it's the amount of love that goes with our honesty and our willingness to do whatever it might take to help that person. Third, the father celebrates at a banquet, even if his elder son isn't there. An important part of confronting others is that we are not dependent on their changing and that we can still celebrate and receive life whether they change or not. Our ability to celebrate is an act of trust in God, knowing that he is the Savior and the one who changes hearts. All we can do for others is to give them our honest unconditional love. The rest is up to the Lord.

Just as we need to love others honestly and unconditionally, we need to love parts of ourselves in this way too. Often we treat part of ourselves as the elder brother treated the prodigal. We say to ourselves, "Go away, anger . . . get out, sexual feelings . . . stay away, tiredness . . ." We substitute many things, depending on what parts of ourselves make us uncomfortable. But the Lord wants us to welcome all of our feelings and the energy behind those feelings. Before St. Paul was converted, he was an angry man who used his anger to persecute Christians. After Paul met the Lord, Jesus did not take away Paul's anger but rather helped Paul to use the energy behind it to spread the Gospel throughout the world. When we share our feelings with Jesus, he doesn't take them away from us, but rather uses the energy behind them to help us love him and others more.

There's a way of being with each of our feelings and letting the Lord speak to us through them. For example, when I have strong sexual feelings I share them with the Lord and I say to him, "Let me use the energy behind these feelings in the way you want me to." Sometimes my sexual feelings are telling me that I need to relate to someone in an intimate way, and so I have a quiet conversation with another. Sometimes my feelings are telling me that I need to feel every cell of my body, and so I go jogging. Other times, the Lord is speaking through my sexual feelings to tell me that I need to be creative, and so I go and do some cooking. I find that whatever I am feeling, I can make friends with my feelings by sharing them with the Lord and asking him to reveal to me what it is that my feelings need in order to give and receive his unconditional love.

A baby learning to walk is an image of how change in ourselves or another happens easiest through unconditional love. A loving mother doesn't kick her baby from behind until it stops crawling and gets up and walks. Instead, she first loves her baby no matter what it does. When the child is old enough to walk, the most important thing a mother does is look into its eyes as it takes that first step toward her. It's the amount of love a child feels that gives it the security and courage to try the strange experience of walking. Honest love needs to have as much love as a mother has for her baby, so that a person can take a first step by looking into loving eyes.

I. Group Experience

A. Common Opening Prayer (5 minutes)

B. Video or Audio Tape: "Healing Through Honest Love" (30 minutes)

How can we confront another in a way that is loving and healing?

1. We can confront in a way that will be healing only when we love that person and when we have died to ourselves by seeing how we are like him or her (e.g., Dennis and Pat).
2. Going through the five stages of forgiveness can help us to confront in love (e.g., story of the prodigal son).
   a. Denial Stage: at the beginning of the story the father says and does nothing.
   b. Anger Stage: the father becomes angry at the prodigal for leaving home but channels his anger into discovering more creative ways of communicating.
   c. Bargaining Stage: the father cancels his bargain by saying, "I'll be with you if you change or not."
   d. Depression Stage: seeing that we have the same problem. The father runs to his son and offers a gesture of reconciliation, acknowledging that both have made mistakes.
   e. Acceptance Stage: the father knows he can be closer to the prodigal now than if the hurt had never occurred. Thus, he is ready to face the hurt with his elder son.
   When we have gone through these stages we are ready to confront. We can confront others only when we love them as if they were members of our own family and so would do anything for them to help them grow. A person can change only because of the amount of love that comes with our honesty.
3. We need to welcome home the prodigal in ourselves, receiving our feelings with love rather than treating them like the prodigal and getting rid of them.
4. We can make friends with all of our feelings, letting the Lord use the energy behind them to help us give and receive his love.
5. Honest love means loving as much and as patiently as a mother teaching her baby to walk.

Closing Prayer: asking the Lord to help us love a person whom we want to change.

C. Silent Reflection (3 minutes). Quiet time to get in touch with what part of today's tape moved your heart most deeply.

D. Guided Journaling (Optional — 10 minutes). See Lesson 3.

E. Companion Sharing (5 minutes minimum for each person to share his or her reaction to today's tape and to the past week).

1. Share with your companion as much as you wish of what is in your heart after seeing this week's tape. Perhaps you will want to share what you have just written during the guided journaling.
2. Share with your companion how you have experienced the Lord's presence in your life during the previous week. You may wish to share the journal response from last week that touched you the most.
3. What are you most grateful for now and how do you need Jesus' help?

F. Companion Prayer (since the purpose of this prayer is healing, you may wish to pray over your companion for about 10 minutes). Lay your hands on your companion and pray as Jesus would for about 10 minutes. Let the words and silences in your prayer be those of Jesus as he is already praying in your heart. Give thanks to Jesus for what your companion is most grateful for and pray for whatever healing your companion most needs. Close your prayer by praying that your companion receive the grace of this lesson: *to give honest and unconditional love.* Then let your companion pray over you.

G. Group Sharing (Optional —15 minutes minimum). Take two minutes of silence to ask what has been most difficult and what has been most helpful in your prayer and journaling this past week. Share your reflections with the larger group. Close with a prayer thanking the Lord for the breakthroughs and for discovering the blocks where he is already bringing forth further growth.

H. Closing Snack and Celebration (Optional). An open-ended time to enjoy one another and to continue sharing.

II. Home Experience

A. **Daily Healing Prayer** (10 minutes). Each day choose one of the following healing or contemplation in action prayers and pray it for at least 10 minutes. These prayers are only *suggestions*. Perhaps you will find yourself drawn to pray what is in your heart using varied breathing, a symbol, a repeated word, a melody, a gesture, a drawing, or a piece of clay which you can mold. Although there are many prayers suggested, it would be best to pray only a few of them, parts of them, or to repeat from this or any other chapter the prayer that most moved your heart. Use whatever way you can best give your heart to Jesus and enter into his heart. Perhaps your prayer will be as simple as looking at a beautiful flower and taking in God's love for you. You may wish to begin your prayer by centering yourself, perhaps using the Breath Prayer (see Lesson 1). You may wish to continue with the Embrace Prayer (see Lesson 3, Prayer #2), or a similar prayer of simply resting in God's love.

1. *Prodigal Return* (Tape Prayer)
   a. Prayerfully read how the father welcomes home the prodigal son in Luke 15:20-23: "While he was still a long way off, his father caught sight of him and was deeply moved. He ran out to meet him, threw his arms around his neck, and kissed him. . . . The father said to the servants: 'Quick, bring out the finest robe and put it on him; put a ring on his finger and shoes on his feet. Take the fatted calf and kill it.'" Ask the Father whom he wants you to forgive. Stand with the Father and see this person coming up the road toward you.
   b. Be present with the Father, and through the use of some gesture (perhaps throwing your arms around his neck) welcome the prodigal home. With the Father, hold the prodigal in your arms until you desire all that the Father desires for this person.
   c. Repeat whatever actions are helpful as you begin welcoming with the Father whoever you need to forgive. Do this until you can say every part of the Lord's Prayer for the prodigal, giving him to the Father.

2. *Prayer for Jesus' Anger*
   a. Share with Jesus one way in which you feel you have been treated unjustly by another (perhaps a lie, a broken contract, taking what was yours, etc.).
   b. Just as Jesus was angry at the mistreatment of the man with the withered hand, see how Jesus is angry at the way in which you have been mistreated. He hates the sin and injustice and doesn't want it to happen again.
   c. Ask Jesus to give you the gift of his righteous anger at seeing one he loves mistreated. Then ask him how he wants to help you and be with you, just as he helped the man with the withered hand.

3. *Paradise Prayer*
   a. With Jesus on the cross, look over at the good thief and say, "This day you will be with me in paradise." Repeat this until you, like Jesus, want to give everything possible to the good thief.
   b. Ask Jesus who has hurt you that he wants you to forgive. Repeat the same words with Jesus until you want to give everything possible to the person who has hurt you.

4. *Music Prayer*
   a. With Jesus, listen to your favorite music or song.
   b. Bask in it, as if it is coming from the heart of God just for you.
   c. Play it or sing it again, but this time let it come from your heart toward a person that you are trying to love.

5. *Stations of the Cross*
   a. Make or recall the stations of the cross and let each draw you more deeply into the unconditional forgiveness Jesus gave at each step up Calvary.
   b. When you reach the twelfth station, forgive one person with Jesus.

6. *Plant Prayer*
   a. Let Jesus show you one person who needs love or forgiveness.

b. Hold a flower or plant and let it represent that person, since both share some qualities (fragility, etc.).
c. Spend a few minutes with Jesus loving that plant/person.

7. *Martha Prayer*
a. Read how Jesus confronts Martha (Luke 10:38-42) until you have a feeling for how Jesus confronts.
b. Let Martha's place be taken by someone you need to confront and see if you can sense how Jesus responds.

CONTEMPLATION IN ACTION PRAYERS

Take a minute and ask for the grace to give honest and unconditional love. Then do one of the following:

8. Take someone out to dinner with whom you need to be lovingly honest. Spend the time really loving and enjoying that person. If honest confrontation comes naturally from your deepest love for that person, perhaps try expressing your feelings.
9. Read John 2:13-25, where Jesus sees injustice and cleanses the temple. Ask Jesus to show you one situation that needs to be changed (for example, a child needing attention, a lonely neighbor, an upcoming legislative bill that needs a letter to Congress, a way in which you or another are being treated unjustly). Feel Jesus' anger at seeing someone being hurt. Then let Jesus show you what he would do to the correct the situation, and take the first step in what he wants you to do about it.
10. Spend the day trying to really listen to and enjoy a person whom you find difficult to love and want to change.

B. Daily Journal (5 minutes)

1. Share with Jesus when during this prayer or during the day your heart was deeply moved—perhaps a moment of being grateful for or of longing for healing in *giving honest and unconditional love.*
2. Write in your journal how Jesus responds (what he seems to do or say in response to what you have told him). If you can't

get in touch with Jesus' response, write what most moves you as you speak to to him or what are the most loving words you want to hear.

OPTIONAL HOME EXPERIENCES

C. Personal Reflection Questions

1. When have you really loved another person? Did this lead to hurts? To honest love? Why or why not?
2. When have you been able to confront another person effectively? What helped?
3. Whom might you need to confront soon with honest love? Are you able to listen to them and feel their pain and experience what their world is like? What changes would you want from them? Are you able to love them even if they don't change? Are you able to see any place where your love as fallen short? Can you see any growth coming out of this hurt?
4. What feeling (tiredness, anger, shame, fear, sexual passion, etc.) do you like least? In what way have you been able to become aware of this feeling and use it as a drive to love others more?
5. When have you experienced the difference between anger that leads to loving and anger that becomes hostility (doing or wishing harm to another)?

D. Scripture Readings

Matthew 18: Confrontation in a Christian community.
Luke 10:38-42: Jesus confronts Martha.
Luke 15:11-32: The prodigal son.
John 21: Jesus confronts Peter and loves him, despite Peter's imperfect response.

E. Additional Readings

Healing Life's Hurts, pages 167-169. Role of the five stages of forgiveness and the Beatitudes in honest love.
Learning To Forgive, by Doris Donnelly (New York: Macmillan, 1979).
Feeling and Healing Your Emotions, by Conrad Baars (Plainfield, N.J.: Logos International, 1979).

All of the readings in the preceding three lessons (5, 6 and 7).

Note: You may want to use the following meeting as a Gratitude Session. See Appendix G for suggested format. After the Gratitude Session, you may wish to take a vacation in order to rest and integrate the experience of the course before going on to Lesson 9.

Lesson Nine
HEALING BY LIVING THE EVENTS IN JESUS' LIFE

INTRODUCTION

Often when I pray with people who are struggling, the Lord doesn't take the struggle away immediately. Usually those people experience a sense that Jesus is there taking them through the struggle. But when a person's struggle seems too great and when Jesus doesn't seem to be there at all at first, the Bible can help. Select a passage on a time when Jesus was in the middle of a similar struggle. Once people can focus on Jesus rather than just feel their own pain, and once they know how Jesus moved through his struggle, then they can move through their own struggle.

I (Matt) had an experience of this during my thirty-day retreat two years ago, when I felt unable to pray. I tried everything I knew to change things, but still my prayer was dry. Everyone else around me seemed to be getting a lot out of prayer, and that just made me feel worse. (If you are going through this course with a group, perhaps you feel the same way — as if everyone else is doing better than you.) At first I kept asking the Lord to come and make my prayer better. All I could say was, "Get me out of this! Get me out of this!" But Jesus was waiting for me to say, "Help me to go through this with you, the way you went through the same thing."

What finally helped me was to see how Jesus went through the same thing. In the agony in the garden when he was alone, Jesus too had difficulty praying, and his struggle wasn't taken away. He had to go through it step by step. Jesus cried out, "Father, if it be possible, take this away." That had been my cry during the first part of the retreat. But then came the second part of Jesus'

prayer, "Yet not my will but thine be done." And so I began to pray with Jesus to the Father, "I can't pray, but let me be here for you in it. Let me know that you love me the way you loved Jesus when he was going through the same kind of struggle." That's when I started to feel at peace again. I became aware that I didn't have to earn God's love by perfect prayer. I could be in the midst of a struggle to pray and still know at a completely different level that the part of myself I didn't like — the part of me that was struggling and couldn't pray — was still loved by God. That's the kind of healing that can happen when I enter into where Jesus is struggling and let the way he goes through his struggle bring me into the way I can go through my struggle too.

Sometimes when we enter into a struggle with Jesus, such as dryness in prayer, the struggle doesn't go away immediately, but you have a sense that Jesus is there taking you through it. At other times, the struggle itself goes away. A woman who came to one of our workshops had suffered for many years. Her son had committed suicide by hanging himself, and she blamed herself for his death because she had not loved that son as much as her other children. We led the group through a five-minute prayer and this woman's whole life was changed. She later wrote about her experience: "I saw Jesus covered with perspiration. His body was turning gray because of the lack of oxygen. But something puzzled me. And then I noticed my son was hanging by Jesus' side. Not on a cross — he was hanging from a rope. And then Jesus looked at me, a look full of agony, compassion and love. And he said, 'This day your son will be with me in paradise.' And I really believe Jesus, that that day my son was taken up into heaven. And I want you to rejoice with me and with us over it."

We still hear from this woman's husband, a psychiatrist, who calls us whenever he comes to the United States to tell us what a total change has taken place in his wife. She was healed by entering into a Scripture scene, joining Jesus at the foot of the cross, and letting Jesus do for her what he did for the good thief. As Jesus gave the good thief paradise, he also gave her son paradise.

The tradition of Scripture prayer goes all the way back to Jesus walking with his disciples along the road to Emmaus. The disciples tell Jesus about their struggles, the ways they have been disappointed by the events of the last days. And then they enter into the Scripture that Jesus opens to them, perhaps Psalm 21 where so much of the passion is foretold. Jesus says to them, "Give me your hearts and take on what's in these Scriptures." When they did this, their hearts were changed until they were "burning within them." Thus the disciples were able to return with new hope and vigor to the community where they had been so hurt. Scripture prayer is getting into where Jesus has walked through a struggle like ours and letting him make sense out of it for us as he did for the Emmaus disciples when they gave him their reactions and took on his reactions. Scripture prayer heals us because we're sharing our struggle with someone who loves us and who can walk through that struggle with us.

I find that Scripture prayer can be an everyday experience if I continually ask myself, "What event in Jesus' life is he living out in me right now?" One day last summer I was in a big circus tent having a joyful reunion with six hundred other Jesuits whom I hadn't seen in several years. I could almost hear the Lord saying, "These are my beloved people with whom I am well pleased." I felt as if I were at the transfiguration, and with Moses I wanted to say, "Let's put up a few tents and just stay here forever." Shortly after that I went back home. I was working on the front yard, where I had planted some new grass. A car came down the street and the people inside it threw out some beer bottles, right on my new grass. At that moment, I didn't feel as though I was at the transfiguration any longer. I felt really angry, wanting to throw the bottles back at those people in the car. Angry and disgusted, I stopped working and went inside. I was living out a whole different event in Jesus' life. I felt violated, not respected — and when I asked Jesus "When did you feel the way I feel?" I thought of him on the way to the cross falling down for the third time. I had an image of Jesus feeling violated and not respected as people threw sticks and stones at him. Then I heard Jesus say, "Father, forgive them; they know not what they are doing." Jesus was asking me to grow and be able to forgive even when I felt violated and not respected. So I was able to go back outside and pick up the beer bottles on my new grass and say, "Father, forgive them." I had shared my struggle with Jesus and he took me beyond where I could have gone myself.

You can ask yourself what event Jesus is living out in you right now as you go through this course. Perhaps you have found Scripture prayer helpful before, and as you read this you feel very affirmed, as Jesus did at the transfiguration. Perhaps you can hear the Father saying to you, "This is my beloved son — or daughter — with whom I am well pleased." Or maybe you're saying to yourself, "I've tried all this before and prayer doesn't work and nothing seems to change." If so, you may be feeling like Jesus during the agony in the garden when he got up and down three times, unable to pray and feeling so much desolation. In every experience of your life you can ask Jesus, "What event are you living out inside of me right now?" As St. Paul says, "It's no longer I who live, but Christ lives in me" (Galatians 2:20). Scripture prayer happens when you ask Jesus how he's thinking and feeling inside of you and when you share with him how you're thinking and feeling. Then you begin to walk through life together.

The first step in Scripture prayer which helps you to walk through life with Jesus is to find an event in Jesus' life when he was having an experience like yours. The next step is to read the passage that describes this event. Read it three times: once to understand it with your mind; the second time, to enter into what Jesus is experiencing and to love him in it; the third time, to let Jesus love you and show you how he would go through anything for you. After you have read the passage three times, enter into any part of the scene in any way that you want to. The important thing is not to have a perfect technicolor image of the scene, but to surrender to Jesus and be with him so that you can take on his heart. The scene will be healing for you to the extent that you can be with Jesus, loving and being loved in it. (See Appendix C, "Scripture Prayer Helps," for further suggestions.)

One scene that we can all enter into is Jesus' birth. A psychiatrist who works with schizophrenic children told us that she prays for these children to share Jesus' birth and to be held by Mary and Joseph in that stable. As they begin to experience the perfect love of a mother and a father, missing in their own early years, they stop hallucinating and their condition improves. This psychiatrist discovered Scripture prayer when she herself was being prayed with because she was not comfortable having others hug her. During the prayer she felt as if she were a six-month-old baby cradled in Mary's arms. During the following months she returned to this prayer many times and always felt as if she were being healed in some way, but she did not know how. She only knew that all she wanted to do in prayer was rest in Mary's arms and take in the perfect love of a mother. As she did this, she began to find that for the first time she could let others hug her. So, finally, one day she said to her own mother, "I don't understand why I'm praying this way. Did anything happen to me when I was six months old?" Her mother said, "When you were six months old, you had a rash and you were covered with blisters. For several weeks I could not hold you. No one could touch you because it was too painful for you." Jesus shared his birth with this woman, so that years later, as an adult, she could receive from Mary what she had lost as a six-month-old baby. Whether we enter a scene at Jesus' birth or at his death, he wants to share that part of his life with us and give us all that we need.

I. GROUP EXPERIENCE

A. **Common Opening Prayer** (5 minutes)

B. **Video or Audio Tape:** "Healing by Living the Events in Jesus' Life" (30 minutes)

How can we find Jesus in the midst of a struggle?
1. When we are experiencing a struggle as too big for us, finding a part of Scripture in which Jesus works his way through a similar struggle can help. Sometimes Jesus answers our prayer by leading us through a struggle with him, rather than getting us out of it right away (e.g., Matt's thirty-day retreat).
2. Sometimes entering into a passage of Scripture with Jesus can even bring total healing of our situation (e.g., woman whose son had killed himself and who was able to enter into the passage about Jesus and the good thief).
3. Praying the events in Scripture is an important part of the tradition of the Church, beginning with the Emmaus disciples (e.g., an Ignatian retreat).
4. Why is praying the events in Jesus' life so healing? It's the sharing of our struggle with someone who will listen and lovingly respond that heals us (e.g., A.A., woman afraid of being hit).
5. Scripture prayer can become an everyday experience by asking, "What event in Jesus' life is he living out in me right now?" (e.g., Jesuit reunion, beer bottles on the lawn). Scripture prayer happens when we ask Jesus how he is thinking and feeling inside of us, when we share with him how we are thinking and feeling . . . and we walk through life together.
6. How to pray the events in Jesus' life.
   a. Read the passage three times:
      First, to understand with the mind.
      Second, to love Jesus in the scene.
      Third, to let Jesus love us.
   b. Enter into the scene with Jesus, taking on his heart.
7. One scene we may all need to enter into is Jesus' birth (e.g., woman who had a rash as a six-month-old baby and needed to be held by Joseph and Mary).

Closing Prayer: to experience ourselves with Jesus being held as an infant by Joseph and Mary.

C. **Silent Reflection** (3 minutes). Quiet time to get in touch with what part of today's tape moved your heart most deeply.

D. **Guided Journaling** (Optional—10 minutes). See Lesson 3.

E. **Companion Sharing** (5 minutes minimum for each person to share his or her reaction to today's tape and to the past week).

1. Share with your companion as much as you wish of what is in your heart after seeing this week's tape. Perhaps you will want to share what you have just written during the guided journaling.
2. Share with your companion how you have experienced the Lord's presence in your life during the previous week. You may wish to share the journal response from last week that touched you the most.

3. What are you most grateful for now and how do you need Jesus' help?

F. **Companion Prayer** (since the purpose of this prayer is healing, you may wish to pray over your companion for about 10 minutes). Lay your hands on your companion and pray as Jesus would for about 10 minutes. Let the words and silences in your prayer be those of Jesus as he is already praying in your heart. Give thanks to Jesus for what your companion is most grateful for and pray for whatever healing your companion most needs. Close your prayer by praying that your companion receives the grace of this lesson: *that your thoughts, feelings and actions be joyful reminders of Jesus' presence within you.*

G. **Group Sharing** (Optional—15 minutes minimum). Take two minutes of silence to ask what has been most difficult and what has been most helpful in your prayer and journaling this past week. Share your reflections with the larger group. Close with a prayer thanking the Lord for the breakthroughs and for discovering the blocks where he is already bringing forth further growth.

H. **Closing Snack and Celebration** (Optional). An open-ended time to enjoy one another and to continue sharing.

II. Home Experience

A. **Daily Healing Prayer** (10 minutes). Each day choose one of the following healing or contemplation in action prayers and pray it for at least 10 minutes. These prayers are only *suggestions*. Perhaps you will find yourself drawn to pray what is in your heart using varied breathing, a symbol, a repeated word, a melody, a gesture, a drawing, or a piece of clay which you can mold. Although there are many prayers suggested, it would be best to pray only a few of them, parts of them, or to repeat from this or any other chapter the prayer that most moved your heart. Use whatever way you can best give your heart to Jesus and enter into his heart. Perhaps your prayer will be as simple as looking at a beautiful flower and taking in God's love for you. You may wish to begin your prayer by centering yourself, perhaps using the Breath Prayer (see Lesson 1). You may wish to continue with the Embrace Prayer (see Lesson 3, Prayer #2), or a similar prayer of simply resting in God's love.

You may wish to begin your prayer with "Scripture Prayer Helps" (Appendix C), using whatever suggestions you find helpful for entering into Scripture prayer.

1. *Healing Our Birth by Sharing Jesus' Infancy* (Tape Prayer)
   a. Picture the stable in Bethlehem where Jesus was born. See Mary and Joseph each in turn pick up Jesus and tenderly love him.
   b. See your parents standing next to Mary and Joseph, holding you as an infant. Let Mary hold you and fill you up with all the love your mother was unable to give you from the time you first came into her womb. Then let Joseph's strong hands cradle you and fill you up with the love and security your father was unable to give.

2. Jesus wants to share every part of himself with us. What do you most need from him (e.g., his childhood, his family, his compassion, his courage, his righteous anger, his perfect manhood, etc.)? Find a passage that speaks to you of what you most need. Read the passage prayerfully, asking Jesus to give you that part of himself.

   Jesus gives us Mary as our mother. She, too, will share with us every part of herself. What do you most need from her (e.g., her love for Jesus or Joseph, her trust of the Father, her perfect femininity, etc.)? Find a passage that speaks to you of what you most need from Mary, and ask Jesus to share his mother with you in this way.

3. *Prayer Through Touch*
   Choose an event in Scripture where someone touches Jesus (e.g., Mary holding the infant Jesus or her crucified son, Luke 7:36-50, Luke 8:40-48, etc.).
   a. Through the way you touch and stroke him, reverently hold Jesus. Express how much you love him.
   b. Through the way Jesus touches you, experience his infinite love for you.

4. *Prayer Through a Word*
   Choose an event in Scripture where there is a key word spoken to Jesus or to someone close to him (e.g., Mary's "Yes" to the angel, a time when Jesus says "Father" or "Peace"). Listen to whatever words in the passage you need to take into your spirit, such as, "As the Father sent me, I send you."
   a. Enter into the mystery of the word, and into a deep silence in the presence of Jesus, the Word. Listen to the word being said to Jesus or to someone close to him and let it roll into your spirit with its power and life.
   b. When your whole spirit vibrates with it, slowly say the word just as deeply as it was said in the passage. Give a deeper part of yourself each time you say it until you are sending it forth with your whole heart just as Mary did with her total "Yes."

5. *Prayer Through a Gaze*
   Choose an event in Scripture where Jesus is looking at someone (e.g. at Mary at his feet in Luke 10:38-42, at Zacchaeus in Luke 19:1-10, at John and Mary in John 19:25-27, at Peter in John 21, etc.).
   a. Just as a mother can spend hours lovingly gazing at her baby without a word, look at Jesus in the scene. Let the way you smile and look at him say all.
   b. Then let Jesus look at you and drink in all that his face says.

6. *Prayer Through Walking*
   Choose an event in Jesus' life where he is walking (e.g., to heal Jairus' daughter, to Lazarus' family, with determination to Jerusalem, up Calvary, etc.).
   a. Make a pilgrimage to a church or find a special spot where you can walk (in your imagination or with real steps) with Jesus until you feel his pace and all that makes him move faster or slower.
   b. Continue taking in Jesus' heart, with each step moving you deeper and deeper into what Jesus is experiencing.

7. *Prayer Through Resting*
   Take your favorite Scripture passage and read it three times: once for meaning, once to love Jesus, and the third time to be loved by Jesus. Enter into the scene at the point where you felt most loved by Jesus and just rest in that love.

8. *Prayer Through Breathing*
   Choose an event in Jesus' life and ask Jesus to reveal to you all that he takes in from the Father and all that he gives to others in that event.
   a. With Jesus breathe in from the Father all the compassion, courage, clarity of truth — whatever is needed. Use a word if it helps you.
   b. Then, with Jesus, breathe out all that he gives to the others in the scene. Use a word if it helps (e.g., "Peace," "Your sins are forgiven," etc.).
   c. Continue to do this, becoming more like Jesus with each breath until you are aware only of being Jesus. As you become Jesus, follow his heart in being with the Father and with others.

9. *Living with Jesus Now*
   a. Ask for the gift of discovering and appreciating what event Jesus is living out in you now.
   b. Review the last day. What event or events focus for you the growth and struggle of the last day?
   c. Share that event with Jesus and then ask him when in his life he experienced the same thing and how he grew from it.
   d. Let him share with you the similarities and differences between how he experienced that event in his own life and how he lives it out in you now. Let him tell you which of the feelings and thoughts that you experienced were his also.
   e. If you are still struggling to love and forgive someone, allow Jesus to say and do those things which will help you take the first step in becoming whole.

Option: You might repeat this exercise, but instead of reviewing the past day, review the past year, or a period of your life (e.g., childhood, adolescence), or the event in your life that most cripples you.

10. *Loving with Jesus*
Pick out a person you would like to be able to love more. Ask Jesus for the gift of knowing how he lives in that person.
   a. Let Jesus reveal to you one way or one event that shows how that person is growing or struggling.
   b. Let Jesus share with you an event in his life when he experienced the same thing.
   c. Let him share with you the similarities between how he experienced that event in his own life and how he experiences that event as he lives it out in that person. Let him tell you which of the feelings and thoughts that person experiences are Jesus' feelings and thoughts.

11. *Struggling with Jesus*
Read a passage of Scripture where Jesus is struggling (e.g., in prison, dying, thrown out of town, etc.).
   a. Ask him where or in what people in your city he is going through the same struggle now.
   b. (Optional) If you wish, make a pilgrimage to that place in your city. As you take each step, ask for the gift of experiencing how Jesus now struggles within those people.
   c. Ask Jesus to show you the next simple step he wants you to take in caring for him in that situation.

12. *Jesus Living in the Key Events of Our Life*
   a. Ask for the gift of seeing how Jesus has lived in your life.
   b. In one column, write down four or five key events of growth and struggle in your life. In the next column, put down the event in Jesus' life where he grew and struggled in the same way.

   Example:

My key moments of growth and struggle	Jesus' key moments of growth and struggle
Death of John	Death of Lazarus
General Confession	Baptism by John
South America	Agony in Garden
Healing of Pauline	Healing of Cripple

   c. Let Jesus share with you the similarities and differences between how he experienced that event in his life and how he experienced that event as he lived it out in you.
   d. Walk with Jesus through one of these events in his life and take in all you need to heal the event in your own life. For example, into the abandonment that I felt at John's death, I take in Jesus' conviction that the Father never abandons him but always hears him.

13. *Sharing Jesus' Struggle*
   a. Get in touch with a way in which you are struggling, and also a moment in Jesus' life when he struggled in the same way.
   b. Listen to how Jesus prayed to the Father in that time of struggle.
   c. Get in touch with how Jesus within you is now praying to the Father in the midst of your struggle. Pray Jesus' prayer in just the way that he is already praying it within you.

14. *Praying with Jesus*
   a. Recall the time when you had the most difficulty praying, or a time when you wished you could pray as well as someone else.
   b. Read the account of Jesus' agony in Mark 14:32, where his prayer is dry and restless and he tries three times to get others to pray with him. Eventually he will feel so distant from the Father that he will cry out, "My God, my God, why have you forsaken me" (Mark 15:34).
   c. Let him share with you how he grew and struggled during that time of dryness, and how he grows and struggles in you in your own time of dryness in prayer.

CONTEMPLATION IN ACTION PRAYERS

Take a minute and ask for the grace to have the thoughts, feelings and actions of Jesus. Then do one of the following:

15. Prayerfully read Galatians 2:19: "It is no longer I who live, but Christ lives in me." Ask for the gift of seeing how Jesus is alive in another person. Then share with that person what event of Jesus' life you see Jesus living out in him or her today.

16. Get in touch with something you are struggling with. Ask Jesus to help you see which of the feelings and yearnings in that struggle are his. Then allow Jesus to say and do those things for you that will bring you a step closer to wholeness. Finally, visit someone else with the same struggle and let yourself be Jesus for that person as you say and do the things that will bring that person closer to wholeness.

17. Ask Jesus to show you how to really enjoy him. Then enjoy him in a friend. Spend a moment at the end of the day enjoying Jesus as you enjoyed your friend.

18. Hold a baby and get in touch with how Mary or Joseph held Jesus, or what Jesus experienced as he held a big finger in his powerless hand.

19. Before going to sleep, imagine yourself in Jesus' life as a child sleeping on his knee, John leaning against his heart at the Last Supper, an apostle breathing in peace in the upper room, etc. Let this enter into you as you fall asleep. When you wake up, immediately try to recall the same scene and rest in it again for a moment.

B. Daily Journal (5 minutes)

1. Share with Jesus when during this prayer or during the day your heart was deeply moved—perhaps a moment of being grateful for or of longing for healing in *having the thoughts, feelings and actions of Jesus.*

2. Write in your journal how Jesus responds (what he seems to do or say in response to what you have told him). If you can't get in touch with Jesus' response, write what most moves you as you speak to him or what are the most loving words you want to hear.

OPTIONAL HOME EXPERIENCES

C. Personal Reflection Questions

1. What passages of Scripture have meant the most to you at difficult times in your life? What did they draw out of you, invite you to?

2. What event (or Gospel story) in Jesus' life do you enjoy recalling most? When in your life have you most allowed Jesus within you to live in that same way?

3. In the nativity (crib) scene, how would you enter into it now? Who would you be? What would you say? Where would you place yourself? Is this different from the way you would have entered into the scene one year ago? Five years ago?

4. Have you ever experienced gifts coming from dryness in prayer? What helps or hinders you in receiving such gifts?

5. Who is the person in your life most like Jesus? In what ways is that person like Jesus? When was Jesus most like that person?

6. When have you experienced healing from being with a person who was suffering in the same way you were? Have you ever experienced your suffering becoming worse by being with a person who was suffering in the same way? What makes the difference?

D. Scripture Readings

Luke 24:13-35: Jesus revealing the Scriptures at Emmaus.
Matthew 6:5-13: Pray to the Father in secret.
Matthew 7:7-12, 15-23: The power of prayer that leads to the Father.
Luke 4:1-21: Jesus' prayer for forty days of self-denial and silent listening to his scriptural mission.
Luke 6:12-15: Praying all night over the Father's choices.
Luke 22:29-46: Prayerfully stating his will, yet surrendering to the Father.
John 17: Jesus praying to the Father for us.

E. Additional Readings

Reading Scripture as the Word of God, by George Martin (Ann Arbor: Word of Life, 1975).
When the Well Runs Dry: Prayer Beyond the Beginnings, by Thomas Green (Notre Dame: Ave Maria, 1979).

Lesson Ten
HEALING BY DISCOVERING OUR SIN

INTRODUCTION

Why is it that our crime rate soars and packs our prisons, and that the rate of mental illness has soared to such an extent that the mentally ill now occupy one out of six hospital beds? Dr. Karl Menninger, psychiatrist and founder of the world-famous Menninger Clinic, answers in *Whatever Became of Sin?* that our prisons and mental institutions are bulging because modern man cannot discover his sin.[1] Menninger pleads that we again make the healthy discovery that we are sinners, because a sinner is one who says, "I am *responsible* for my unloving actions and I can *change.*" When we hurt ourselves or another, we have a choice of ignoring it and letting the destructive pattern continue, or of recognizing the evil and correcting it. Dr. Menninger states three options for altering a destructive pattern of behavior. The first option is imprisonment, on the assumption that we are responsible and can't reform; the second option is mental hospitalization, on the assumption that we are mentally ill and don't know the evil we are doing. But the third and only healthy option is to see ourselves as healthy and responsible sinners who want to change and can change. The power to change comes when, as healthy sinners, we hate the sin and love the sinner. If we do not hate our sin, we become insensitive to our sin rather than anxious to correct it. If we do not love the sinner, we become depressed and scrupulous with no power to correct our destructiveness. The discovery of our sin, then, is a healthy discovery because it means we see our destructiveness, take responsibility for it, and, with God loving and empowering us, take steps to change the evil that can be changed.

It is healthy but difficult to discover our sin.

One of the easiest ways for me (Dennis) to get in touch with my sinfulness and especially what I cannot forgive in myself is to see where I overreact to another. Very often I overreact to the evil in another because the evil is in me. I call this overreaction "sawdusting,"[2] because Scripture says: "Why do you look at the speck of sawdust in your brother's eye and pay no attention to the plank in your own eye? How can you say to your brother, 'Let me take the speck out of your eye,' when all the time there is a plank in your own eye? You hypocrite, first take the plank out of your own eye and then you will see clearly to remove the speck from your brother's eye" (Matthew 7:3-5).

An example of sawdusting happened to me two years ago when I was making my thirty-day retreat in an inner city neighborhood where many transients live. I noticed that every time I saw one of these transients coming toward me, I would cross the street so we wouldn't have to meet. I wondered what my reaction meant, and at liturgy one day I decided to pray about the transients. At first I thought, "There's no sawdusting going on here because I'm so different from those transients. They feel hopeless. They're depressed. They've given up on life. They don't work and they drink. I'm not depressed. I haven't given up on life. I work . . . once in a while, and I don't drink. I'm not like those transients at all."

But as I experienced more what life was like for the transients, it became apparent to me that the reason many of these people were hopeless was that life had demanded too much from them, and so they dropped out. Likewise the reason that I crossed the street was because I feared that these transients would demand too much from me. I was afraid that they would ask me for more help than I could give to them, and so I dropped out by

---

1. Karl Menninger, M.D., *Whatever Became of Sin?* (New York: Hawthorn, 1973).
2. Sawdusting includes not only projection (when the evil

seen in another is not there but really within oneself), but also objective perception of evil that is actually there within another as well as in oneself.

crossing the street. We were both the same; we each had our ways of "dropping out" when life's demands were too great. One of the most healing things I did during my retreat was to bake some cookies to share with the transients. As we ate cookies together that evening in friendship, I could begin to forgive the side of myself that drops out. When I am sawdusting, usually my first reaction is, "I'm not like those people at all. I'm very different from those transients." But if I look at my attitudes and feelings, I find out how much I am like them. My attitudes and those of the transients were the same: I didn't want any more to do with people who demanded something from me. My feelings were the same: those of fear and isolation. I find that the easiest way for me to get in touch with my sawdusting and sinfulness, with my feelings and attitudes that need to be changed, is to ask who it is that I most avoid.

But when I (Matt) am not in touch with my sawdusting, I can get in touch with my sinfulness most easily by thinking of it as ingratitude. For example, two things I am grateful for are that the Lord often hears my prayers for healing and that I have a close relationship with my brother Dennis. These gifts the Lord has given me, and sin is any way in which I am ungrateful for these gifts or abuse them. I can abuse the gift of praying for people when I overuse it and get exhausted so I can't pray for anyone. Or I can underuse it when I walk past a person for whom the Lord wants me to pray. Since others are also gifts to me, I also sin when I overuse or underuse their gifts. For example, my relationship with Dennis is a gift and I sin when I call him to pray too much or too little with others. In any way his gifts fail to grow, our relationship has less life and fails to grow. So, if I want to get in touch with my sinfulness, all I have to do is find my gifts by asking, "What am I grateful for?" I can find my sins if I am aware of my gifts. A gift is given to love with, and sin is any way that I fail to love by overusing or underusing a gift.

Just as I can find out what my sins are by looking at my gifts, so too I can find out what my gifts are by looking at my sins — because both sin and gift come from the same drive. A drive becomes a gift when its energy is used to love and a sin when its energy is not used to love. For example, Peter had an impetuous drive to be first. He was the first to get in trouble by walking on water, by claiming he would never desert Jesus even if all others did, and by defending Jesus with his sword in the garden. This drive to act first was the source of his sinful pride that made him rely too much on his own initiative and too little on God's until, left to his own strength, he denied Jesus. But when the risen Jesus meets Peter on the lakeshore (John 21), Jesus doesn't ask Peter to squelch his desire to be first but simply to channel it into loving leadership for feeding his sheep. In the same manner, Jesus asks us to take the twisted drive behind sin and let that drive become the gift it was meant to be by loving as Peter did.

Perhaps the main reason the Lord wants us to look at our sins is so that we will know where our gifts are. The time when I (Dennis) sinned the most in my life was when I went to South America to live in a community and teach in a school. The people in that community didn't have much hope and thus they didn't communicate with each other. For the first month or two I tried to bring everyone together. But finally I got angry and disgusted. I gave up on the school and the community and decided to do what I wanted. So I spent the next eight months traveling around South America. During that time I experienced most of the capital sins. I was full of pride, putting myself first and saying, "I don't care about anyone else." I felt the most sexual temptations of any time in my life. I was angry and I was slothful.

But the same drive that led to my sins led to my gifts. Most of my gifts that I value developed from that sinful time in South America when I struggled with my drive of intimacy in the midst of loneliness and discouragement. For instance, one gift I value is that of building community. Several times Jesuits have asked me to be "superior" of a community. The "superior" is the name we give to the person responsible for building community and bringing people together. I can do this well because after I returned from South America, I began to develop the gifts I needed to build close communities so that fewer people would have to go through what I did. Another gift I value is my prayer life. But it was South America that made me become serious about prayer. Living such an isolated life there, I realized that unless I had a steady relationship with Jesus, I might just as well leave the Jesuits and get married. Thus many of the gifts that I have today came out of the most sinful time in my life.

An example which brings together the ideas of sawdusting and of sin and gift is the Pieta, Michelangelo's statue of Mary holding Jesus. A few years ago an angry person took a hammer and mutilated Mary's face. That man had so much darkness in him that he could look at a beautiful work of art and see in it something that had to be destroyed. Sawdusting is when the darkness inside of us jumps out toward another person and we say, "There's evil there." We want the other to change or even be destroyed, when really the evil is inside of us, and we're just like what we see in the other person. The damage to the Pieta also illustrates the idea of sin and gift, because what made it such a traumatic event for the whole world was that it was so beautiful, so gifted that the least little mark was a tragedy. The more we see our beauty and our giftedness, the more we will also know our sin. If we don't see our gifts, then we won't know that even a little mark is a tragedy in God's eyes. Perhaps the most beautiful thing about the Pieta is that it shows what God does with sin. God repairs sin, and he brings out more beauty than before. Many master artists worked on the Pieta to repair it so that now you can't tell that it was damaged, and it even has a whole new beauty. That's the way sin is with us. It can bring forth a whole new beauty that's inside of us if we just let ourselves be loved by the Lord.

While many master artists have looked at the Pieta and chosen to treasure it as a gift, a madman looked at that same Pieta and chose to destroy it. Each time we remember a sinful event in our life, we are offered the same choice: to choose to treasure the event as gift or to choose to destroy it. In the story of the prodigal son, two people look at the same event of the prodigal coming home and react very differently. For the elder brother, it's a devastation. For the father, it's the greatest gift. The father can say, "Yes, I hate the destruction that happened here through sin. But gifts are coming out of it. Now my son and I can be closer than we ever were before." The challenge is to look at our sin and see the gift that the Lord sees and promises to bring forth. "We know that God makes all things work together, for the good of those who love him" (Romans 8:28).

I. Group Experience

A. Common Opening Prayer (5 minutes)

B. Video or Audio Tape: "Healing by Discovering Our Sin" (30 minutes)

Why is it that if we don't forgive another, the Father cannot forgive us?
1. In the story of the prodigal son, the elder brother will not forgive the prodigal. The elder brother has projected his sin onto the prodigal.
2. We can get in touch with our own sinfulness by seeing who it is that we over-

react to or avoid, for that is the person in whom we see our own darkness (e.g., inner city transients, woman who disliked communists).
3. Sin is ingratitude for our gifts and abuse of them. If we want to find out what our sins are, we can look at our gifts. If we want to discover our gifts, we can look at our sins — for they are twisted drives which were originally given to us as gifts by the Lord (e.g., Mary Magdalene, Pieta).
4. The most important reason for us to look at our sin is to discover where our gifts are. The most sinful times in our lives can become the most gifted because those are the times when Jesus meets us, forgives us, and gifts us (e.g., Dennis in South America).

Closing Prayer: to accept Jesus' forgiveness and to be grateful for the gift of one part of our body.

C. Silent Reflection (3 minutes). Quiet time to get in touch with what part of today's tape moved your heart most deeply.

D. Guided Journaling (Optional — 10 minutes). See Lesson 3.

E. Companion Sharing (5 minutes minimum for each person to share his or her reaction to today's tape and to the past week).
1. Share with your companion as much as you wish of what is in your heart after seeing this week's tape. Perhaps you will want to share what you have just written during the guided journaling.
2. Share with your companion how you have experienced the Lord's presence in your life during the previous week. You may wish to share the journal response from last week that touched you the most.
3. What are you most grateful for now and how do you need Jesus' help?

F. Companion Prayer (since the purpose of this prayer is healing, you may wish to pray over your companion for about 10 minutes). Lay your hands on your companion and pray as Jesus would for about 10 minutes. Let the words and silences in your prayer be those of Jesus as he is already praying in

your heart. Give thanks to Jesus for what your companion is most grateful for and pray for whatever healing your companion most needs. Close your prayer by praying that your companion receive the grace of this lesson: *to recognize how he or she is tempted to sin, especially by overusing or underusing gifts.* Then let your companion pray over you.

G. **Group Sharing** (Optional — 15 minutes minimum). Take two minutes of silence to ask what has been most difficult and what has been most helpful in your prayer and journaling this past week. Share your reflections with the larger group. Close with a prayer thanking the Lord for the breakthroughs and for discovering the blocks where he is already bringing forth further growth.

H. **Closing Snack and Celebration** (Optional). An open-ended time to enjoy one another and to continue sharing.

II. Home Experience

A. **Daily Healing Prayer** (10 minutes). Each day choose one of the following healing or contemplation in action prayers and pray it for at least 10 minutes. These prayers are only *suggestions*. Perhaps you will find yourself drawn to pray what is in your heart using varied breathing, a symbol, a repeated word, a melody, a gesture, a drawing, or a piece of clay which you can mold. Although there are many prayers suggested, it would be best to pray only a few of them, parts of them, or to repeat from this or any other chapter the prayer that most moved your heart. Use whatever way you can best give your heart to Jesus and enter into his heart. Perhaps your prayer will be as simple as looking at a beautiful flower and taking in God's love for you. You may wish to begin your prayer by centering yourself, perhaps using the Breath Prayer (see Lesson 1). You may wish to continue with the Embrace Prayer (see Lesson 3, Prayer #2), or a similar prayer of simply resting in God's love.

1. *Pieta Prayer* (Tape Prayer)
   a. With Mary at the foot of the cross, hold the cold, torn body of Jesus and feel his wounds. Do this until you share Mary's deeper anguish — that Jesus has given his last drop of blood and yet those he healed still reject him and his forgiveness.
   b. Tell Mary that you want his death to make a difference to you. Hold Jesus, and with the words, "Lord Jesus, mercy," breathe in Jesus' forgiveness. With a sorrow that grows with each breath, hunger for his mercy as you hunger for air. Let your breath filled with Jesus' mercy flow into and cleanse each part of your body that Jesus has gifted and that you have abused. Ask Jesus to reveal the sin of each part of your body. For example, how much have you used your ears, mouth, hands, etc. for listening, speaking or reaching out too much or too little? Let your breath cleanse with mercy your ears, mouth, hands, heart, reproductive organs — each part where Jesus reveals sin.
   c. As you breathe Jesus' mercy into each part, consecrate that part and its gifts to the Father.
   d. Look at Mary and soak up her smile as she sees Jesus living in you.

2. Every sin is the distortion or misuse of what was originally given to us as a gift by the Father. (See example on p. 70.)
   a. Ask Jesus to help you get in touch with what you feel is your greatest sin.
   b. Ask Jesus to reveal to you the gift that lies beneath this sin.
   c. Ask Jesus to redeem this part of you, restoring what you feel is your sin to the gift that it was originally intended to be.
   d. With your breathing, inhale the light of Jesus, receiving his gift with each breath. Exhale the fear, darkness and hurt that have caused this gift to become distorted and sinful.

3. *Prayer for Healing Sexuality*
   a. Read Luke 7:36-50, the story of the penitent woman, whose "many sins must have been forgiven her, or she would not have shown such great love." Kneel at the feet of Jesus and

listen to the Pharisees point out all the times you have misused your sexual energy and fallen into sin.

b. Rejoice with Jesus that he has forgiven you a debt of five hundred rather than fifty so that you can love him that much more.

c. Thank Jesus for that same sexual energy that now gifts you with the power to love him intimately.

d. Take a deep breath and draw in the love of the Spirit. Ask the Spirit to protect and heal your sexual energy so that you can intimately love him and others.

4. *Sin and Gift Prayer*
   a. Read John 21:15-20. Peter denied Jesus three times by not using his gift of courage. In John 21, Jesus invited Peter to use the gift of courage to love him and feed his sheep.

   b. While on the lakeshore, look Jesus in the eye and ask him to reveal to you the gifts you have for feeding his lambs and sheep.

   c. Ask Jesus to reveal to you how, like Peter, you can underuse or overuse each gift to hurt yourself or another. You may wish to write down the sins that occur when you underuse or overuse a particular gift.

   d. Like Peter, tell Jesus how you love him and depend on him to call forth your gifts.

5. Prayerfully read Isaiah 41:17-19 and Isaiah 35:1.

   "The afflicted and the needy seek water in vain. I, the Lord will answer them. I will turn the desert into a marshland and the dry ground into springs of water. I will plant in the desert the cedar and olive together with the pine."   Isaiah 41:17-19

   "Let the wilderness and the dry lands exult, let the wasteland rejoice and bloom, let it bring forth flowers like the jonquil, let it rejoice and sing for joy."
   Isaiah 35:1

   Think of a desire or drive in your life that you experience as a problem or an affliction and that makes you feel dry and barren. With gesture, become a parched seed buried in the barren desert

sand. When you are ready to allow your desire or drive to become a gift, feel the springs of fresh water crack the earth around you. Begin to break through the soil and gradually become a blossoming flower or a tree with uplifted branches. Allow your blossoming flower or uplifted branches to bask in the sun (the light of Christ).

6. *Elder Brother Prayer*
   a. Prayerfully read the reply of the elder brother to his father in Luke 15:29-31: "For years now I have slaved for you. I never disobeyed one of your orders, yet you never gave me so much as a kid goat to celebrate with my friends. Then, when this son of yours returns after having gone through your property with loose women, you kill the fatted calf for him."

   b. Choose one person you need to forgive and, like the elder brother, tell the Father what you don't like about that person. Include what behavior (sold all the property, associated with immoral people) and attitudes (doesn't give a damn about anyone, thinks he or she is the center of the universe, etc.) you don't like.

   c. Let the Father show you the feelings (sadness, anger, loneliness, etc.) in that person's heart that trigger such attitudes and behaviors.

   d. Ask the Father to reveal to you when you have experienced the same feelings (perhaps even in regard to this person you need to forgive). Let the Father show you how those feelings lead to similar attitudes and perhaps to unloving behavior.

   e. Let the Father draw you both close to himself so you can both receive his forgiveness.

7. *Darkness/Light Prayer*
   a. Prayerfully read John 12:46: "I, the light, have come into the world, so that whoever believes in me need not stay in the dark any longer."

   b. Sit in a dark room and let the Lord reveal to you the one thing you like least about yourself. Close your eyes and let him show you how this sin is a hurt or frightened place within you that needs his light and healing. Perhaps the Lord may even show you in what part of your body this darkness especially resides.

c. When you are ready to let Jesus, the light of the world, enter into this part of you, light a candle or sit in the sun and say, "Jesus," breathing him in while soaking up his light.

8. *Scripture Sinner Prayer*
Take your favorite Gospel story of a sinner (Zacchaeus, Peter, adulterous woman, Matthew, etc.) and let yourself become that sinner encountering Jesus. You might want to do this for the Gospel sinner that you resemble the most.

CONTEMPLATION IN ACTION PRAYERS

Take a minute and ask for the grace to recognize how you are tempted to sin, especially in overusing or underusing gifts. then do one of the following:

9. Prayerfully read Matthew 6:15: "If you do not forgive others, your heavenly Father will not forgive you." Then get in touch with what part of yourself you like the least. In order to be able to receive the Father's forgiveness for that part of yourself, do something kind today for a person who reminds you of that part of yourself.

10. Prayerfully read Matthew 25:25, about the man who buried the master's talents: "Out of fear I went off and buried your thousand silver pieces in the ground." Then use a gift or talent you have neglected, such as making something you enjoy but seldom take the time to make. Do it with love and enjoyment rather than concern to make it perfectly or to get it finished.

B. Daily Journal (5 minutes).

1. Share with Jesus what gift you used most today and how you are tempted to sin especially by over-using or under-using your gifts.
2. Write in your journal how Jesus responds

(what he seems to do or say in response to what you have told him). If you can't get in touch with Jesus' response, write what most moves you as you speak to him, or what are the most loving words you want him to say to you.

OPTIONAL HOME EXPERIENCES

C. Personal Reflection Questions

1. If you were to describe the person who irritates you the most, what traits would he or she have? What negative traits in that person are also in you?
2. A gift used too much or too little becomes a sin. What is the gift that is hardest for you to use well (e.g., the gift of listening—you can listen too much or too little)?
3. When were you hurt most? What gifts did you develop as a result? What sins did you develop as a result?
4. Each sin comes from a drive that can be directed into a gift with which to love. For example, Paul's zealous drive to persecute Christians became redirected into zeal for spreading the Gospel. Peter's desire to always be first became redirected into the gift of leadership. Can you identify how your main sins as well as your gifts for sharing love come from the same drive?
5. What gifts developed from your sinful moments?

D. Scripture Readings

2 Samuel 12:1-25: Our judgments of others reveal our own sins.
Sirach 27:30—28:7: Forgive your neighbor.
Matthew 18:21-35: The unforgiving servant is not forgiven
Luke 7:36-50: Projection by Simon the Pharisee; the gift of love.
Luke 18:9-14: The Pharisee and the tax collector.
Luke 19:11-27: Parable of the use of talents.

E. Additional Readings

Healing Life's Hurts
Chapter 9, "Third Stage: Bargaining." Bargaining as projection of our own

strengths and weaknesses, in which we demand of another what we have become proud of being able to do, or ask another to make up for the ways in which we most need to change and grow.

Chapter 10, "Fourth Stage: Depression." The stage of depression comes when we move from demanding that others change to asking how we need to change.

Healthy depression leads us to be angry at our unloving actions while still loving and forgiving ourselves as God does.

On the Road to Spiritual Wholeness, by Flora Wuellner (Nashville: Abingdon, 1978), especially Chapter 2, "Our Hidden Wholeness."

See page 67, column 2, #2:

Every sin is the distortion or misuse of what was originally given to us as a gift by the Father. For example:

The sin of:	May be an abuse of the gift of:
Pride	Leadership (e.g., Peter).
Covetousness	Having deep desires (e.g., the good thief who wanted heaven).
Lust	Intimacy (e.g., Mary Magdalene).
Anger	Zeal to change what needs to be changed (e.g., Paul).
Gluttony	Communion; a hunger and thirst for life within.
Envy	Seeing gifts and growth in another; affirming others (e.g., Joseph's brothers in Genesis).
Sloth	Integrity (e.g., parable of the two sons in Matthew 21:28-32).
Fear	Sensitivity; awareness of what needs to be done (e.g., woman with the hemorrhage).
Stubbornness	Perseverance (e.g., man who keeps knocking in Luke 11:5-9).
Guilt	Sensitive conscience; loving much because you've been forgiven much; deep relationship with Jesus as a loved sinner (e.g., woman at the feet of Jesus in Luke 7:36-50).

Lesson Eleven
HEALING BY ACCEPTING GOD'S FORGIVENESS

INTRODUCTION

Whenever St. Ignatius desired to have consolation, he would simply recall all his sins. The most important thing about sin is the choice it presents to us. When we sin, we can become depressed, withdrawn and even suicidal. We can say, "That's the end of it," and that was Judas' choice. Or when we sin we can say, "Now I can be closer to the Lord than ever before," and that was Peter's choice (John 21). When Peter could receive forgiveness for having betrayed the Lord three times, he was ready to follow Jesus at a new and deeper level. In Luke 7:47, we're told that the woman who anointed Jesus' feet loved much because she had been forgiven much. We can love the Lord much when we know how much he has forgiven us.

The time when I (Dennis) felt most forgiven and thus wanted to love much was when I made my general confession, soon after entering the Jesuits. After that confession I knew that Jesus had forgiven me much, and I was so grateful that all I could say to him was, "I'll go anyplace for you, anywhere and anytime." That experience changed my life. People in Alcoholics Anonymous will recognize the fifth step of the A.A. program in what I am saying. In this step, alcoholics review their whole life and confess to another person and to God the things of which they are most ashamed. Although even before we sinned God gave us forgiveness by Jesus' death on the cross, confession helps us to *receive* and to experience at a deep level God's constant forgiveness, especially when we find it hardest to rejoice with a Father who has forgiven us a debt of five hundred rather than

fifty. If you've been a great sinner, then you have an opportunity to become a great lover.

Confession is meant to be healing and to make us great lovers, but so often it's just a repetition of the same old sins and we leave without feeling the power to change. Confession's healing power comes not only when I confess my sins, but also when I confess whatever sin I am most ashamed of — whatever I consider to be the worst part of me. Such was my experience in third grade when I (Matt) made one of my most healing confessions. I had many sins that I was going to confess. I hadn't taken out the garbage on time, I hadn't washed the dishes when I was supposed to . . . there were a whole lot of things my mother had asked me to do that I hadn't done right. I was trying to find a name for all these sins, something that expressed disobedience to parents.

The word that I thought was the right one was "adultery." I thought adultery was disobeying adults. Sister never explained what it was; we were just taught that it was a really big sin, the kind that made your soul turn black. So here I was, in third grade, and I had already committed adultery. When the next Saturday came, I planned my strategy while waiting in the confession line. My strategy was to try a "sandwich" confession — that's where you say two small sins in a loud voice and hope the priest doesn't catch the big sin that you whisperingly sandwiched in between. So, when it came time to start my confession, I said, "Bless me, Father, for I have sinned. It has been three weeks since my last confession. Since then my sins are, I missed my morning prayers three times, committed adultery five times and fought with my brother three times." There was a long pause and I knew I was caught. The priest said to me, "Well, how old are you?" I said, "I'm in third grade." He said, "That's what I thought. I don't think you committed adultery. But if you did, I want you to know that Jesus really loves you and he forgives you." I felt a whole new freedom come into me. I had put what I thought was the worst sin you could ever commit into the Lord's hands, and he had forgiven me. Confession is as healing for me today as it was in third grade whenever I tell the Lord the worst things about myself and let myself receive his love and forgiveness. Even if I am not really a sinner, I can feel like one and be healed as I let the Lord love me where I feel the most shame. My deepest sin is not the action I commit, but letting my shame separate me from God's healing forgiveness (Mark 3:28-29).

The Tape Prayer for this lesson is the "Prodigal Prayer" in which we try to experience what it's like to be welcomed back home after we've done what we have felt most ashamed of, just as the prodigal son was welcomed home after he had done the most shameful act he could do — treat his father as if he were already dead by asking for his inheritance and spending it all. Even after such a great offense, the father in the prodigal son story could still joyfully welcome his son home. When we were in Korea recently, we learned about the kind of fatherly love that can forgive the worst offenses in a son. We noticed that there were many strong and growing Christian communities in Korea, and when we asked what helped these communities to develop we were told about a play called "Love's Atom Bomb." This play is based on a true story which began in 1948, when the communists came down and overran a village. When Pastor Son returned to the village from the leper colony where he worked, he found that a communist had murdered both of his sons. A few days later the communist who had killed his sons was caught and sentenced to death. Pastor Son went over to the jail where the prisoner was, and he said, "If you put this boy to death it won't bring back my sons. I want you to release him to me so that I can raise him in my family and he can do the work my sons wanted to do." The prisoner was released and raised in Pastor Son's family. Eventually he went to the seminary and worked in the leper colony. When the murderer's family heard what had happened to their son, they went to visit Pastor Son. They couldn't understand such compassion, and they wanted to learn what made it possible for Pastor Son to forgive the murderer of his own children. And so Pastor Son sent his daughter to live with this family for a few years, and the whole family became Christians.

The idea of loving our enemies is unique to Christianity. As Christians we can love our enemies because we have a Father who loves us when we act like an enemy to him. We have a Father whose sun shines on the just and the unjust, who loves even unrepentant sinners as much as he loves those who are perfect. Our Father does not turn from us but we as sinners can turn away from his constant, healing love. When we are scrupulous or feeling as if we must earn God's mercy, we are proudly playing God by refusing his ever-present mercy.

Our Father invites us to find the moment in our life when we haven't been aware enough of his mercy, the moment we are most ashamed of and don't want anyone to know about. Then we can receive his healing love in that moment just as Pastor Son was able to love the boy who murdered both his sons.

I. Group Experience

A. Common Opening Prayer (5 minutes)

B. Video or Audio Tape: "Healing by Accepting God's Forgiveness" (30 minutes)

How can we experience most fully the depth of God's love for us?
1. When we have sinned, we have an opportunity to be closer to the Lord than ever before. We can discover the depth of God's love for us by experiencing his forgiveness for the things we are most ashamed of (e.g., Peter, Dennis' general confession).
2. Confession is healing when we bring the worst side of ourselves to the Lord, receiving his forgiveness and extending it to others (e.g., Matt's third grade confession). We hate the sin and love the sinner.
3. Loving our enemies is an idea unique to Christians. We can conceive of this only because we have a Father who loves us even when *we* are the enemy (e.g., Pastor Son).

Closing Prayer: experiencing ourselves as the prodigal who needs forgiveness and as the Father who offers it unconditionally.

C. Companion Prayer I (5 minutes). After listening to the tape, pray with your companion to receive God's forgiveness. Take a few moments of silence to ask Jesus to reveal to you the prodigal part of yourself, the part you are most ashamed of. Then let the person on the right be the Father and the person on the left be the prodigal. If you are the Father, without using words welcome home the prodigal. If you are the prodigal, soak in the love of the Father welcoming you home. After 5 minutes of silent prayer, reverse roles. (See Luke 15:11-32.)

D. Companion Sharing (5 minutes minimum for each person to share his or her reaction to today's tape and to the past week).

1. What part of today's tape moved your heart most deeply?
2. Share with your companion how you have experienced the Lord's presence in your life during the previous week. You may wish to share the journal response from last week that touched you the most.
3. What are you most grateful for now and how do you need Jesus' help?

E. Companion Prayer II — Optional (since the purpose of this prayer is healing, you may wish to pray over your companion for about 10 minutes). Lay your hands on your companion and pray as Jesus would for about 10 minutes. Let the words and silences in your prayer be those of Jesus as he is already praying in your heart. Give thanks to Jesus for what your companion is most grateful for and pray for whatever healing your companion most needs. Close your prayer by praying that your companion receive the grace of this lesson: *to be able to accept God's forgiveness.* Then let your companion pray over you.

F. Group Sharing (Optional — 15 minutes minimum). Take two minutes of silence to ask what has been most difficult and what has been most helpful in your prayer and journaling this past week. Share your reflections with the larger group. Close with a prayer thanking the Lord for the break-

throughs and for discovering the blocks where he is already bringing forth further growth.

G. Closing Snack and Celebration (Optional). An open-ended time to enjoy one another and to continue sharing.

II. Home Experience

A. Daily Healing Prayer (10 minutes). Each day choose one of the following healing or contemplation in action prayers and pray it for at least 10 minutes. These prayers are only *suggestions.* Perhaps you will find yourself drawn to pray what is in your heart using varied breathing, a symbol, a repeated word, a melody, a gesture, a drawing, or a piece of clay which you can mold. Although there are many prayers suggested, it would be best to pray only a few of them, part of them, or to repeat from this or any other chapter the prayer that most moved your heart. Use whatever way you can best give your heart to Jesus and enter into his heart. Perhaps your prayer will be as simple as looking at a beautiful flower and taking in God's love for you. You may wish to begin your prayer by centering yourself, perhaps using the Breath Prayer (see Lesson 1). You may wish to continue with the Embrace Prayer (see Lesson 3, Prayer #2), or a similar prayer of simply resting in God's love.

1. *Prodigal Prayer* (Tape Prayer)
   You may wish to pray this prayer alone, or with a person other than the companion you prayed it with during the group meeting.
   a. Ask Jesus to reveal to you the prodigal part of yourself, the part you are most ashamed of.
   b. Read Luke 15:11-32 and decide whether you want to be the father or the prodigal. If you are the father, without using words welcome home the prodigal. (If you are alone, do this in your imagination and perhaps with gestures. If you are with another, express yourself non-verbally.) If you are the prodigal, soak in the love of the father as he welcomes you home.
   c. Reverse roles.

2. *Prodigal Prayer in Proxy*
   Repeat the Prodigal Prayer. Instead of
   doing it with the prodigal part of yourself, imagine yourself doing it with a person you find hard to forgive.
   a. Be God the Father loving that person.
   b. Become that person and allow your-
      self to be loved by God the Father. (To
      become that person you may wish to
      use parts of the Becoming Another
      Prayer in Lesson 1.)

3. *Prayer for Receiving the Grace of This
   Lesson*
   Ask Jesus to give you his knowledge of
   how loved and accepted he is by the
   Father. Breathe it in with every breath
   and breathe out all the blocks in yourself
   to receiving the Father's love and acceptance. (You may wish to pray this prayer
   with Mary instead of Jesus.)

4. *Stone Cross Prayer*
   a. Ask the Lord to reveal to you every sin
      of your life.
   b. Take a bag and collect stones, one to
      represent each of these sins. Perhaps
      you might choose larger stones for
      what you consider larger sins.
   c. Feeling the weight of the stones,
      thank Jesus for dying on the cross to
      take away all our sins and for opening
      you to his mercy every time you con-
      fessed your sins.
   d. As a sign of your willingness to stop
      focusing on the burden of guilt which
      Jesus forgave from the cross, use all
      the stones to build a cross.
   e. When the cross is completed, pray
      that every cross will remind you that
      you can love Jesus a lot because he
      has forgiven you a debt of $500 rather
      than $5 ("In consequence I say to you,
      her sins, which are many, have been
      forgiven; therefore she loves much.
      But he who is forgiven little, loves
      little"! Luke 7:47).

5. *Letter to Peter*
   a. Prayerfully read Mark 14:66-72.
   b. Write a letter to Peter to convince him
      that he is forgiven.

6. *Shower Prayer*
   a. Prayerfully read Psalm 51:3-4.

"Have mercy on me, O God, in your
goodness; in the greatness of your
compassion wipe out my offense.
Thoroughly wash me from my guilt
and of my sin cleanse me."
   b. Ask the Lord to reveal to you any past
      sins which he has already forgiven
      when you confessed them, but which
      still cause you to feel unworthy and
      distant from him.
   c. Take a shower and let the Lord's heal-
      ing waters continue to wash and soak
      especially the one part of your body
      which you feel has most hurt him and
      others, so that you experience more
      deeply how he has already forgiven
      you.

7. *Healing by Accepting God's Forgiveness*
   Look back at your life, at the times when
   you have hurt another.
   a. Within the diamond on p. 170 write the
      names of five people you have hurt.
   b. Put a circle around those who are not
      closer to you now.
   c. Pick one of these. Tell Jesus how you
      feel about hurting that person. Be
      honest and express all your anger so
      that Jesus can heal it.
   d. When you can figure out why you may
      have hurt that person, put a vertical
      line through the name (to indicate
      that you were not reacting just to that
      person but to other pressures too).
   e. When you feel that you can forgive
      both yourself and that person to the
      degree that Jesus has already for-
      given both of you, draw a horizontal
      line through the name. Pray for this
      forgiveness to deepen.
   f. When you can see some good coming
      out of the hurt (some ways both you
      and that person grew), X out the
      name.
   g. When you can think of some way to
      build a bridge to that person, draw a
      triangle around the name. You have
      begun to forgive that person and your-
      self and allowed God to enter the
      situation with his healing.
   h. Thank Jesus for the growth and for
      beginning the healing.

8. *Jesus Washing Your Feet*
   a. Prayerfully read John 13.

b. Let yourself be Peter by getting in touch with how you need forgiveness. Then let Jesus wash your feet. Feel the cool water and the gentleness of his touch. Perhaps Jesus says something or perhaps he just silently expresses everything in the loving way he washes your feet.

9. *Celebrating Forgiveness*
   a. Read how the Father celebrates forgiveness:

   "He will exult with joy over you,
   he will renew you by his love;
   he will dance with shouts of joy for
        you
   as on a day of festival."

   (Zephaniah 3:18)

   b. Exult with joy and dance the Father's dance for you. Experience how he celebrates your forgiveness.

CONTEMPLATION IN ACTION PRAYERS

Take a moment and ask for the grace to accept God's forgiveness. Then do one of the following:

10. *Confession*
    Find someone you trust very much and share with that person something about yourself that is hard for you to love and to forgive yourself for. Or go to the sacrament of reconciliation, asking to receive forgiveness and healing in this area of your life.
11. Prayerfully read Luke 19:1-10, about Zacchaeus paying back those he had defrauded ("Zacchaeus stood his ground and said to the Lord: 'I give half of my belongings, Lord, to the poor. If I have defrauded anyone in the least, I pay him back fourfold' "). Then make reparation to someone you have hurt. For example, you might rebuild that person's reputation, return what was taken, etc.
12. Prayerfully read Luke 15:22 about the celebration the father threw for his prodigal son. ("The father said to his servants, 'Quick! Bring out the finest robe and put it on him; put a ring on his finger and shoes on his feet. Take the

fatted calf and kill it. Let us eat and celebrate because this son of mine was dead and has come back to life.' Then the celebration began.") When you have experienced yourself as forgiven, celebrate with a special meal or other recreation.

B. Daily Journal (5 minutes)

1. Share with Jesus when during this prayer or during the day your heart was deeply moved — perhaps a moment of being grateful for or of longing for healing in *accepting God's forgiveness.*
2. Write in your journal how Jesus responds (what he seems to do or say in response to what you have told him). If you can't get in touch with Jesus' response, write what most moves you as you speak to him or what are the most loving words you want to hear.

OPTIONAL HOME EXPERIENCES

C. Personal Reflection Questions

1. What is the most prodigal part of yourself, the part you are most disappointed in? How does your body express that disappointment (e.g., posture, tiredness, illness)? What do your interior voices say to that disappointment (e.g., "Try harder"; "You should be perfect"; "You can't change"? See *Healing Life's Hurts,* pages 144-145.) How do your actions express your disappointment with yourself (e.g., depression, withdrawal, overextension)?
2. When did you feel that you could love a lot because you were forgiven a lot?
3. When did you feel most forgiven? How were you different after that experience?
4. When is it hardest for you to hate the sin and love the sinner in yourself?
5. What was the most healing confession in your life? Why was it so healing?

D. Scripture Readings

Luke 7:36-50: The sinner is closer to God than the perfect Pharisee.
Luke 15:11-32: The prodigal son.

Psalm 32: Happy the man whose fault is forgiven.

Psalm 51: Have mercy on me, O God.

Isaiah 49:15-16: God loves us as a mother loves a weak infant.

E. Additional Readings

Healing Life's Hurts

Chapter 10, "Fourth Stage: Depression." The stage of depression comes when we move from demanding that others change to asking how we need to change. Healthy depression leads us to be angry at our unloving actions, while still loving and forgiving ourselves as God does.

Chapter 13, "Everyday Prayer for Healing One Memory." Example of a prayer for healing one memory using all the five stages of forgiveness.

Healing of Memories, Chapter 11, "Healing of Memories and Confession." This chapter shares how the sacrament of reconciliation can be a celebration of new freedom instead of a routine time of repeating the same sins.

IMPORTANT REMINDER: IF YOU ARE PLANNING ON USING THE FOOTWASHING SERVICE TAPE AT THE NEXT MEETING, BRING A PITCHER WITH WARM WATER, A BASIN AND A TOWEL. COME PREPARED TO HAVE YOUR FEET WASHED.

Lesson Twelve
FOOT WASHING SERVICE

INTRODUCTION

Washing feet is like a sacrament, but no one denomination has claimed it and so it belongs to all of us. A sacrament is an action of Jesus that he asks us to repeat in order to give his love. When he washed his disciples' feet, Jesus requested, "As I have done so you must do for one another" (John 13). As with all sacraments, washing feet is an opportunity to receive the healing love of Jesus.

Why did Jesus choose to wash feet as a way of communicating his healing love? In Jesus' time, the feet were the part of the body that was considered the worst, the most defiled. They were the last part of yourself that you would want anyone to touch. Feet were defiled and considered unclean not just because they had picked up dirt but because a person might have walked where lepers had walked. Before entering a house as a guest, Jews would wash their feet not only to get them clean but also as a sign of respect for the host lest they bring inside all the defilement carried by the feet. Thus to wash the defiled feet of another was a sign of the most outstanding love and respect. Simon Peter washed the feet of Jesus as a special sign of respect because Jesus was a rabbi and a very special person. Washing another's feet was a way of saying, "I'll do anything for you, even wash your feet. That's how much I respect you." When we let another wash our feet in a footwashing service, we're bringing the part of ourselves that we're most ashamed of to the Lord and letting his cleansing and renewing love be mediated to us.

When we wash each other's feet we are being Peter and Jesus for one another as we give and receive the Lord's love and forgiveness. We can also wash feet in proxy for others. At one conference we gave for women religious, a psychiatrist wandered into the footwashing service. That psychiatrist washed feet all night long. One sister after another would grab him, asking him to be the father who had neglected them, or the brother they hadn't gotten along with, or a doctor who had mistreated them. The beautiful thing about this was that the psychiatrist had had all these kinds of problems with daughter, sister, etc., and as he extended the Lord's forgiveness to the sisters on behalf of father, brother, etc., the cancer he had throughout his body went into remission. So, if you ask others to be Jesus for you and wash your feet, you bring them into healing too. Their healing will happen especially as you invite them to love you in the ways they may never have been able to love the person in their own life whom you represent. As they wash your feet and offer Jesus' forgiveness to you, they will also discover how deeply Jesus has forgiven them too. Contrition comes not so much from knowing how much evil we have done as by knowing how much we are loved. The footwashing in the Gospel of John took place because "he loved his own in this world and would show his love for them to the end" (John 13:1). "Once you know all these things, blest will you be if you put them into practice" (John 13:17).

Note: This tape is optional. We suggest that you use it if you are interested in deepening your experience of forgiveness in the way that Jesus did for his apostles, through foot washing. By being Peter and allowing someone to be Jesus washing your feet, you can experience deep forgiveness and come to appreciate why Jesus said, "But if I washed your feet, then you must wash each other's feet" (John 13:15). If you are not planning to have a foot washing service, then this tape should be omitted.

I. Group Experience

A. Common Opening Prayer (5 minutes)

B. Video or Audio Tape: "Foot Washing Service" (30 minutes)
Giving to Jesus the prodigal part of ourselves that needs to be cleansed.
1. Foot washing is an unofficial sacrament for all Christians, belonging to no one denomination. In Jesus' time, foot washing was a sign of outstanding love (John 13).
2. We can wash each other's feet on behalf of others, being Peter and being Jesus for one another (e.g., hurts between father and daughter, mother and daughter, handicapped and "healthy").
3. We can wash one another's feet in proxy for others because Jesus is in us all (e.g., psychiatrist and nuns).

Note: If you have the videotape, you may wish to view the entire tape and then proceed to "Instruction II" under "C" below. If you are listening to the audio tape, you may wish to listen to the first portion of the tape, on what foot washing meant for Jesus. What follows on the tape are three foot washings (between father and daughter, between mother and daughter, between a handicapped and a "healthy" person). Since much of what happens in a foot washing is non-verbal, we suggest that those listening to the audio tape turn it off before these three foot washings (after the first 7 minutes) and proceed with the service according to Instructions I and II below.

C. Foot Washing Service

(Materials needed: pitcher with warm water, towels, basin)

Instruction I:
  a. Get three sets of volunteers representing different hurts (e.g., mother-daughter, father-daughter, husband-wife, handicapped-"healthy," Protestant-Catholic, priest-lay, man-woman, doctor-nurse, etc.).

  b. Let the first set of volunteers come forward. One person sits in a chair and the other gets ready to wash his or her feet. As the person in the chair represents Peter, let that person say several sentences about what he or she is sorry for so that all present can get in touch with how they also need forgiveness for acting in similar ways. Then let the other person (who represents Jesus) wash "Peter's" feet.

  c. When the first person's feet have been washed, let the two people switch positions so that the person who was Peter is now Jesus, ready to wash the other's feet.

  d. After all three sets of volunteers have washed feet, then invite everyone else to wash feet according to Instruction II below.

Instruction II:

Decide who it is that you have hurt and most want to ask forgiveness from. If the one you hurt is present, tell that person how sorry you are and let him or her wash your feet. If the person is not present, have someone who reminds you of that person wash your feet. To maintain a prayerful atmosphere, perhaps have a tape recorder playing religious songs in the background.

D. Closing Snack and Celebration
Just as the father celebrated the return home of the prodigal by killing the fatted calf and celebrating with a party, end the foot washing service with a party welcoming one another home.

II. Home Experiences

A. Daily Healing Prayer (10 minutes)

Each day, choose one way to celebrate the forgiveness you have received. You may wish to go out to dinner or do something you have been putting off for a long time that you would enjoy. If you also wish to pray, celebrate by returning to prayer experiences in the previous chapters during which you felt most loved.

B. Daily Journal (5 minutes)

1. Share with Jesus when during your prayer or the day you most experienced yourself as the prodigal celebrating your return home to the father.
2. Write in your journal how Jesus responds (what he seems to do or say in response to what you have told him). If you can't get in touch with Jesus' response, write what most moves you as you speak to him, or what are the most loving words you want him to say to you.

Lesson Thirteen
HEALING THROUGH INTERCESSION

INTRODUCTION

Intercession is a simple way that we can pray for anybody, anywhere, anytime. Jesus gives us examples of intercessory prayer when he prays for the centurion's servant and the Canaanite woman's daughter (Matthew 8:5-13; 15:21-28). Both these people were among the lowest classes of Jewish society. In Jesus' time women had little status in Jewish society, and the Canaanite woman and her daughter were not only women but pagans as well. The centurion was a Roman in charge of the divisions that were occupying Jerusalem, and his slave, under Roman law, had no rights and could be put to death by his master. Yet Jesus is so eager to heal that the centurion can say to him, "Only say the word and my servant will be healed. You don't even have to bother to come." In intercessory prayer, Jesus is showing us that he wants to touch the people who are smallest, who are hurting the most.

When we lived at Bethany House of Intercession with Fr. George Kosicki for one year, we always prayed for three gifts so that our intercessory prayer might be more like Jesus' prayer. These gifts are compassion, a listening heart, and *joyful* intercession.

Compassion is the first gift needed for intercessory prayer. Many of the priests who came to stay at Bethany were struggling with problems like alcoholism, depression, broken relationships, etc. They had come for healing themselves. We blessed each of them for the gift of compassion and told them to forget about themselves for three days. We asked them to focus instead on praying for a person who was suffering in the same way. If they were alcoholics, we asked them to pray for other priests who were struggling with alcohol-

ism. If they were depressed and ready to give up, we asked them to pray for other priests who were depressed and ready to give up. We found that after three days of mainly praying intercessory prayer, most of the priests had received the healing they needed. Their own wounds were touched and healed as they learned through intercessory prayer how much Jesus loved another person who was just like themselves. When a depressed priest could, through his intercession, let Jesus love another depressed priest, the intercessor learned that Jesus loved him in his depression too. When we pray for another who is like ourselves, we catch Jesus' love and desire to be there and heal. The easiest way to receive healing is to pray for someone who is just like ourselves and to pray with that deep compassion of Jesus.

A listening heart is the second gift needed for intercessory prayer. As compassion begins to make us one with the person for whom we are interceding, we begin receiving the gift of a listening heart. The gift of a listening heart happens when our heart, Jesus' heart, and the heart of the person for whom we are interceding become one. An example of one way to receive a listening heart is Leo. In the first and second lessons, "Simple Ways To Pray" and "Simple Ways To Pray (Follow-Up)," we speak about a man named Leo. In the film "Simple Ways To Pray," Leo prayed for his seventy-seven-year-old father, Frank. Frank grew up in Mexico during the 1920's revolution, when the Church had often sided with the wealthy. Frank came from a poor family, and because of his experience in Mexico he wanted nothing to do with priests or with religion. Leo thought that Frank might die soon, and he was concerned about his father's soul. During the prayer we asked Leo to try to become Frank by holding his hands the same way, adjusting his posture to be like Frank's, and letting his whole body become just like Frank's. After letting his whole body become like Frank's, Leo allowed his heart to begin feeling the concerns and worries in Frank's heart. By taking on the posture and even the feelings of another, Leo was trying to intercede like Jesus who, as high priest, interceded by becoming like us in all things but sin (Hebrews 2:17; 4:15).

After the prayer, Leo told us that he really did become his father and experienced Jesus and some other unknown person coming to love him. The prayer and Jesus' love were so real that Leo knew his father had received Jesus' love and would be saved. The gift of a listening heart means that our heart is listening to two hearts, the suffering heart of the person we are praying for and the interceding, loving heart of Jesus.

When we asked Leo later what had happened to Frank since the prayer, he told us that Frank was as anti-clerical as ever. But, for three years before the prayer, Frank had become increasingly senile. He would wander around Chicago, thinking he was back in Mexico and looking for his childhood places. Frank would also have nightmares and fits of anger. After the prayer, Frank's senile behavior disappeared and has not returned. Many times we think that our prayers aren't answered because we don't get what we asked for, e.g., Frank was as anti-clerical as ever after Leo's prayer. But each time we pray with a listening heart, Jesus can take the next simple step in filling that person with new life. The gift of a listening heart means allowing our heart to listen to the hearts of other persons until we enter their painful world and there meet Jesus. If we take both steps, becoming the person and then letting Jesus fill that person with new life, when we finish the prayer our listening heart will not be full of pain but full of new life. New life comes to us too because as we pray for another, Jesus is looking lovingly at us and filling us with new life, and because as we become another we find Jesus already praying through the Spirit in the heart of the person we bring to him.

Joyful intercession is the third gift needed for intercessory prayer. When we have listened to Jesus praying through the Spirit in the heart of another, then we can pray with joy as we experience Jesus filling that person with new life. This doesn't mean that we have to wait until we're in a joyful mood to pray for others; we can pray out of our pain, too, as did the priests at Bethany. But the mark of genuine intercession is what it does to us: Are we led into the joy and confidence of the Lord, or do we leave prayer still in the pain? Do we leave with more of a focus on the problem or on the Problem Solver? We have a friend named Rose Trujillo who developed cancer and was given six months to live. She began to pray out of her pain for other cancer victims and for priests. Rose lived for four years rather than six months, and the only times she was without pain were when she was interceding for others. When she was praying, she was receiving so much love and strength from the Lord that she was almost oblivious to pain, and her will to live increased. Many people leave a period of intercession all worn out and in the same sad shape as the person they've prayed for, thinking that this is the lot of an intercessor. But the Lord's way of intercession is that we leave prayer not with self-centered pain but with more of his love and hope than when we began.

Sometimes praying for another *will* involve pain. My mother woke up one night with a shooting pain in her right leg. She recognized this as the kind of pain that her ill father had been having, and she got up and began to say a rosary for him. As she finished the rosary, the phone rang and she was told that her father had just died. I think that the pain my mother felt did indeed come from the Lord. It caused her to be up and praying for my grandfather as he was dying; it led her into more love rather than into discouragement and into herself. Sometimes we may really be called to share in the pain of another person. But the sign of whether it comes from Jesus is that the pain leads us to compassionately reach out to others and to become more closely united with God. If through intercessory prayer we take on pain and suffering that wear us out and close us in on ourselves, then we should not be doing intercession. When we're praying Jesus' prayer, we are growing and receiving love — that's the mark of joyful intercession.

Sometimes, even when we pray joyful intercession with compassion and a listening heart, the person for whom we are interceding doesn't change at all. Even Jesus prayed for many people who, as far as we know, never changed. Some of them may even have been the ones who took him away and crucified him. We are not promised that everyone we pray for will be changed; what we are promised is that as we reach out to people *we* will be changed and become more whole.

Our cousin, Sr. Mary Jane Linn, discovered this when spending the last years of her life in full-time intercession for our ministry. She told us once how her gift of intercession began. She had been

81

working in a home for elderly and infirm sisters. One day she went to visit a sister named Gratia. Gratia had been hanging on for years and years, and Mary Jane sensed that she needed to be released to die. One day Mary Jane asked Gratia what she would like to do before she died. Gratia answered that she wanted to be reconciled with a friend Michael, but no one knew how to locate him. Mary Jane said to Gratia, "It's 9:30 in the morning, and I don't have anything else I need to do for a while. I'm going to stay here with you and pray that your friend Michael comes, and I'm not going to leave your room until he does come." Mary Jane began to pray, and at noon a man came to the door. It was Michael. After Gratia and Michael had been together, Mary Jane asked Michael how he had decided to come that day. Michael said, "I was doing my work this morning. I had a lot of things to do, but Gratia's name kept coming to my mind. I kept on saying, 'No, I've got all this to do.' But her name kept coming. And about 10:00 a.m. I said, 'I'm not getting any work done.'" And so Michael got into his car and drove the two hours it took to get to Gratia, who, after reconciling herself with Michael, died two hours later. The point of this story is not that every time we pray, something will happen like Michael coming. The people we pray for have free will, and Michael could have decided to keep working that morning. The point is that intercession is the powerful prayer of Jesus in us interceding, and the Father is always sending an answer even when people don't respond to his answer.

The Tape Prayer for this lesson is "Becoming Another," sometimes called the "Shoe Prayer" or "Moccasin Prayer." The Sioux Indians have a prayer that says, "Great Spirit, grant that I may never criticize another until I have walked a mile in his moccasins." In this prayer they are asking to know what a person is feeling inside before judging him. That's the gift of intercession — to really understand what it's like to be the person we're praying for and to pray the prayer that Jesus is already praying in that suffering heart.

I. Group Experience

A. Common Opening Prayer (5 minutes)

B. Video or Audio Tape: "Healing through Intercession" (30 minutes)
How do we pray for someone who is far away or who is not ready to receive our prayers?

1. There is a simple way to pray for anybody at any time. Jesus wants to heal the poorest, littlest people through intercession (e.g., the centurion's servant).
2. How do we pray intercessory prayer? We need three gifts:
   a. Compassion (e.g., Bethany House of Prayer, Leo and Frank).
   b. A listening heart (e.g., Leo and Frank).
   c. *Joyful* intercession (e.g., Rose Trujillo).
3. When we pray intercessory prayer for someone who is like us, we are often healed too.
4. Praying for others doesn't mean asking for suffering — it means growing in love (e.g., Matt's mother).
5. When we pray for someone, there is no guarantee that the person will change — but *we* will change every time we reach out (e.g., Mary Jane Linn and Michael).

Closing Prayer: By becoming like us in everything but sin, Jesus was able to intercede for us before the Father. In the Shoe Prayer, by experiencing what it feels like to be another, we can pray the intercessory prayer to the Father that Jesus is praying within that person right now.

C. Silent Reflection (3 minutes). Quiet time to get in touch with what part of today's tape moved your heart most deeply.

D. Guided Journaling (Optional — 10 minutes). See Lesson 3.

E. Companion Sharing (5 minutes minimum for each person to share his or her reaction to today's tape and to the past week).

1. Share with your companion as much as you wish of what is in your heart after seeing this week's tape. Perhaps you will want to share what you have just written during the guided journaling.
2. Share with your companion how you have experienced the Lord's presence in your life during the previous week. You may wish to share the journal response from last week that touched you the most.

3. What are you most grateful for now and how do you need Jesus' help?

F. **Companion Prayer** (since the purpose of this prayer is healing, you may wish to pray over your companion for about 10 minutes). Lay your hands on your companion and pray as Jesus would for about 10 minutes. Let the words and silences in your prayer be those of Jesus as he is already praying in your heart. Give thanks to Jesus for what your companion is most grateful for and pray for whatever healing your companion most needs. Close your prayer by praying that your companion receive the grace of this lesson: *to intercede with the mind and heart of Jesus.* Then let your companion pray over you.

G. **Group Sharing** (Optional — 15 minutes minimum). Take two minutes of silence to ask what has been most difficult and what has been most helpful in your prayer and journaling this past week. Share your reflections with the larger group. Close with a prayer thanking the Lord for the breakthroughs and for discovering the blocks where he is already bringing forth further growth.

H. **Closing Snack and Celebration** (Optional). An open-ended time to enjoy one another and to continue sharing.

II. Home Experience

A. **Daily Healing Prayer** (10 minutes). Each day choose one of the following healing or contemplation in action prayers and pray it for at least 10 minutes. These prayers are only *suggestions*. Perhaps you will find yourself drawn to pray what is in your heart using varied breathing, a symbol, a repeated word, a melody, a gesture, a drawing, or a piece of clay which you can mold. Although there are many prayers suggested, it would be best to pray only a few of them, parts of them, or to repeat from this or any other chapter the prayer that most moved your heart. Use whatever way you can best give your heart to Jesus and enter into his heart. Perhaps your prayer will be as simple as looking at a beautiful flower and taking in God's love

for you. You may wish to begin your prayer by centering yourself, perhaps using the Breath Prayer (see Lesson 1). You may wish to continue with the Embrace Prayer (see Lesson 3, Prayer #2), or a similar prayer of simply resting in God's love.

1. *Becoming Another* or *Shoe Prayer* (Tape Prayer)
   a. Prayerfully read Hebrews 2:14: "Surely he did not come to help angels, but rather the children of Abraham: therefore he had to become like us in every way, that he might be a merciful and faithful intercessor before God on their behalf."
   b. Ask Jesus what one person he would like you to intercede for. Then ask him for the grace to intercede by becoming like that person in every way but sin.
   c. Let your body be molded into the body of the person for whom you hear Jesus asking you to pray. Ask Jesus to help you to experience what he wishes you to experience. Perhaps he will help you to feel the person's problems until your heart beats as anxiously or as lethargically as that person's heart. Let these problems mold your forehead, face, jaws, shoulders, back, hands and feet. Let your entire body resemble that person's body. Note how your body expresses that person's fears, anger, guilt, loneliness, discouragement, etc.
   d. When you are in touch with how that person needs healing, pray the prayer which Jesus within that person prays to the Father for healing. (Perhaps this prayer is only one or two sentences.)
   e. As that person, let the Father lay his hand on and begin to heal you until you have no more burdens to breathe out to him, but instead find yourself breathing out his healing love.
   f. Close by praying the Lord's Prayer in the way that Jesus within you now prays.

2. *Prayer for Receiving the Grace of This Lesson*
   Watch Jesus on the cross interceding for us. Ask him for the gift you need to inter-

cede with him (e.g., compassion, joy, a listening heart, a love that gives without asking for return). Perhaps you might ask Mary to teach you how to be interceding at the foot of the cross.

3. Choose something you often struggle with (e.g., alcoholism, poverty, depression, an uninteresting job, physical illness) and intercede for someone who has the same struggle.

4. Read Luke 7:1-10 and, like the centurion, bring before Jesus someone who is in need. Then say the name "Jesus," with each breath drawing in another dimension of his presence. Now with the eyes of Jesus see the person you are interceding for and feel Jesus' compassion. When you are filled with Jesus' compassion, see yourself laying your hand upon that person and see that person filled with light and strength as you breathe Jesus' life into him or her.

5. Sit in the sun that gives life and pours forth from the Father, who lets it shine on the just and the unjust (Matthew 5:45). Bask in all the life that comes from the Father, and then let it flow through you to a person for whom you wish to pray.

6. Read the newspaper and intercede for one person you read about that Jesus puts in your heart.

7. Stand in the place of another and receive the Eucharist for that person. You might want to do this for several days, taking that person to the Eucharist in your heart each day for a different period of his or her life.

8. Before falling asleep, relax each part of your body as a sign of trust in the Lord. Ask that the person you are praying for will be able to let go and trust in the Father too.

CONTEMPLATION IN ACTION PRAYERS

Take a moment and ask for the grace to intercede with the mind and heart of Jesus. Then do one of the following:

9. Reach out and help someone in the way you would like the Lord to help another person that you are worried about. Be for one person what you would like the Lord to be or do for another person whom you can't help. For example, if you are praying for someone far away who is depressed, you might listen lovingly to a discouraged person at home, or affirm another who is uncertain. Ask Jesus within you to be present to the distant person too.

10. Today as you do an activity (e.g., jog, cook, drive) ask Jesus that another person might have more life. For example, you might drive down the same roads you do each day, but make a point of enjoying the scenery today with the hope that the other person might have more joy.

11. Prayerfully read Matthew 6:10: "If God can clothe in such splendor the grass of the field which blooms today and is thrown on the fire tomorrow, will he not provide much more for you, O weak in faith." Then spend some time gardening, giving the Father's care to the plants and to another person whom you carry in your heart.

B. Daily Journal (5 minutes)

1. Share with Jesus when during this prayer or during the day your heart was deeply moved — perhaps a moment of being grateful for or of longing for healing in *being able to intercede with the mind and heart of Jesus.*

2. Write in your journal how Jesus responds (what he seems to do or say in response to what you have told him). If you can't get in touch with Jesus' response, write what most moves you as you speak to him or what are the most loving words you want to hear.

OPTIONAL HOME EXPERIENCES

C. Personal Reflection Questions

1. What experiences have you had that lead you to believe in the power of intercessory prayer? What experiences lead you to question it?

2. Some intercessors suffer for the person they are raising up in prayer. When is this suffering good (e.g., as when Jesus wept over Jerusalem)? When is this suffering an obstacle or a temptation to be worn down as an intercessor? Should you ever ask to suffer?

3. When should you try to change God's mind as Abraham did (Genesis 18:16-33)

and as Mary did at Cana (John 2:1-12) and when are you not to do so? When does God's will include your request?

4. How do you know that you are praying with the mind and heart of Jesus as he is interceding? What qualities does your prayer have at such times? What helps you to pray with his mind and heart?

5. Why don't people always change when you intercede for them?

D. Scripture Readings

Luke 7:1-10: The intercession of the centurion.

Mark 7:24-30: The intercession of the Canaanite woman.

John 14:12-15: Whatever you ask in my name (i.e., with my mind and heart) I will do.

Job 7:10: Job is restored after he prays for his accusers.

Hebrews 4:14-16: We have a compassionate high priest interceding for us.

1 John 5:14-17: Ask and God will give life to the sinner.

1 Timothy 2:1-6: Intercession is pleasing to God, especially for authorities.

Romans 8:26: The Spirit intercedes for us in our weakness.

Luke 22:31: Jesus intercedes for Peter.

Philippians 1:1-10: Paul's intercession for the Philippians.

Ephesians 3:14-21: Paul's prayer of intercession for the readers of his letter.

E. Additional Readings

Healing Life's Hurts, Chapter 12, "Eucharist: Healing a Memory." This chapter speaks about how intercession at the Eucharist can be helpful to you.

The Healing Light, by Agnes Sanford (Plainfield, N.J.: Logos, 1976). Classic book about the power of intercessory prayer.

Lost Shepherd, by Agnes Sanford (Plainfield, N.J.: Logos, 1971). This book presents in novel form Mrs. Sanford's teachings about interecessory prayer.

Lesson Fourteen
PHYSICAL HEALING (TRADITION)

INTRODUCTION

Healing happens to the extent that we are Jesus loving another. When Jesus went to heal Jairus' daughter, he brought with him his friends Peter, James and John, and the girl's parents (Luke 8:49-56). Perhaps he brought his friends and the girl's parents because they were the ones who loved deeply either him or the little girl. We find that healing occurs more often where there is more love because God, the source of all healing, is love.

Three people especially have the gift of healing because they usually have the gift of loving more deeply. These three people are: the person who is a close friend of the one who is sick, a person who has been healed through prayer of the illness we are praying for (e.g., if we are praying for a back problem, someone who through prayer has been healed of a back problem), and a person who struggles with the same problem (e.g., someone who is still suffering from difficulty with a back problem). A close friend can pray more deeply than a stranger the "heartfelt prayer" that heals the sick (James 5:15-17). So, too, a person healed of the same illness can pray with more loving expectation, and a person who is struggling with the same illness can pray with more loving compassion than someone who has never had that same illness. We can all pray for physical healing, but Jesus will heal through our prayers usually to the extent that we love and are like him.

Physical healing is my favorite kind of prayer because it is when I feel most like Jesus. When praying for the sick, I am praying in the way that Jesus spent the majority of his prayer time, and I begin feeling his love and his compassion for the sick. Jesus had so much love and compassion that he couldn't walk past a sick person, not even a leper, without reaching out his hand to heal. According to the Jewish law in Jesus' time, he should have stayed one hundred and fifty feet downwind from lepers. Yet he had to reach out and touch lepers because the love and compassion of the Father filled his heart. Jesus healed not to prove that he was God, but *because* he was God and he had to reach out as the Father had to reach out. To be Jesus is to have his compassion for the sick and to let his healing prayer come into our hearts.

Jesus did not keep his compassion for the sick to himself. When he sent out both his twelve apostles and his seventy-two disciples, he told them to teach, preach and heal (Matthew 10:1-8; Luke 10:1-9). In his last words on earth Jesus commissioned all believers to go forth, to lay their hands on the sick, and to pray for them to recover (Mark 16:15-20). The early Church took this commission seriously and considered healing prayer as the primary means of evangelizing. When telling the story of Jesus, early Christians laid hands on the sick to show that Jesus was real and loved his people. Even though the early Christians were repeatedly thrown into prison on account of praying for healing, they continued their healing ministry. They couldn't just speak about a loving God without also showing his healing love (Acts 4).

Healing, rather than just speaking of God's love, remained an essential part of Christian life from the time of the first apostles until the fourth century. Lay people were given blessed oil to anoint members of their family for healing. But a change in the attitude toward healing began during the time of the Emperor Constantine in the fourth century. The conversion of Constantine meant that the state now accepted Christians and rarely martyred them for their faith. With this end to the age of martyrdom, Christians thought that they needed another way to suffer for Christ. So they began to look upon illness as a way of offering their bodies to the Lord. Manichaeism and other heresies reinforced these attitudes as Christians considered the body as an evil to be controlled by fasting and living in the desert. These heresies began to predominate over Jesus' own Hebrew attitudes of the goodness of the created world and of the unity of body, mind, and soul. Since the soul was now considered more important than the body, Christians prayed for spiritual healing but not for physical healing. Thus the idea of redemptive suffering entered the Church and grew until all illness was seen as redemptive — a cross to be suffered rather than healed through prayer.

Augustine promoted redemptive suffering by writing that the Church needed miracles of healing in the beginning in order to convince people to believe, but that, once established, the Church no longer needed miracles of healing. A few years later, Augustine wrote another book, *Retractions,* in which he retracted all he had said about healing no longer being needed. He had changed his mind because during the preceding two years he had seen over seventy major miracles take place in his own cathedral. But despite Augustine's rediscovery of healing, the healing ministry got lost again. Because of the many abuses and the magical attitudes of some lay people toward healing, and especially toward anointing of the sick, the Church insisted that priests, and not lay people, become the ordinary ministers of the anointing of the sick. But because of the rampant plagues priests had time only to anoint and to visit the dying on their deathbeds.

As Christians knew that the Church imposed severe penances for sins, they waited until they were on their deathbed before going to confession. Thus the sacrament of the anointing of the sick lost its meaning as a sacrament of healing, and it became the sacrament of extreme unction through its association with confession and deathbed anointing. This situation continued in the Church until the time of Vatican II.

Vatican II rediscovered the sacrament of the anointing of the sick as a sacrament of healing and made four major changes in the guidelines for celebrating it. First, Vatican II restored the sacrament as primarily a prayer for healing rather than a prayer for a peaceful death. Second, anointing of the sick became the prayer of the whole community rather than of only the priest and the patient alone in a hospital room. Therefore, doctors, nurses, and family members may be included in the celebration of the sacrament. Third, every act of love and care for a sick person is considered a part of the sacrament. Thus, when a doctor lovingly prescribes medicine or prays for his patient, he is extending the celebration of the sacrament. Praying to heal the sick is not only for "charismatics," but is an extension of the sacrament of the anointing of the sick. Such prayer is just as essential in living out that sacrament as forgiveness is in living out the sacrament of reconciliation. The fourth change emphasized that the sacrament of the anointing of the sick can be repeated many times for a sick person. The Church tells us to keep extending the healing love of Jesus by praying again and again.

Each time I pray, I am not certain exactly what will happen. If I pray, for instance, for a person in a wheelchair, I don't know whether he will walk after one prayer. What I do know is that every time I pray the Lord will take the next simple, loving step with that person. I saw what some of those steps could be while praying for a friend, Joe. Three of the other people praying with me for Joe were doctors, and since Joe had scoliosis of the back, the doctors had traced out on Joe's back how the backbone needed to be readjusted. We prayed for about fifteen minutes, but with no visible healing.

We asked Joe, "Is anything happening?" He said, "Well, I'm feeling peaceful. And it hasn't gotten any worse. Usually if I sit this long it gets worse." The first two things that usually happen when we pray for healing are that the person feels peaceful and the infirmity does not get any worse. These are both gifts easy to overlook. Since the healing usually deepens each time we fill the person with more and more of Jesus' love, we put our hands on Joe's back again and prayed a while longer. Then we asked Joe, "Is there anybody you need to forgive?" At first he said, "No," but after a few more minutes of prayer he thought of three people to forgive. As Joe forgave these people, the pain in his back began to disappear and he could bend his back more freely. Those are usually the next two loving steps in physical healing: the pain goes away, followed by movement being restored. The final step is structural change. By the end of the prayer, Joe's backbone had readjusted itself as perfectly as the doctors had traced out on his back. Although some healing (as in the case of a religious sister mentioned later in this chapter) happens through just one prayer and can effect a physical change for which there is no natural explanation, most healing, as in Joe's case, happens through repeated prayer which speeds up the natural processes of healing. Everytime I pray with someone like Joe, the Lord will take the next loving step even if I don't know what that next step is.

Although for years Joe's back pain had made it difficult for him not to center in on himself, he called that back pain "redemptive" and had prayed little for the next step of healing. Often we say that an illness is redemptive when ninety percent of the time it isn't. Physical pain, such as Joe's back, usually causes us to center in on ourselves, and to the extent we do so, it is not redemptive. An illness is only redemptive to the extent that it helps us move out to others and to God.

One example of a redemptive illness would be that of a friend named Larry who is blind. We made our thirty-day retreat under Larry because he is one of the most perceptive spiritual directors we know. Larry's blindness is redemptive because it has helped him to hear hearts and thus to open himself to others and to God. One day Larry wondered if he should go to a famous healer who had come to town and ask for healing. We asked him "Would you be able to give and receive more love if you could see?" He said, "I know that God can heal. . . . But I don't think I could give and receive more love right now if I could see. My blindness is a big part of how God uses me."

If we prayed with Larry, we're not certain that his sight would be restored because we agree that God uses Larry's blindness. But we do know that God would take the next loving step with Larry. Perhaps the next step would be for Larry to hear hearts even more sensitively and perceptively than he does now. If so, his blindness would be even more redemptive to the extent that it opened him up more to God and to others. So, every time we pray for healing, we know that the Lord will take the next loving step in opening the person to give and receive more love either by making the illness more redemptive or by physical healing.

If so much can happen through prayer for physical healing, why is it sometimes so hard for me to reach out and pray? I saw how I resist praying for healing when I gave a thirty-day retreat to a religious sister with genetic neural damage in her ears. She had to lip-read what I said. I thought, "Maybe if I prayed with her God would restore her hearing." But I didn't have much confidence in my prayers for physical healing because some people I had prayed for recently had died. At that time I didn't understand

that death and a resurrected body could be a complete answer to my prayer. So I was discouraged and I thought that if someone else prayed for her, or if she went to a special place, she might be healed. About a year later, I received a phone call from this sister. Some members of her community had prayed with her. Even though she still had genetic neural damage, doctors confirmed that her hearing had been totally restored. The doctors were astounded and so was I. I felt both happy and sad. I was happy that she could hear and sad that I had not reached out to pray for her myself. Ten years later she can still hear perfectly. When I give workshops she sometimes comes and plays songs she has written. Before I can pray for another, I often need to ask Jesus to come and remove the blocks that keep me from loving as he loves and from praying his prayer. When this happens, then I am free to do the kind of prayer I enjoy most — healing the sick by being Jesus.

I. Group Experience

A. Common Opening Prayer (5 minutes)

B. Video or Audio Tape: "Physical Healing (Tradition)" (30 minutes)
Can you believe that Jesus in you can heal another?

1. Healing happens to the extent that we are Jesus for another. Healing comes down to loving, because God is love.
2. Jesus always reached out to heal the sick, and he handed this ministry on to us so that we would know what it was like to have his mind and heart.
3. A summary of the history of healing in the Church and the use of the sacrament of anointing of the sick.
4. Every time we pray, the Lord will take the next loving step (e.g., Joe Ross).
5. An illness is redemptive only if it helps us to receive love and then to reach out to others and to God (e.g., Larry).
6. Sometimes it is hard for us to reach out and pray for physical healing (e.g., sister with impaired hearing).

Closing Prayer: asking Jesus to remove all the blocks in us to praying for physical healing, especially anything that keeps us from union with him.

C. Silent Reflection (3 minutes). Quiet time to get in touch with what part of today's tape moved your heart most deeply.

D. Guided Journaling (Optional — 10 minutes). See Lesson 3.

E. Companion Sharing (5 minutes minimum for each person to share his or her reaction to today's tape and to the past week).

1. Share with your companion as much as you wish of what is in your heart after seeing this week's tape. Perhaps you will want to share what you have just written during the guided journaling.
2. Share with your companion how you have experienced the Lord's presence in your life during the previous week. You may wish to share the journal response from last week that touched you the most.
3. What are you most grateful for now and how do you need Jesus' help?

F. Companion Prayer (since the purpose of this prayer is healing, you may wish to pray over your companion for about 10 minutes). Lay your hands on your companion and pray as Jesus would for about 10 minutes. Let the words and silences in your prayer be those of Jesus as he is already praying in your heart. Give thanks to Jesus for what your companion is most grateful for and pray for whatever healing your companion most needs. You may also wish to use this time to pray for your companion for physical healing, and then to share your experience of this with one another. Close your prayer by praying that your companion receive the grace of this lesson: *to experience Jesus' compassion for those who are physically sick.* Then let your companion pray over you.

G. Group Sharing (Optional — 15 minutes minimum). Take two minutes of silence to ask what has been most difficult and what has been most helpful in your prayer and journaling this past week. Share your reflections with the larger group. Close with a prayer thanking the Lord for the breakthroughs and for discovering the blocks where he is already bringing forth further growth.

H. Closing Snack and Celebration (Optional). An open-ended time to enjoy one another and to continue sharing.

II. Home Experience

A. Daily Healing Prayer (10 minutes). Each day choose one of the following healing or contemplation in action prayers and pray it for at least 10 minutes. These prayers are only *suggestions*. Perhaps you will find yourself drawn to pray what is in your heart using varied breathing, a symbol, a repeated word, a melody, a gesture, a drawing, or a piece of clay which you can mold. Although there are many prayers suggested, it would be best to pray only a few of them, parts of them, or to repeat from this or any other chapter the prayer that most moved your heart. Use whatever way you can best give your heart to Jesus and enter into his heart. Perhaps your prayer will be as simple as looking at a beautiful flower and taking in God's love for you. You may wish to begin your prayer by centering yourself, perhaps using the Breath Prayer (see Lesson 1). You may wish to continue with the Embrace Prayer (see Lesson 3, Prayer #2), or a similar prayer of simply resting in God's love.

1. *Healing Our Blocks to Praying Like Jesus* (Tape Prayer)
   a. As you read your favorite Scripture passage in which Jesus heals the sick, ask to have Jesus' compassion to heal.
   b. Place your hand on your heart and ask that your heart have Jesus' prayer in it so that Jesus can use your heart to heal now.
   c. Let fall into your hand all the blocks that make it impossible for you to believe that Jesus' healing compassion is in you and that you could heal someone now. (For example, "Jesus will not heal through me now because . . . my prayers weren't answered in the past . . . because he only heals through other more holy people . . . because this illness is too

serious . . . because this illness is not serious enough for him to care . . . because there isn't enough time . . .because I am sick . . . etc.) When all the blocks are in your hand, throw them away. As all these blocks leave your heart, inhale "Jesus" and become him with his compassion for the sick.

d. As you become Jesus, inhale and pray the word "Abba" while hungering with Jesus that through your hands the Father may be glorified.

2. *Prayer for Becoming the Body of Christ*
   a. Prayerfully read St. Paul's testimony about Jesus living in him: "The life I live now is not my own; Christ is living in me" (Galatians 2:20).
   b. Tense your right hand, giving to the Father every cell in that hand. As you relax your right hand, ask that every cell of it be no longer yours but Jesus' cells.
   c. Continue to do this with the rest of your body, part by part.

3. *Scripture Prayer for Becoming Jesus*
   a. Read your favorite Gospel healing story.
   b. Watch Jesus as he acts in this story until you feel his compassion and desire to heal the sick.
   c. Ask Jesus to anoint you so that you may have his same compassion and desire to heal the sick.
   d. Pray for one sick person.

4. *Scripture Prayer for Receiving Jesus' Healing Love*
   a. Read your favorite Gospel healing story.
   b. Let yourself take the place of the sick person in the story and soak up Jesus' healing love.

5. *Loving God's Creation*
   a. Prayerfully read Wisdom 11:24—12:1 "For you love all things that exist, and have loathing for none of the things which you have made, for you would not have made anything if you had hated it. How would anything have endured if you had not willed it? Or how would anything not called

forth by you have been preserved? You spare all things, for they are yours, O Lord, who loves the living. For your immortal spirit is in all things."
   b. Find a created thing which you find especially beautiful (e.g., a flower, leaf, shell, bird, snowflake, cloud, lake, bug, stone, etc.).
   c. Gaze at it for several minutes, asking the Father to give you all the love for creation that he poured forth in making this part of it. Let the object you gaze at tell you of the Father's love for all that he has made.
   d. Ask that you be able to see the same beauty, fragility and goodness in other people that you can see at this moment in this one created thing. Ask that you be able to experience God's love for the very cells of their bodies, as you now experience his love for the part of creation that is before you.

6. *Tension Prayer*
   a. Ask Jesus to show you what part of your body is most tense and what problems have created the tension.
   b. Ask Jesus what can be done about these problems.
   c. Breathe in Jesus' strength to change what can be changed and breathe out to Jesus what cannot be changed.

CONTEMPLATION IN ACTION PRAYERS

Take a moment and ask for the grace to experience Jesus' compassion for those who are physically sick. Then go and do one of the following:

7. *Visiting the Sick*
   a. Read the story of Mary's visit to Elizabeth (Luke 1:39-56).
   b. Visit one person who is sick or in a nursing home. See if you can make this visit not out of charity but because you enjoy being with that person, as Mary enjoyed being with Elizabeth.

8. *Letter Writing*
   a. Read Jesus' words to those he was about to leave (John 15:9-17).
   b. Write a letter to one person who may

die soon and say to that person what is really in your heart.

B. Daily Journal (5 minutes)

1. Share with Jesus when during this prayer or during the day your heart was deeply moved — perhaps a moment of being grateful for or of longing for healing in *experiencing Jesus' compassion for those who are physically sick.*
2. Write in your journal how Jesus responds (what he seems to do or say in response to what you have told him). If you can't get in touch with Jesus' response, write what most moves you as you speak to him or what are the most loving words you want to hear.

OPTIONAL HOME EXPERIENCES

C. Personal Reflection Questions

1. When were you most ill and how did that keep you from giving and receiving love? What would you have wanted someone to do who visited you?
2. What helps you to pray for another for physical healing?
3. What makes it difficult for you to pray for another for physical healing?
4. Whom do you know who has a physical illness which is redemptive? In what ways do they use their illness to give and receive love with God and others? In what ways have you seen illness to be an evil that God generally wants to heal?
5. What abuses of physical healing prayer have you seen? How would you avoid them?

D. Scripture Readings

Mark 16:15-20: Jesus commissions all believers to heal.

Acts 4:1-34: Healing despite imprisonment.
James 5:13-16: Anoint the sick with oil.
Colossians 1:24: Some suffering may be redemptive, helping us to love God and others.
Colossians 1:15-20: All created things hold together in Christ.
Wisdom 11:24-12:1: God loves everything that he has made.

E. Additional Readings

Healing Life's Hurts
Chapter 4, "Physical Healing Through Healing a Memory." Emotional stress causes physiological changes in our bodies and can lead to physical illness. As we receive the Lord's love and peace, our emotions are healed and our bodies are directly affected, even healed completely.

Healing, by Francis MacNutt (Notre Dame: Ave Maria, 1974).
The Power To Heal, by Francis MacNutt (Notre Dame: Ave Maria, 1977).
The Prayer That Heals: Healing Prayer in the Family, by Francis MacNutt (Notre Dame: Ave Maria, 1981).
To Heal as Jesus Healed, by Barbara Shlemon, Dennis Linn and Matthew Linn (Notre Dame: Ave Maria, 1978).
The Healing Light, by Agnes Sanford (Plainfield, N.J.: Logos International, 1976).
Fearfully and Wonderfully Made: A Surgeon Looks at the Human and Spiritual Body, by Dr. Paul Brand and Philip Yancy (Grand Rapids: Zondervan, 1980).

Note: You might also want to borrow the film, "The Embattled Cell," from your local chapter of the American Cancer Society. This film, which is available free of charge, shows live human cancer cells and live white blood cells attacking the cancer cells.

Lesson Fifteen
PHYSICAL HEALING (PRACTICE)

INTRODUCTION

Praying for healing is very simple — it's just being a source of Jesus' love for another. I learned how simple healing can be when I was in India, praying for physical healing with Francis Mac-Nutt and Barbara Shlemon who have well-known healing ministries. A bishop came asking for prayer, and since the others were busy, another priest and I had the bishop all to ourselves. I thought, "This is great! I'll pray for this bishop and he will get healed. Then he will tell his priests that healing is real and parishes will come alive all over India." The bishop had a heart problem causing swelling in his legs. So I began to pray for the swelling in his legs to go down. I prayed for a few minutes but there was no change. I kept praying, trying every way I knew, even asking the bishop if he needed to forgive anyone. But nothing seemed to help. The bishop was in the same bad shape at the end as when we began, perhaps even worse, because of all I was going through. Finally I stopped and sat down exhausted. I felt useless and wondered if some block in me was keeping the Lord's love from working through me.

While I was sitting down and feeling useless, two men carried in a twenty-eight-year-old woman named Pauline D'Sousa. About six months before, she had been in a train wreck outside of Bombay. In that wreck all her accompanying friends had died while yelling for help. In fact, of the sixty passengers, she was the only survivor on her train car. It had taken three hours to remove passengers from the wreckage and, in the process, a blow torch had cut through the nerves in Pauline's knee. Since then, Pauline had no sensation in her right leg below the knee. Thus she could not walk normally and had to wear special shoes with braces. The accident had also wrenched her back, and so she was in constant pain even with her back brace. In addition, she was depressed and unable to sleep because she constantly heard the two trains crunching together and her friends screaming for help. Pauline had tried many doctors since the train wreck, but none could help her any further.

I ignored Pauline because I was still feeling discouraged after praying with the bishop. I also thought that because of the severity of her injury, Pauline would need some special people like Barbara or Francis to pray for her. But they were still busy, and so a couple of us, including the bishop, decided to get started with Pauline until someone else could take over. When we met Pauline, we discovered that she couldn't speak English. So all my ideas of what inner healing prayer I could say to help heal Pauline's trauma were useless. All we could do was to try like Jesus to hold her and to love her. We prayed that way in total silence for about five minutes.

Then we asked her, through an interpreter, what she was experiencing. I had to ask her because I don't usually know exactly what God is doing. I've learned that I don't need dramatic words of knowledge to pray. All I need is Jesus' love. When I don't know what is happening, I just ask the person and then pray for more of whatever is happening to continue. Pauline said, "I felt like Jesus was holding me. He came out of a bright light and for the first time in six months all my depression and anxiety are gone. I feel free." We had been praying for Jesus to hold her and to give her his peace. So we prayed for more peace. When we asked Pauline five minutes later what was happening, she said, "I feel as though my foot is buzzing. I'm beginning to have sensation in it."

So we switched to praying for the right foot. After five minutes, she could move her big toe. Five more minutes of prayer, and she could move all her toes. After another five minutes, she could move her whole foot normally. We hadn't even thought of praying for Pauline's back, but that was healed too. In thirty minutes the Lord had healed her back, her foot, and all her depression. During the past five years none of Pauline's symptoms have returned.

We were amazed that so much healing happened to Pauline. But we should not have been amazed because the deepest healings Pauline experienced happen every time we pray with Jesus' compassion for the sick. Every time we pray, focusing not on techniques or results but on loving the sick as Jesus did, all involved in the prayer experience three things: first, more peace than before the prayer; second, a closer community than before; third, a deeper sense of being Jesus. The peace Pauline experienced was so deep that it permanently banished her depression and anxiety that drugs and therapy had not touched. Finally, the sense of community between us, even though we spoke different languages, was deeper than words could express. We knew in our hearts why Jesus wanted to call the woman with the flow of blood "daughter," the closest relationship possible (Luke 5:34). Then, too, when we prayed for Pauline, we knew what it meant to be Jesus, who spent two-thirds of his days allowing the Father's healing love to touch his sick children. Growth in peace, community and being Jesus are the deepest gifts given in healing prayer. They are always given when we focus on loving as Jesus and receiving his love.

Although these three gifts are always given, I had never seen so much physical healing happen as well. After praying with Pauline, I stood back and thought, "I don't understand this. Why, when I prayed with deep faith for the bishop, did no physical healing seem to happen? How come, when I prayed with hardly any faith for Pauline, she was healed? I have thought of two reasons which now help me to understand that strange evening. The first reason has to do with my attitude. When I was praying with the bishop, I was focused more on finding the right technique, since nothing worked. In contrast, when I was praying with Pauline, because she could not speak English, I could not use any techniques and had to focus on losing myself in Jesus and trying to be him for Pauline. In praying for Pauline, I had no faith in my prayer but only in Jesus' love. But the second reason why so much happened to Pauline

was her attitude. Pauline was so confident of receiving Jesus' love that she had come that night carrying a paper sack containing her sandals. She believed that if someone prayed for her, she would not need her big therapeutic shoes. Healing is most likely to happen not only when the persons praying can let Jesus' love flow through them, but when the one receiving prayer can, like Pauline, soak up that love and expect that love to heal.

Praying with the healing love of Jesus is so simple that we can pray, as in Pauline's case, without even using words. If we are praying for another, all we have to do is let ourselves become Jesus. "To become Jesus" means that it is "no longer I who live but Jesus who lives in me" (Galatians 2:20). So, for instance, when we reach out to pray, we can try to reach out with the same compassion as Jesus, even asking him where he would place his hand, and how he would place it. Then it is just a matter of letting Jesus' love flow from our hearts, through our hands, and into the person. As we become Jesus, we will know if there is anything we are to say or do to give his love, or if we should just silently be Jesus loving.

If we are receiving prayer, all we need to do is to soak up Jesus' love. Perhaps a helpful image to soak up Jesus' love is that of being stretched out on a beach with the warm sun radiating our whole body as we allow the healing light of Jesus gradually to fill us. Sometimes it helps to breathe in Jesus' love and breathe out any darkness, but unless we feel something keeping us from receiving Jesus' love, we don't even need to do that. We don't need to think about anything; we only need to receive Jesus' love. If we are praying for healing or if we are receiving prayer, what heals is Jesus' love. As this love flows into every cell of our body, we become Jesus. To the degree we are Jesus, we are healed and heal.

I. Group Experience

A. Common Opening Prayer (5 minutes)

B. Video or Audio Tape: "Physical Healing (Practice)"

How to pray for physical healing.
1. Praying for healing is simple because healing is loving another and being Jesus for that person, rather than focusing on knowing the right techniques or having extraordinary gifts (e.g., Bishop, Pauline). If we love as much as Jesus, we

will know how Jesus would pray and the next loving step that he would take.

2. Healing can happen when there is a person who can let the Lord's love flow through himself or herself and a person who can receive that love.
3. Healing is being Jesus with every cell of our body.

Prayer for healing by silently giving and receiving Jesus' love.

C. Two Options for Remainder of Group Experience: Do one or both of the following.

Option I: If your companion wishes prayer for physical healing, be Jesus for him or her, praying to the Father. After finding out what your companion wants prayer for, place your hand on him or her in the way that Jesus wants to. Pray for your companion for 5 minutes in absolute silence. Then ask your companion what he or she is experiencing (e.g., peace, lessening of pain, healing of a relationship, etc.). Then pray for 5 more minutes in any way you wish, asking the Father to deepen the healing that he has begun.

Option II: Do the Companion Sharing ("D" below) and Companion Prayer ("E" below).

D. Companion Sharing (5 minutes minimum for each person to share his or her reaction to today's tape and to the past week).

1. What part of today's tape moved your heart most deeply?
2. Share with your companion how you have experienced the Lord's presence in your life during the previous week. You may wish to share the journal response from last week that touched you the most.
3. What are you most grateful for now and how do you need Jesus' help?

E. Companion Prayer (since the purpose of this prayer is healing, you may wish to pray over your companion for about 10 minutes). Lay your hands on your companion and pray as Jesus would for about 10 minutes. Let the words and silences in your prayer be those of Jesus as he is already praying in your heart. Give

thanks to Jesus for what your companion is most grateful for and pray for whatever healing your companion most needs. Close your prayer by praying that your companion receive the grace of this lesson: *to be Jesus praying for the sick.* Then let your companion pray over you.

F. Group Sharing (Optional—15 minutes minimum). Take two minutes of silence to ask what has been most difficult and what has been most helpful in your prayer and journaling this past week. Share your reflections with the larger group. Close with a prayer thanking the Lord for the breakthroughs and for discovering the blocks where he is already bringing forth further growth.

G. Closing Snack and Celebration (Optional). An open-ended time to enjoy one another and to continue sharing.

II. Home Experience

A. Daily Healing Prayer (10 minutes). Each day choose one of the following healing or contemplation in action prayers and pray it for at least 10 minutes. These prayers are only *suggestions.* Perhaps you will find yourself drawn to pray what is in your heart using varied breathing, a symbol, a repeated word, a melody, a gesture, a drawing or a piece of clay which you can mold. Although there are many prayers suggested, it would be best to pray only a few of them, parts of them, or to repeat from this or any other chapter the prayer that most moved your heart. Use whatever way you can best give your heart to Jesus and enter into his heart. Perhaps your prayer will be as simple as looking at a beautiful flower and taking in God's love for you. You may wish to begin your prayer by centering yourself, perhaps using the Breath Prayer (see Lesson 1). You may wish to continue with the Embrace Prayer (see Lesson 3, Prayer #2), or a similar prayer of simply resting in God's love.

1. *Prayer for Becoming Jesus* (Tape Prayer)
   a. Prayerfully read St. Paul's testimony about Jesus living in him: "The life I live now is not my own; Christ is living in me" (Galatians 2:20).
   b. Hold your hand up to Jesus and ask that it be his healing hand.

c. When you begin to experience Jesus' compassion for the sick, place your hand on the forehead or the diseased part of your body or another person's body. Be attentive to placing your hand as Jesus would, with the same care and gentleness and in the same place.

d. Pray in silence. Perhaps as you inhale and exhale you may wish to pray the word "Abba." Allow the healing light of Jesus to flow through your hand and to flood the diseased area with his peace, strength and health.

2. *Praying with the Sick*
Choose one person who is ill and pray with that person for five minutes each day. Record what you experience the Lord doing in both of you.

3. *Intercessory Prayer at a Distance*
Choose a friend who is physically ill and at a distance.
a. Prayerfully read the story of the centurion's servant (Matthew 12:5-14).
b. Repeat the centurion's request for his servant, on behalf of your friend who is ill: "Lord, I am not worthy that you should come to me; say but the word and my friend will be healed."
c. Hear Jesus' reply and visualize your friend glowing with Jesus' peace and healing light, especially in the diseased area.
(You may wish to say this prayer at the Eucharist, when the entire Church says the centurion's prayer immediately before receiving Holy Communion. Then let Jesus come to your sick friend by receiving Holy Communion on behalf of that friend.)

4. *Becoming Another*
Choose a friend who is physically ill and at a distance. Intercede for that friend by doing the Becoming Another prayer (see Lesson 1).

CONTEMPLATION IN ACTION PRAYERS

Take a moment and ask for the grace to be Jesus praying for the sick. Then do one of the following:
5. Take a person who is elderly or infirm out for a ride.

6. Look at the face of a sick person until, like Mother Teresa, you know that you are seeing the face of Jesus.
7. Visit a sick person with the same care that Jesus or Mother Teresa would.

B. Daily Journal (5 minutes)

1. Share with Jesus when during this prayer or during the day your heart was deeply moved—perhaps a moment of being grateful for or of longing for healing in *being Jesus praying for the sick.*
2. Write in your journal how Jesus responds (what he seems to do or say in response to what you have told him). If you can't get in touch with Jesus' response, write what most moves you as you speak to him or what are the most loving words you want to hear.

OPTIONAL HOME EXPERIENCE

C. Personal Reflection Questions

1. What helps you to forget about yourself and just experience Jesus praying within you and loving a sick person? What Scripture passage best reveals to you how Jesus prays with the sick?
2. As you pray with the sick, what thoughts and obstacles hinder you?
3. When have you seen an emotional healing also bring physical health? How do you know whether to pray for an emotional healing before praying for physical healing—or vice versa? In the person for whom you are praying, is it the body or the mind that is most blocking the giving and receiving of love?

D. Scripture Readings

Mark 3:1-6: Healing is so central to Jesus' ministry that it must even be done on the sabbath.
1 Corinthians 12:9: Healing as a gift of the Spirit.
1 Corinthians 12:27-13:13: Healing must be subject to the greater gift of love.
Luke 4:18-19: Jesus proclaims his identity in terms of healing.

E. Additional Reading
Same as in previous lesson, "Physical healing (Tradition)."

Lesson Sixteen
HEALING THE ENVIRONMENT

INTRODUCTION

Sometimes when the Lord has physically healed us, our first thought is, "I hope this lasts!" Though we don't know how we are going to feel tomorrow, we do know that if the Lord healed our backache today and we wake up tomorrow with a painful back, the Lord can heal that back again. Prayer for healing usually is a process, as it was in Mark's story of the blind man at Bethsaida (Mark 8:22-26). Jesus prayed for the man once, and the man's sight was restored enough that he could see shapes of people that looked to him like trees walking. So Jesus prayed again and this time the man's sight was restored completely. Unlike Jesus, too many people pray once, "claim their healing," and quit praying for more healing that the Lord wants to continue through the process of prayer.

A professor of spirituality in Rome told us how he learned that physical healing is often a process. He said, "About two months ago I prayed for a blind man. As I prayed, his sight improved. So I kept praying. But then his sight left him, and he was as blind as when we began. I didn't know what was happening, but I did know that Jesus had used our prayer and could make him well. So I told the man and his wife to go home and pray for each other for five minutes every day for two months and then come back to see me again. They came back a week ago, and the man could see perfectly. But this was not the deepest healing. He told me that their marriage had been falling apart. The deepest healing was that the process of being Jesus for each other for five minutes every day had reawakened in them an awareness of how much they really loved each other, and their marriage

was now healed." If Jesus takes his time in healing us, it's usually because he knows we need more love, and usually because someone needs the experience of giving us that love by being Jesus for us. Throughout the whole healing process, we can give and receive Jesus' love — and that's always going to be healing.

Healing the family is important not only in beginning the healing process but also in maintaining the healing we receive. When we were working on the Sioux reservation, we would take people into Minneapolis for the regional charismatic conference and they would receive prayer. Through this prayer, Jesus healed many of their physical illnesses. But then they would return home to the reservation and to many family problems. Within a few months they would become sick again. (Maybe that is why Jesus took the Bethsaida blind man out of the village and told him not to go back.) So we began to work on healing the relationships in their families. In those homes where relationships were healed as love deepened, people stayed well physically. Healing happens when we're surrounded by an environment of love.

Not only the entire family but also doctors and nurses make up an important part of that healing environment of love. Dr. Larry Samuels, who works in nuclear medicine, told us that after he began to pray over his work he could more readily find hairline bone fractures that other nuclear medicine specialists had missed. Another friend, a nurse in a prenatal unit, must insert IV tubes into tiny babies. This is very difficult to do because babies' veins are so small. Our friend has developed a reputation for being able to insert IV tubes on the first try, and when the doctors are having difficulty they will call her in to help. Her secret is that, in front of all the doctors, she will hold up the IV needle and say, "Lord Jesus, just guide my hand and help me to insert this needle because this little child is yours and you love it." The Lord wants to use doctors, nurses, and all the other means of healing that he has created.

Medicine is a special means that the Lord uses to heal. In inviting his disciples to anoint with oil, Jesus was inviting them to use the most common medicine of his time (Mark 6:13). Too many think that it is an act of faith to throw away medicine rather than to bless it and use it as Jesus did. Many nurses bless medicine for the same reason they bless food — so that it will bring health. A nurse, or anyone else, can say a prayer over medicine, such as, "Lord Jesus, you made this medicine. I ask you to bless it so that it will have its full healing effect with no harmful side-effects. I ask this in the name of the Father, the Son and the Holy Spirit." Nurses who bless pain medication in this way have told me that their patients usually need one-third less medication.

Praying for the whole environment — whether praying for the entire family on the Indian reservation or for pain medication in a hospital — is the way that Jesus prayed. Jesus prayed not only to heal people but to heal the whole environment, as when he calmed the storm at sea (Mark 4:35-41). Agnes Sanford, an Episcopalian laywoman, also prayed to heal the whole environment. Agnes spent the last years of her life living in California, right on the San Andreas earthquake fault line. A seismologist would tell her when there was danger of an earthquake and in what direction the earth needed to shift. Every morning she would pray for the Lord's peace and light to enter the shifting earth and for any strong shock waves to be calmed and moved out to sea.

Praying for the whole environment includes not only praying for the natural elements (e.g., sea or earth's fault) but also for plants and animals. In India we met a Jesuit who was living in a poor village. He told us how he had healed a dying water buffalo by pouring a bottle of holy water down its throat and praying over it. He said, "I thought that water buffalo would keel right back over and die. But it's been well ever since I prayed for it. And not only that, but now all the people in the village are bringing me their dogs and cats and chickens and other animals whenever they get sick — and I do the same thing. I just pour holy water over them all, and I pray, and they get well too. I don't understand it . . . all I know is it works!" The Lord has put the whole of creation into our

hands and we can exercise that stewardship by praying for our physical environment.

Not just our physical environment but also our social environment is healed when we forget about ourselves and reach out in prayer. While in India, we gave a retreat for priests and ended with a healing service open to all. About four thousand people came — laypeople, Hindus, Muslims, everyone. We told them to turn to the person next to them and to pray for each other. Touchables reached out to untouchables, Hindus prayed for Muslims or Christians, men and women (who do not usually touch each other in that culture) were touching and praying for each other. The love of Jesus drew people together who otherwise might never have loved or touched each other. Social barriers broke down as people reached out across those barriers, and many were physically and emotionally healed.

Religious barriers also fell. After the people had prayed for one another, we invited them to go to a priest if they still needed healing. We found that there was no easier way to evangelize those Hindus and Muslims than for them to see priests standing out in the rain for two hours, wanting to be there with the love of Jesus for as long as they were needed. When the Hindus and Muslims saw such love, they perceived the essence of Christianity and many conversions took place. Such love affected not only the Hindus and Muslims, but also the priests. The next day priests told us how they had experienced Jesus' love for the poor, for women, for Hindus, for untouchables as never before and how social barriers had been erased for them. And the other thing they said was, "We got physically healed just in the act of reaching out." Priests who the day before had arthritis, and whose illness would ordinarily have become more severe in the rain, had been healed. When we reach out for another person, the Lord not only will heal us physically but will also heal our social environment.

Not only can physical healing heal our social environment, but healing our social environment can lead to a deeper gift of physical healing. Several years ago a man named Ralph had an accident while loading a truck. His back was crushed and the doctors told him that he would never work again. So the government gave Ralph a full disability pension for the rest of his life. However, Ralph had some friends who took him to the prayer meeting in Newburgh, New York. This prayer group prayed many times for him, and gradually his back was healed. Ralph went to the disability office to report that since Jesus had healed his back he could work and would not need disability checks anymore. But the government people said that after such an accident Ralph's back could never be well. He couldn't convince anyone in the disability office that his back was well. So Ralph just kept receiving checks in the mail.

With checks still coming in the mail, Ralph didn't need a paying job and so he decided to use his time to serve the Lord. His prayer group had a garden where they grew food for the poor. When the garden wasn't in season, he searched for other sources of food to give away. Meanwhile, he had begun praying for other people to be healed the way he was. As Ralph's prayers were answered, the people he prayed for offered him food to give to the poor. One man, whose son Ralph had prayed for and who had been healed of a drug problem, gave Ralph six-hundred dozen English muffins each week to give to the poor. With so much food piling up, Ralph went to the prayer group and said, "I need a truck to take all this food to the poor." A lady in the prayer group who had been healed of cancer offered to buy Ralph a truck. The more Ralph reached out to pray for the needs of others, the more food he received for the poor. When Ralph takes the food to the poor, he prays for them, so they not only have food but they also know the Lord's peace and healing. The whole prayer community in Newburgh has learned to reach out, going into homes in the inner city and bringing love and friendship as well as food. The more this community reaches out to change the social environment of the poor, the more Jesus blesses them with the gift of healing and of deep deliverance prayer. This was promised long ago: "This, rather, is the fasting that I wish: releasing those bound unjustly, untying the thongs of the yoke; setting free the oppressed, breaking every yoke; sharing your bread with the hungry, sheltering the oppressed and the homeless; clothing the named when you see them, and not turning your back on your own. Then your light shall break forth like the dawn, and your wound shall quickly be healed; your vindication shall go before you, and the glory of the Lord shall be your rear guard" (Isaiah 58:6-8).

Our wounds shall "quickly be healed" as we reach out to heal the whole environment.

I. Group Experience

A. Common Opening Prayer (5 minutes)

B. Video or Audio Tape: "Healing the Environment" (30 minutes)

Continuing to pray for our healing and extending the healing power of the Lord . . . all over.

1. Healing is a process that often takes time (e.g., Jesus and the blind man, couple in Rome). Claiming a healing that is not present may keep us from using the medicine and further prayer through which Jesus wants to complete our healing.
2. Our healing may not last if we return to an unloving environment (e.g., Indian reservation).
3. We can pray for healing of the whole environment. We can pray for doctors, nurses and medicines (e.g., Dr. Larry Samuels, nurse and IV tubes for babies). We can pray for all of nature (e.g., Francis MacNutt's tree, Agnes Sanford and the San Andreas fault, Indian water buffalo).
4. Praying for healing is the best way to evangelize (e.g., St. Francis Xavier and the children of India).
5. Healing happens when we reach out to others — even the healing of whole social structures (e.g., Indian villagers who shared their food with the hungry, priests' retreat in India, Ralph and his community in New York).

C. Silent Reflection (3 minutes). Quiet time to get in touch with what part of today's tape moved your heart most deeply.

D. Guided Journaling (Optional — 10 minutes). See Lesson 3.

E. Companion Sharing (5 minutes minimum for each person to share his or her reaction to today's tape and to the past week).

1. Share with your companion as much as you wish of what is in your heart after seeing this week's tape. Perhaps you will want to share what you have just written during the guided journaling.
2. Share with your companion how you have experienced the Lord's presence in your life during the previous week. You

may wish to share the journal response from last week that touched you the most.

3. What are you most grateful for now and and how do you need Jesus' help?

F. **Companion Prayer** (since the purpose of this prayer is healing, you may wish to pray over your companion for about 10 minutes). Lay your hands on your companion and pray as Jesus would for about 10 minutes. Let the words and silences in your prayer be those of Jesus as he is already praying in your heart. Give thanks to Jesus for what your companion is most grateful for and pray for whatever healing your companion most needs. Close your prayer by praying that your companion receive the grace of this lesson: *giving life to the sick and to the whole environment.* Then let your companion pray over you.

G. **Group Sharing** (Optional—15 minutes minimum). Take two minutes of silence to ask what has been most difficult and what has been most helpful in your prayer and journaling this past week. Share your reflections with the larger group. Close with a prayer thanking the Lord for the breakthroughs and for discovering the blocks where he is already bringing forth further growth.

H. **Closing Snack and Celebration** (Optional). An open-ended time to enjoy one another and to continue sharing.

II. Home Experience

A. **Daily Healing Prayer** (10 minutes). Each day choose one of the following healing or contemplation in action prayers and pray it for at least 10 minutes. These prayers are only *suggestions*. Perhaps you will find yourself drawn to pray what is in your heart using varied breathing, a symbol, a repeated word, a melody, a gesture, a drawing, or a piece of clay which you can mold. Although there are many prayers suggested, it would be best to pray only a few of them, parts of them, or to repeat from this or any other chapter the prayer that most moved your heart. Use whatever way you can best give your heart to Jesus and enter into his heart. Perhaps your prayer will be

as simple as looking at a beautiful flower and taking in God's love for you. You may wish to begin your prayer by centering yourself, perhaps using the Breath Prayer (see Lesson 1). You may wish to continue with the Embrace Prayer (see Lesson 3, Prayer #2), or a similar prayer of simply resting in God's love.

1. *Praying Light into the World* (Tape Prayer)
   a. Sense Jesus before you saying, "I am the light of the world. No follower of mine shall ever walk in darkness; no, he shall possess the light of life" (John 8:12).
   b. Ask Jesus to show you how he wishes to bring the light of life into your corner of the world. Perhaps he wants you to pray for a person, a place (office, classroom, etc.) or a thing (tree, animal, medicine, etc.), asking that it be filled with his healing light.
   c. Imagine the creative light of the Father flowing through you as you let yourself be Jesus. Let this light flow into the person, place or thing that you wish to fill with the loving presence of God. Continue letting the light flow through you until you sense that whatever you are praying for is glowing and glorifying the Father.

2. *Health Prayer*
   a. Thank God for each part of your body that is healthy.
   b. Surrender each part to him. If you wish, consecrate each part to God for his use with the sign of the cross.

3. *Persevering in Soaking Prayer*
   a. Ask Jesus to show you the face of one physically ill person who needs your prayer for an entire week.
   b. Pray every day for that person, in the way that Jesus leads your heart.
   c. Record the moment when you were most like Jesus, with his compassion and desire to heal the sick. Record how the Spirit moved you to pray at that moment (e.g., for the person to be filled with light or love, for inner healing, the gift of redemptive suffering, deliverance from evil spirits, a resurrected body, etc.).

4. *Blessing Medicine*

Bless the medicine in your medicine cabinet, asking that it have no harmful side-effects and that it be used for Jesus' healing. You may also wish to say a short prayer asking Jesus to work through your doctor as well as through medicines.

5. *Blessing of Oil*

Have a priest bless oil for lay use with the blessing in the back of this book (see Appendix J). Use the oil to pray for one person.

6. *Anointing with the Name of Jesus*

Song of Songs 1:3 says, "Your name is oil poured out." The name "Jesus" (Yeshuah in Hebrew) means "Yahweh saves" or "healing of Yahweh." The "healing of Yahweh" refers to the whole person — body, mind and spirit. With the name of "Jesus" that brings health, anoint each part of your body while imagining his healing oil soaking into it. For example, if you have a headache, just say "Jesus" and experience his oil penetrating and warming each cell in your head until it is whole. When you sense that it is time, move on to another part of your body. You might want to intercede for a sick person who is far away by picturing that person in your mind, focusing on the part of that person's body that is not whole. Anoint the corresponding part of your own body with the healing name of Jesus.

CONTEMPLATION IN ACTION PRAYERS

Take a moment and ask for the grace to give life to the sick and to the environment. Then do one of the following:

7. *Feeding the Sick*

Bring to a sick person something you have baked or some other food he or she would appreciate. While bringing the food, say an informal prayer asking that the Lord bless the food and that it bring health.

8. *Listening to the Sick*

a. Read John 5:1-15 and see how Jesus listens to the sick.

b. Visit a sick person and listen to him or her until you compassionately understand how his world looks through that person's eyes.

c. When you feel moved by compassion, you might ask if the sick person wishes prayer, and pray for him or her out of the love in your heart. If the person is uncomfortable with receiving prayer now, just promise to keep him or her in your own prayers.

9. *Healing by Reaching Out*

a. Read Isaiah 58:5-11, where God promises to heal our wounds more quickly if we reach out to the needy.

b. Ask the Lord what needy person he wants you to reach out to, and how.

10. *God Loving in Creation*

Prayerfully read Luke 12:22-31.

a. Let the Father's love flow through you into a flower or plant as you hold it for 5 minutes.

b. Now hold the flower or plant for another 5 minutes and let yourself be loved by the Creator as he gifts you with it. Absorb all his love.

B. Daily Journal (5 minutes)

1. Share with Jesus when during this prayer or during the day your heart was deeply moved — perhaps a moment of being grateful for or of longing for healing in *giving life to the sick and to the environment.*

2. Write in your journal how Jesus responds (what he seems to do or say in response to what you have told him). If you can't get in touch with Jesus' response, write what most moves you as you speak to him or what are the most loving words you want to hear.

OPTIONAL HOME EXPERIENCES

C. Personal Reflection Questions

1. What would you say to a person who told you to claim your healing and throw your medicine away? How does pretending that an unhealed illness is healed prevent you from using the medical and spiritual means that the Lord uses to

heal? Is faith in our own faith the same as faith in God's love?

2. Have you ever experienced being healed as you forgot about yourself and reached out to another? Did you ever have pain go away while you were praying for another?

3. When have you most experienced how much God loves his creation? When have you experienced God loving you through his creation?

D. Scripture Readings

Sirach 38:1-15: The Divine Physician works through the doctor.

Isaiah 58:6-11: The fasting that heals wounds by caring for the poor.

Mark 8:22-26: The progressive healing of the blind man.

Colossians 1:15-20: All creation is to be filled with Christ and made one in him.

E. Additional Readings

The Power to Heal, by Francis MacNutt (Notre Dame: Ave Maria, 1977).

Creation Waits, by Agnes Sanford (Plainfield, N.J.: Logos International, 1977). Encourages us to believe in our power to pray for the earth.

NOTE: You may want to use the following meeting as a Gratitude Session. See Appendix G for suggested format. After the Gratitude Session, you may wish to take a vacation in order to rest and integrate the experience of the course before going on to Lesson 17.

Lesson Seventeen
DELIVERANCE PRAYER (TRADITION)

INTRODUCTION

In grade school we would give up candy during Lent. One nun taught us that if the evil one tempted us to eat candy, all we had to do was brush him off our shoulders and say, "Get out of here, Satan! I don't want you." I can remember walking by the store and looking at all the candy inside — and then brushing Satan off my shoulder and saying, "Get out of here, Satan!" The surprising thing is that it worked, even with all my desire for candy. But her approach was a bit simplistic because temptation can arise not only from the devil but also from the world (mouth-watering ads for an "indescribably delicious Almond Joy") and the flesh (a hungry stomach). But there was a truth in what she told us; we do have power over the evil one.

Jesus lives within us and he has given us power over the evil one. The power to command, in Jesus' name, the evil one to leave us alone is what we call deliverance prayer. We call this deliverance prayer because we are asking to be delivered from the power of the evil one. Deliverance prayer differs from exorcism prayer which is used when our whole person is entirely under the control of Satan, as in the case of the Gerasene demoniac who "screamed and gashed himself with stones" and whom "no one had proved strong enough to tame" (Mark 5:1-9). On the other hand, deliverance prayer is used when only a part of our personality (as in some cases of uncontrollable anger, sexual deviations, deafness, etc.) is under the influence of the evil spirit. Such was the case of the woman "who for eighteen years had been possessed by a spirit which drained her strength" making it impossible for her to be erect (Luke 13:10). Whereas an official exorcism has to be performed by someone appointed by the bishop, any loving mature Christian can pray deliverance prayer. Deliverance prayer is the kind of prayer that we are praying every time we end the "Our Father" saying "Deliver us from evil."

Jesus and the people of his time prayed for deliverance from evil spirits and expected the prayer to work. When the Pharisees attacked Jesus for doing exorcisms, they did not question that he was really casting out evil spirits. They were simply accusing Jesus of doing it through the wrong power (Mark 3:22-27). The defeat of Satan through deliverance prayer was so evident that Jesus used it as proof for the coming of God's reign (Luke 11:20). Scripture scholars tell us today that the scriptural accounts of Jesus' power over Satan are among those passages most readily authenticated as actual historical events.[1]

Jesus gave his disciples and us his same power over Satan. In the story of the epileptic boy (Mark 9:14-29) Jesus encourages his disciples to fast and pray for power over evil spirits. On another occasion, the disciples return to share their successful deliverances (Luke 10:17-20). Finally, at the end of Mark's Gospel, Jesus commissions all his followers to take authority over evil spirits (Mark 16:17).

The prayer said by his followers throughout the early Church, the "Our Father," originally said: "Deliver us from the evil one." Not until around the time of Augustine was the common usage, "Deliver us from evil." The early Christians expected that when they prayed the "Our Father," the Father would deliver them from the

---

1. For theological views on deliverance see, Dennis Linn and Matthew Linn, *Deliverance Prayer* (Ramsey, N.J.: Paulist Press, 1981).

evil one's power. The traditions of the Desert Fathers and of saints such as the Cure d'Ars and St. Francis of Assisi testify to real encounters with Satan and an even more vivid awareness of having Jesus' authority to resist evil. The rite of baptism is an example of how Jesus hands on his power to us. The sacrament of baptism includes prayers for exorcism, and the new adult rite has a special exorcism prayer. This additional prayer is for adults previously involved in a non-Christian religion where they may have met not just the loving God whom many religions seek but also the forces of evil which only Jesus can fully overcome.

In 1972, Pope Paul VI stated that "the greatest need in the Church today" is that we recognize and overcome the reality of the devil who is not just an idea or social construct but "an effective agent, a living, spiritual being, perverted and perverting."[2] Throughout the ages the Church has dealt with the evil one through everything that brings Jesus' life into a person, such as the sacraments, and through deliverance prayer which directly commands the evil one to leave. Today more than ever, we need to exercise wisely this power of deliverance because so many people have become involved with the occult or with drugs, thus lowering the will's resistance and opening themselves to the evil one's influence.

Deliverance prayer requires wise caution, as Cardinal Suenens lately reminded us. As we become aware of this kind of prayer, we may overuse it and begin to focus on Satan rather than on Jesus. An overemphasis on solving all through deliverance prayer may also keep us from using medicine and psychiatry or from taking action on justice issues. We may abdicate personal responsibility for our actions and say, "Satan made me do it," rather than drawing on what power we do have to choose what is right in any given situation. It is as dangerous to find Satan everywhere as it is to ignore him completely.

Given these cautions, the reality of deliverance prayer is being recognized not only by many Scripture scholars and spiritual theologians, but also by members of the psychiatric and counseling professions. In 1974 an English medical journal, *The Practitioner,* discussed deliverance prayer as one possible help in treating schizophrenia. In 1978 *The Archives of Sexual Behavior* published a study of a man who had a female gender identity and wanted to have an operation to become a transsexual. Through deliverance prayer his gender identity was changed and the operation was unnecessary. This study was reprinted in our book, *Deliverance Prayer*, which discusses many additional ways in which psychological and sociological research can be integrated with the spirituality of deliverance prayer.[3]

Recently we learned about a dramatic example of the power of deliverance prayer to help those who have psychological problems. We visited a therapist in Connecticut who had been working with thirty-two of his patients for two years or longer. He invited a woman, known for her gift of discerning spirits, to evaluate each of these patients. Without being told anything of the patient's history, she was able to correctly diagnose the problem and its roots and to indicate if an evil spirit were connected to the problem. In twenty-eight of the thirty-two cases, this woman discerned an evil spirit connected with the problem that the person was experiencing. After deliverance prayer, all but one of these twenty-eight patients were released from their emotional illness within three months.

What is the relationship between evil spirits and emotional illness? The common illness of depression, for example, has many possible causes. A depression may have a primarily physical cause as with hypoglycemia. Of course, depression may be caused by emotional factors and some depression may be caused by spiritual factors (i.e., unforgiveness or perhaps the spirit of depression). Any given case of depression may be caused by one or any combination of these factors. So I would not approach a depressed person and say, "You have a spirit of depression. Spirit, I command you to leave." I would not do this because, first of all, such an accusation might fill the person with fear, and, second, I cannot always be sure that the cause of the depression is an evil spirit. However, if I suspected the presence of an evil spirit, what I might do is pray silently, commanding the spirit to leave. On the one hand it is important not to overuse deliverance prayer or

2. "Deliver Us From Evil," General Audience of Pope Paul VI, Nov. 15, 1972 reprinted in *L'Osservatore Romano* (Nov. 23, 1972).

3. Dennis and Matthew Linn, *Deliverance Prayer* (Ramsey, N.J.: Paulist Press, 1981). Also in *Feeling and Healing Your Emotions* Dr. Conrad Baars, a Catholic psychiatrist, mentions simple ways that he uses deliverance prayer with his patients.

to frighten people by telling them that they have evil spirits. On the other hand, it is important to know that sometimes evil spirits are involved in cases of emotional illness and it can be helpful to command them to leave in the name of Jesus.

It is easier to command evil spirits to leave if we know how they entered. Evil spirits enter us by three main doors: emotional wounds, sin, and occult activity. The majority of spirits enter through festering emotional wounds such as those of fear, anger, guilt, or resentment that are left by deep emotional hurts. For example, a person who has been hurt by an alcoholic father may be opened to a spirit of anger and then experience much persistent anger, e.g., against his father, authority figures, other alcoholics etc. These emotional wounds can remain open doors for spirit activity unless inner healing occurs by experiencing Jesus loving us and then helping us to forgive those who have hurt us. When dealing with a spirit of anger, for example, we ask what deep hurt caused this angry reaction and how Jesus wants to enter the scene of that hurt to help us to love and to forgive. Are there any other hurts that fuel this reaction and need healing? As Jesus heals those hurtful events, the wound is healed, and the spirit must leave. Healing the wound closes the door, thus preventing the spirit's return.

The second door inviting spirits is labeled "sin." For example, if we continually tell lies, we gradually lose our will power to tell the truth. This weakening of our will can invite a spirit of deceit that will not go away until the will is strengthened by true contrition, confession of the sinful pattern, and a desire to tell the truth with the help of Jesus. Usually, under the sinful pattern is a hurt needing healing. For instance, perhaps our habit of telling lies occurs especially when trying to make additional financial gains, such as lying about earnings on income tax returns. Behind these lies may be a need for extra financial gains in order to insulate us from painful memories of childhood poverty. When Jesus, through inner healing prayer, heals that hurt and when we confess the pattern of sin and open ourselves to Jesus' healing forgiveness, then the spirits invited by our sinful pattern must leave. One of the most powerful ways of closing sin's door is through the sacrament of reconciliation where we ask for forgiveness for our sin and for holding on to emotional wounds rather than forgiving those who hurt us.

Besides emotional wounds and sin, the third door inviting spirits is occult activity. By occult activity is meant the seeking of power or guidance from sources opposed to Jesus Christ such as ouija boards, seances, and non-Christian religions.

Is everything non-Christian to be condemned as the occult? The Second Vatican Council encourages Catholics to find the good in non-Christian religions and not just condemn every facet of their teachings. It is obvious that many non-Christians grow spiritually with the power to love as did Mahatma Gandhi through the Hindu religion. The more a non-Christian religion recognizes a God of love, the more God who is love can use it. If a religion calls its followers to love one another and a loving God, then it may be a step toward the true God and eventually perhaps to embracing the full revelation of Christianity. Religions may serve much as the custom of dating does, providing occasions to learn about the process of loving. But once you have found the one God chose for you from eternity and you make a total commitment in marriage, you can no longer romantically flirt with others. So, too, a committed Christian will often find that former non-Christian practices compromise a total commitment to Jesus Christ and what previously led to Jesus Christ now leads away. Of course, non-Christian religions may also have elements that can hurt, such as curses, seances, or gods who are evil and must be kept away by sacrifices to them. Both totally condemning as occult or approving everything in non-Christian religions is a strategy of the evil one.

Occult bondage can occur even when we have not actively participated in an occult activity. For instance, we can inherit this bondage from a previous generation, as Scripture states (Exodus 20:3-6). Occasionally, too, we can be victims of an occult curse, pact, or seal put on us three times in mockery of the Trinity, and thus it helps to renounce the occult bondage three times.

We can break occult bondage through three steps. First, heal any hurts that may have led us to seek occult power, and in prayer return to the time that the occult choice was made and choose Jesus. Second, confess and receive forgiveness for any involvement. Third, renounce the involvement and form new bonds with Jesus. For example, "Through the power of the cross, I renounce any occult involvement (name it specifically) in which I or my ancestors have participated. In the name of Jesus, I break all bondage, and I command any spirit to go peacefully and directly to Jesus. With my whole heart I give my life entirely to Jesus." This deliverance prayer has added depth if we say it at the Eucharist where the blood of Jesus can break the most powerful occult bonds and forge more powerful bonds to Jesus.

While prayer against occult involvement is not often needed, deliverance prayer may be needed often. When we first began to speak about deliverance, we noticed a lot of fear in ourselves — fear that people would react badly, or that we would have more people to minister to than we could handle. What we did was simply to say, "Spirit of fear, in Jesus' name I bind you, and I command you to leave." The fear lifted and we were free to speak publicly about deliverance prayer. If we are attentive, we will notice that we are praying for deliverance in our daily prayers, as in the "Our Father" or the prayer that used to be said after the Eucharist, "St. Michael the Archangel, defend us in battle." We can pray these simple deliverance prayers alone or with friends. It can be as simple as gathering all the members of the family or community together in the morning before each one goes off to work or to school and asking that each be protected from the evil spirit for that day.

We can also pray deliverance prayer for people who are not present just as Jesus did for the Canaanite woman's daughter (Matthew 15:16-29). One way to do such intercessory prayer is to imagine the healing light of Jesus filling that person as we command the evil one to leave that person alone. We can do this not only for individuals in our families or communities but also for entire cities. We have a friend who works in a parish in Houston, Texas. Houston had one of the highest murder rates in the United States — in 1980, around one thousand murders a year. The greatest number of murders in Houston are committed on Friday night. Our friend gathered the members of his parish together on a Friday night and led them in a procession around the block, praying for the whole city as they went. He was leading them in many prayers, including a prayer of deliverance, saying, "Spirit of murder, in Jesus' name I bind you, and I command you to leave." For the next twenty-four hours, there were no murders committed in the city of Houston. He tried this a second time, on another Friday night, with the same results. We have the power to free ourselves, to free others, and to free whole cities from the power of evil by commanding Satan to leave in the name of Jesus. "Master, even the demons are subject to us in your name" (Luke 10:17).

I. Group Experience

A. Common Opening Prayer (5 minutes)

B. Video or Audio Tape: "Deliverance Prayer (Tradition)" (30 minutes)

The Lord has given us the power to command the evil one to leave us alone.

1. Jesus exercised the power to deliver people from evil spirits. He gave this same power to the apostles and to all Christians.
2. Deliverance prayer requires caution, prudence and deep union with Jesus.
3. Some members of the psychiatric profession are recognizing the role of evil spirits in mental illness and the power of deliverance prayer (e.g., clinic in Connecticut).
4. A simple, silent prayer for deliverance is often all that is needed.
5. We can become open to evil spirits in three ways:
   a. Deep hurts (e.g., Indian woman and Krishna). This is the most common way that evil spirits gain power in our lives. The solution is inner healing, which closes the door through which the spirits can enter.
   b. A pattern of sin (e.g., Mary Magdalene). The solution is to confess the sin and receive God's power to change.
   c. Involvement with drugs or the occult. The person needs to renounce the involvement and invite Jesus in its place.
6. Most deliverance prayer is an everyday experience in which we pray for ourselves or others (e.g., the Our Father).
7. We can pray for deliverance not only for individuals, but for entire cities (e.g., parish in Houston).

Closing Prayer: for Jesus to deliver us in one area of our lives in which we compromise on our commitment to him.

C. Silent Reflection (3 minutes). Quiet time to get in touch with what part of today's tape moved your heart most deeply.

D. Guided Journaling (Optional — 10 minutes). See Lesson 3.

E. Companion Sharing (5 minutes minimum for each person to share his or her reaction to today's tape and to the past week).

1. Share with your companion as much as you wish of what is in your heart after seeing this week's tape. Perhaps you will want to share what you have just written during the guided journaling.

2. Share with your companion how you have experienced the Lord's presence in your life during the previous week. You may wish to share the journal response from last week that touched you the most.

3. What are you most grateful for now and how do you need Jesus' help?

F. **Companion Prayer** (since the purpose of this prayer is healing, you may wish to pray over your companion for about 10 minutes). Lay your hands on your companion and pray as Jesus would for about 10 minutes. Let the words and silences in your prayer be those of Jesus as he is already praying in your heart. Give thanks to Jesus for what your companion is most grateful for and pray for whatever healing your companion most needs. Close your prayer by praying that your companion receive the grace of this lesson: *to be delivered from the evil one in times of temptation and struggle.* Then let your companion pray over you.

G. **Group Sharing** (Optional — 15 minutes minimum). Take two minutes of silence to ask what has been most difficult and what has been most helpful in your prayer and journaling this past week. Share your reflections with the larger group. Close with a prayer thanking the Lord for the breakthroughs and for discovering the blocks where he is already bringing forth further growth.

H. **Closing Snack and Celebration** (Optional). An open-ended time to enjoy one another and to continue sharing.

II. Home Experience

A. **Daily Healing Prayer** (10 minutes). Each day choose one of the following healing or contemplation in action prayers and pray it for at least 10 minutes. These prayers are *suggestions*. Perhaps you will find yourself drawn to pray what is in your heart using varied breathing, a symbol, a repeated word, a melody, a gesture, a drawing, or a piece of clay which you can mold. Although there are many prayers suggested, it would be best to pray only a few of them, parts of them, or to repeat from this or any other chapter the prayer that most moved your heart. Use whatever way you can best give your heart to Jesus and enter into his heart. Perhaps your prayer will be as simple as looking at a beautiful flower and taking in God's love for you. You may wish to begin your prayer by centering yourself, perhaps using the Breath Prayer (see Lesson 1). You may wish to continue with the Embrace Prayer (see Lesson 3, Prayer #2), or a similar prayer of simply resting in God's love.

1. *Deliverance Prayer*
   a. Before a crucifix, prayerfully read Acts 4:12: "There is no salvation in anyone but Jesus, for there is no other name in the whole world given to men by which we are to be saved."
   b. Let the Lord reveal to you an area of compromise in your life — a way in which your heart is divided. It may be remnants of occult activity, a habit of sin, or a hurt that you hold on to.
   c. Before the crucifix upon which Jesus overcame all compromise and triumphed over evil, take authority over that entire area of your life by praying the following prayer of command: "In Jesus' name, I take authority over anything in me that is evil. I bind all (mention the area, e.g., anger, fear, guilt, lust) and command it to leave and be conquered by Jesus."
   d. See Jesus conquering all upon the cross. Breathe in Jesus' power with the words, "Lord, Jesus Christ," taking in all that you need and exhaling the area of compromise with a word describing it (e.g., "anger," "fear," "guilt," "lust"). Do this until you sense the Lord's presence filling you with new freedom.

2. *Prayer for Receiving the Grace of This Lesson.*
   Ask Jesus to give you his ability to resist the evil one in times of temptation and struggle. Breathe it in with every breath and breathe out all the blocks in yourself to resisting evil. (You may wish to pray this prayer with Mary instead of Jesus.)

3. *Cleansing with the Blood of Jesus*
   a. As you receive the Eucharist, let

Jesus' precious blood cleanse you as it joins your blood. Let it remove all the impurities from your body as you breathe out all that is not of Jesus.

b. Let Jesus bond you to himself as his precious blood fills you. Surrender all by repeating, more deeply each time, "Lord Jesus Christ."

c. Another time, you may wish to receive the Eucharist on behalf of someone who needs freedom. As you stand in for that person repeat the above.

4. *Walking on Water*
   a. Read Matthew 14:22-33 and get in touch with how you are like Peter, who is fearful to walk in a new way.
   b. When you are in touch with your fears, focus on Jesus until you can hear him say, "Come." See what happens as you walk toward Jesus while focusing on his strength and protection. Don't get wet feet!

5. *Prayer for Protection*
   Begin and end the day with a prayer for the Lord's protection. When you feel hassled or tired during the day, ask for and see Jesus protecting you. You may wish to use the following prayers:

   Prayer to St. Michael the Archangel
   St. Michael the Archangel, defend us in the day of battle. Be our safeguard against the wickedness and snares of the devil. May God rebuke him, we humbly pray, and do you, O prince of the heavenly host, by the power of God thrust down to hell Satan and all evil spirits who prowl about the world seeking the destruction of souls. Amen.

   St. Patrick's Breastplate
   Christ be with me, Christ before me, Christ behind me, Christ in me, Christ beneath me, Christ above me, Christ on my right, Christ on my left, Christ where I lie, Christ where I sit, Christ where I arise.
   Christ in the heart of every man who thinks of me, Christ in the mouth of every man who speaks of me, Christ in every eye that sees me, Christ in every ear that hears me.

CONTEMPLATION IN ACTION PRAYERS

Take a moment and ask for the grace to be delivered from the evil one in times of temptation and struggle. Then do one of the following:

6. Take a moment to ask Jesus to make you a source of his light. Then sunbathe or sit under a lamp while filling yourself with the Lord's light. When you are filled, radiate his light in all directions by breathing out "Jesus" and seeing the persons and places you are praying for filled with light.

7. Read about your patron saint and ask for his or her help and protection.

8. Take a shower and let the water become the living water of Jesus washing all evil from you and bringing you new life in the ways that you thirst for it (John 4:13-14).

B. Daily Journal (5 minutes)

1. Share with Jesus when during this prayer or during the day your heart was deeply moved — perhaps a moment of being grateful for or of longing for healing in *being delivered from the evil one in times of temptation and struggle.*

2. Write in your journal how Jesus responds (what he seems to be or say in response to what you have told him). If you can't get in touch with Jesus' response, write what most moves you as you speak to him or what are the most loving words you want to hear.

OPTIONAL HOME EXPERIENCES

C. Personal Reflection Questions

1. What makes you believe in the reality of the evil one? What makes you dismiss it?

2. C.S. Lewis says that the devil wants you to either ignore him or see him everywhere. How do you know whether you are focusing too much or too little on the evil one?

3. In the *Spiritual Exercises,* St. Ignatius reveals the devil's strategy:
   a. The devil tries to keep us discouraged and in desolation. Can you identify the mood you are in when you are most open to temptation?
   b. He tempts good people with the good,

such as telling them to be more generous when they are already over-extended. How are you tempted by the good?

c. He is like the commander of any army, looking for the weakest place to attack. What hurts, sinful habits or occult experiences might have opened you to the evil one's power?

d. He likes to keep his moves secret and convince you that your struggles are too shameful or too unimportant to share with a confessor or another. What would be hard for you to share with someone else?

e. He bluffs being powerful but he is really like a person who flees when confronted. Have you ever experienced this? If so, what helped you to see through his bluff?

D. Scripture Readings

Romans 8:35-39: Nothing can separate us from Christ, who conquers all evil.
Ephesians 6:10-18: Actions to fight evil.

Mark 16:15-20: The commission to all Christians to overcome evil.
Mark 9:14-29: Without prayer, the disciples fail to expel the epileptic's demon.
Matthew 6:9-13: Jesus' model prayer for deliverance from evil.
Psalms 62, 68 & 91: Rely on God's protection.
Matthew 7:15-23: Don't focus on demons, but on doing the will of the Father.
Matthew 12:45: Warning that a person must be filled with God's life or demons will return.
Ephesians 3:14-21: Paul's prayer for deliverance into all dimensions of Christ.

E. Additional Readings

Healing, by Francis MacNutt (Notre Dame: Ave Maria, 1974). Chapter 15, "Deliverance and Exorcism."
Deliverance from Evil Spirits, by Michael Scanlan and Randall Cirner (Ann Arbor: Servant Books, 1980).
Deliverance Prayer, by Matthew & Dennis Linn (New York: Paulist Press, 1981).

Lesson Eighteen
DELIVERANCE PRAYER (PRACTICE)

INTRODUCTION

My experience with deliverance prayer began when Norma called me one day. She said, "I've been deeply depressed. I've had all the psychiatric help I can, and I don't know what else to do." Norma added that after her depression began, she became so desperate that she went through primal scream therapy. This opened up such a depth of pain that she wanted to escape in any way she could, and she cried out, "Help me, anyone!" Norma then asked for even Satan to come if it would bring her any relief.

Ever since then, her life had been in turmoil. She could no longer receive the sacraments, pray, or even say the name of Jesus, since being around anything sacred sent her into fits of rage. She left her religious order and was ready to leave teaching too because she feared that she might hurt one of her small pupils in a fit of rage. I had **never talked to anyone as deeply oppressed as** Norma. I began to pray for her, but whenever I said the name "Jesus," either aloud or silently to myself, she flew into a fit of rage. Because of her reaction to the name of Jesus, I thought that the evil one might be the source of her difficulties. I called the chancery to get help from an official exorcist, but I was told that "this problem doesn't exist anymore," and that I should send her to a good psychiatrist. When I said that she had already been to psychiatrists, they suggested that I pray for her myself.

Since the chancery had left the situation in my hands, I knew that it was up to me to help Norma. I also knew that I couldn't do it alone. So, I formed a prayer team, including a skilled professional therapist. As I began to pray, I again saw the reality of Satan's presence. For instance, when

I would pray a written prayer, she would be one sentence ahead of me, saying "No," as if she knew my next thought. I would begin to say, "You are under God's authority," and she would already be saying, "No, I am not subject to God's authority." I decided to give her a test, to be sure that she was not just reading my mind through some kind of psychic ability. I took two identical bottles — one with holy water and one with ordinary water. Without first reading the labels on the bottles myself, I put regular water on her and she did not react. Then I put holy water on her, and she reacted intensely. She also reacted to blessed salt, even just one grain, whereas she did not react to unblessed salt. She always reacted to the holy, a major sign of the evil one's presence.

Norma's reaction to the holy made it virtually impossible for me to pray inner healing prayer. Normally, I would pray inner healing prayer first (i.e., I knew that as a child she had been abandoned by her parents and that hurts such as this might be at the source of her rage), but because of her reaction I had to begin directly with deliverance prayer. So I began the deliverance prayer by binding the evil spirits that seemed to block her. After about two hours of binding the evil spirits and commanding several of them to leave, she was free enough to say the name of Jesus and to invite him into her heart. Once she could use her will to ask for Jesus from within herself, we could pray for inner healing, thus closing the doors of emotional woundedness that had made her vulnerable to the evil one. With these doors closed, we could finish the deliverance prayer by commanding the remaining evil spirits to leave. After this prayer she was able to lead a normal life as a teacher, and she surprised everyone when she returned to her religious order. For the past ten years, Norma has continued to enjoy good health as a teacher and religious sister.

This dramatic and successful experience with Norma made deliverance prayer real for me, but most situations are not so extreme. Norma had virtually no inner freedom, but usually in even the more extreme cases, a person in need of deliverance prayer does have some freedom that he or she can use to build up new life before receiving deliverance ministry. Such a case of building up a person occurred in a mature community that took in Sarah, a woman previously involved in the occult. Sarah had been depressed for most of her life and emotionally hurt in many ways. Community members wisely discerned that, although she did have many evil spirits oppressing her, they should not pray for deliverance right away. They knew that deeper deliverance prayer ideally should be delayed as long as a person is growing in the Christian life. So they led Sarah through a three-year preparation to build herself up physically, emotionally, and spiritually in every possible way — through physical exercise, nutritious food, counseling, loving community, Scripture reading, regular prayer, daily Eucharist, etc. Only after these three years of preparation did they begin to pray for her deliverance. As expected, her deliverance was undramatic and the results lasting. The more life a person has within, the more the evil one is forced out and will stay out. Deliverance then is a sign not that a person is weak and evil but rather that a person has grown much in the life of Jesus that forces out all evil. It follows then there should never be a *deliverance* ministry but only a *healing-deliverance* ministry delivering another into the healing love of Jesus Christ by a full Christian life.

Sometimes, as a person begins living a more committed Christian life, so as to deliver himself or herself more fully to Jesus, deliverance prayer is no longer needed. We have a friend who has such a well-known healing-deliverance ministry that she has a long list of people waiting for prayer. She tells them to go to the Eucharist every day for a month and after the Eucharist to sit in front of the Blessed Sacrament for a half hour of prayerfully loving Jesus and being loved by him. For some this means allowing themselves gradually to be filled from head to toe with the light of Jesus that drives out all darkness. Frequently when these people come back to her after one month, they no longer need deliverance prayer because the evil spirits left as Jesus came. She finds that Jesus even led them to close whichever of the three doors had invited the spirits in. Jesus led those suffering from emotional wounds to forgive and to receive his love, those suffering from sin to confess their sin and be forgiven, and those suffering from occult activity to renounce it, break all bonds, and then forge new bonds with Jesus.

If all the above preparation has occurred to close the doors and to heal a person physically, emotionally, and spiritually, then the spirits will usually be uprooted and further deliverance prayer won't be needed. If still needed, it should first be done silently or with a low key "Our Father" without focusing the person's attention on the presence of spirits. If a person still remains in such bondage so as not to be growing spiritually, as Norma was after I first attempted to pray with her, then prayer by a mature team may be necessary. Such a team should be made up of loving and well-balanced people who enjoy calling forth each other's gifts and who are just as happy eating a pizza with one another as they are in doing deliverance prayer. Too often this ministry attracts just the opposite, "lone rangers" who derive their self-worth from battling with Satan. Such ministers tend to focus on the evil rather than on the goodness in another. Though the evil spirits might leave, they will soon return because such "lone rangers" do not minister love that heals the emotional weakness which opened the person to the evil spirits. Their "battle" ministry only inflicts more wounds on those in need of deliverance prayer. After gathering, the team should pray to be one, and pray for guidance to see if this is the time for deliverance prayer or if other steps are still to be taken to close doors. When it is required and the time has come for the team to pray for deliverance, the prayer follows the pattern of the "Our Father" because that is the prayer of deliverance Jesus taught, and it was the ordinary prayer for deliverance until the time of St. Augustine.

"Our Father who art in heaven, hallowed be thy name": We begin by hallowing and praising the Father until our eyes are focused on God's power and presence rather than on the evil one.

"Thy will be done": We ask the Father how we are to pray and what is the next step. This is a time to begin discerning which spirits are present and need to be cast out. This discernment can come in several ways such as through the words or images that team members receive in prayer, through the behavior of the person being delivered, or through the person's own knowledge of what is oppressing him or her.

"Give us this day our daily bread": Here we ask for the strength that comes from bread, the strength to bind the evil one. Binding the spirits prevents them from interacting with any person (especially the oppressed person) or with any other spirits. For example, if a spirit of anger is present, we might pray, "In the name of Jesus Christ I bind any spirit of anger, and I forbid you to act in any way upon any person or to interact with any other spirit." The power of Jesus is present, and we have only to apply it where it is needed. Not only a direct command in Jesus' name, but also the daily bread of Eucharist has great power to bind evil spirits.

"And forgive us our trespasses as we forgive those who trespass against us": This is a time to pray for inner healing, by giving and receiving forgiveness and by applying the love of Jesus to any emotional wounds. Inner healing is the most important part of deliverance prayer, in which we treat the hurt or habit of sin that opened the person in the first place to the evil one.

"Lead us not into temptation": When people have had a problem with anger or fear or whatever, it is important for them to choose the opposite attitude. When people, for example, have been troubled by fear, I might ask them to imagine themselves as Peter walking on the water and to get in touch with what they fear. Then I might suggest that they reach out for Jesus in all those areas of fear and feel his strong hand. The point is to deliver themselves to Jesus and be bound to Jesus in the very area that had been under the influence of Satan. Lead us not into temptation, but rather really to choose Jesus.

"Deliver us from the evil one": Once the doors of hurt and sin have been closed, we can command the evil spirits to leave. For instance, we can pray, "In the name of Jesus I command you, spirit of anger, to leave peacefully now and go directly to Jesus." Evil spirits will no longer have any roots or any way to hold on to a person if those roots have been pulled up through inner healing, forgiveness, and commitment to Jesus.

"For yours is the kingdom and the power and the glory forever": The "forever" part means that we must continue to bring this person into the Father's kingdom. So after we command the spirits to leave, we fill the person with Jesus' love and power in whatever areas there is need. (Luke 11:24-26).[1] The "forever" also includes follow-up after the deliverance prayer session is over. It is much easier to command spirits out than to keep them out by a committed Christian life. Those who have been delivered from evil spirits need a friend who will stand beside them and lead them more deeply into a committed Christian life through a balanced life of recreation, prayer, sacraments (especially daily Eucharist), Scripture, community—whatever will bring a deeper deliverance into Jesus Christ so that the evil one will have no opportunity to return.

To keep the evil one out, those who have received deliverance prayer need to know two things: first, that they have more freedom, and second, that their feelings are not necessarily going to change. They will have new freedom to choose, but they will also have the same temptations. For example, those who have been delivered from the spirit of lust may still experience strong sexual feelings and sexual temptations. In fact, the more free they are, the more they will feel all of their feelings. But they can choose with more freedom in how to direct those feelings. With sexual feelings, for example, a free person can choose to use those feelings for intimate and committed relationships with Jesus and others rather than for lustful using of people. Deliverance prayer does not exorcise feelings; it enables a person to exercise feelings and use them to choose Jesus.

If any sense of oppression recurs, we do not focus on the evil one but on all the positive growth that is taking place. This fills the heart with gratitude so that we desire to choose the Father even more deeply. The more we are focused on positive growth and gratitude, the more we look at Jesus. The more we look at Jesus, the more the freedom gained in deliverance prayer is going to endure, rooted in peace (Philippians 4:4-9).

For those of us who are called upon to pray deliverance prayer, what matters most is not using the right formula. What matters most is living like Jesus so that the evil spirit is facing not words but Jesus. Deliverance prayer is not deliverance from evil spirits, but deliverance by Jesus Christ into Jesus Christ.

Note: This lesson is optional. Since it deals with "how to" pray deliverance prayer for others, this lesson will be helpful only for those with a mature healing prayer ministry.

I. Group Experience

A. **Common Opening Prayer** (5 minutes)

B. **Video or Audio Tape:** "Deliverance Prayer (Practice)" (30 minutes)

How to pray for deliverance from evil spirits.

---

1. As deliverance prayer demands much compassion and love, sometimes team members may feel drained at the end of the prayer session. Thus it may be important to pray with team members also, thanking the Father for working through them, asking for his continued protection, and asking the Father to fill them with whatever life they need before they return home.

1. Sometimes more than a simple, silent deliverance prayer is needed. Vocal deliverance prayer can do great good or great harm, and should be done only by a team of mature, balanced and loving Christian people who are under pastoral care.
2. What matters most is not deliverance from evil spirits but deliverance into the life of Jesus. The persons receiving ministry should use all of the freedom that they have to build themselves up in their Christian life — through prayer, sacraments, community, etc. (e.g., Dallas community, woman with a spirit of hypocrisy).
3. The Our Father is a model for deliverance prayer.
4. Forgiveness and inner healing are the most important parts of prayer for deliverance.
5. Those who have received deliverance prayer need a friend who can help with follow-up ministry so that they can grow in their Christian life. These persons should use their new freedom to choose how to use their feelings, and should focus on all the new ways in which they are growing and can be grateful to the Lord.
6. The power to pray for deliverance is not in having the right formula, but in being filled with the life of Jesus (e.g., Herman).

Closing Prayer: inviting Jesus, the light of the world, to fill us with his presence.

C. **Silent Reflection** (3 minutes). Quiet time to get in touch with what part of today's tape moved your heart most deeply.

D. **Guided Journaling** (Optional — 10 minutes). See Lesson 3.

E. **Companion Sharing** (5 minutes minimum for each person to share his or her reaction to today's tape and to the past week).
1. Share with your companion as much as you wish of what is in your heart after seeing this week's tape. Perhaps you will want to share what you have just written during the guided journaling.
2. Share with your companion how you have experienced the Lord's presence in your life during the previous week. You may wish to share the journal response from last week that touched you the most.
3. What are you most grateful for now and how do you need Jesus' help?

F. **Companion Prayer** (since the purpose of this prayer is healing, you may wish to pray over your companion for about 10 minutes). Lay your hands on your companion and pray as Jesus would for about 10 minutes. Let the words and silences in your prayer be those of Jesus as he is already praying in your heart. Give thanks to Jesus for what your companion is most grateful for and pray for whatever healing your companion most needs. Close your prayer by praying that your companion receive the grace of this lesson: *to grow ever closer to the Lord.* Then let your companion pray over you.

G. **Group Sharing** (Optional — 15 minutes minimum). Take two minutes of silence to ask what has been most difficult and what has been most helpful in your prayer and journaling this past week. Share your reflections with the larger group. Close with a prayer thanking the Lord for the breakthroughs and for discovering the blocks where he is already bringing forth further growth.

H. **Closing Snack and Celebration** (Optional). An open-ended time to enjoy one another and to continue sharing.

II. Home Experience

A. **Daily Healing Prayer** (10 minutes). Each day choose one of the following healing or contemplation in action prayers and pray it for at least 10 minutes. These prayers are only *suggestions*. Perhaps you will find yourself drawn to pray what is in your heart using varied breathing, a symbol, a repeated word, a melody, a gesture, a drawing, or a piece of clay which you can mold. Although there are many prayers suggested, it would be best to pray only a few of them, parts of them, or to repeat from this or any other chapter the prayer that most moved your heart. Use whatever way you can best give your heart to Jesus and enter into his heart. Perhaps your prayer will be as simple as looking at a beautiful flower and taking in God's love for you. You may wish to begin your prayer by centering yourself, perhaps using the Breath Prayer (see Lesson 1). You may wish to continue with the Embrace Prayer (see Lesson 3, Prayer #2), or a similar prayer of simply resting in God's love.

1. *Light Prayer (Christ Is the Light of the World)* (Tape Prayer)
   a. Cup your hands and reach up until you feel the sun resting in them. Then bring your hands down over your forehead and entire body, bathing every cell with the light of Christ.
   b. With the sun in one hand, gradually move your hand closer to your heart and feel your heart burn within you. After you let the sun rest on your heart, let your hand remove and cast away any darkness (tiredness, sadness, etc.) that might be in your heart.
   c. Using your hands, start at the top of your head and begin to wrap your entire body with protective ribbons of light. Wrap yourself like a mummy, wrapping every part down to the tips of your toes so that no darkness can get through.
   d. Cup your hand in front of your heart and let the light of Christ in your heart fill your hand. Then give that light away to the front of you, to the back and to either side. Give the light by smiling and opening your hands each time you turn to a new direction.

2. *Bless Your Home*
   Bless your home with holy water while praying in your own words and seeing Jesus fill each room with his light. Ask for what each room (or person in that room) needs.

3. *Delivering Another into Jesus*
   a. Ask Jesus to bring to your mind a person that needs his protection. Imagine Jesus placing his hand on one of the person's shoulders, and see your own hand on the other shoulder.
   b. Join Jesus in his prayer for this person, or in filling the person with light.

   c. Continue until the person is so full of Jesus' life that Jesus can step right into the person and walk with him or her.

4. *Praise Protection*
   Praise and thank the Father until you sense his care and protection flooding you.

5. *Mary at the Feet of Jesus*
   a. Read Luke 10:38-42, where Mary sits at the feet of Jesus. Sit at Jesus' feet and ask for the heart of Mary, totally given to him.
   b. Then simply look at Jesus, listen to him and take in his power to take the next step to eliminate an area of compromise in your life where the evil one might have power over you.

CONTEMPLATION IN ACTION PRAYERS

Take a moment and ask for the grace to grow ever closer to the Lord. Then do one of the following:

6. *Blessed Salt*
   Ask a priest to bless salt for your family's use. Bless your house with it by sprinkling it in all the doorways and in each room, commanding the evil one to leave and inviting Jesus' presence and protection. Use the salt for cooking and with meals, being mindful of Jesus' desire to protect you and your family.

7. *Walk into Jesus*
   Take a walk and let each step be a deeper commitment to Jesus. Enjoy the ways that Jesus reveals his care for you.

8. Balanced Life
   Take a moment to ask Jesus what you should enjoy to have a more balanced life. Then enjoy it.

B. Daily Journal (5 minutes)
1. Share with Jesus when during this prayer or during the day your heart was deeply moved — perhaps a moment of being grateful for or of longing for healing in *growing closer to him*.
2. Write in your journal how Jesus re-

sponds (what he seems to do or say in response to what you have told him). If you can't get in touch with Jesus' response, write what most moves you as you speak to him or what are the most loving words you want to hear.

OPTIONAL HOME EXPERIENCES

C. Personal Reflection Questions

1. Deliverance prayer involves not just deliverance from evil but deliverance into Jesus Christ. What one step would help you to grow into a deeper Christian life so that the evil one will have no power over you and you can be like the desert monk, Herman, who freed another just by drinking wine with Jesus?
2. Whom do you know who comes closest to having the maturity needed for the healing/deliverance ministry? What do you need to have this maturity?
3. The first step with anyone who needs deliverance prayer is to have that person grow in a spiritual life of prayer, sacraments, reading of Scripture, etc. What practice has given you so much life that you want to bring another into it?
4. What are the resources in your community that can help in bringing a person into wholeness (e.g., Alcoholics Anonymous, counseling, experts on the occult, Marriage Encounter, etc.)?
5. What has been your experience with deliverance prayer? When have you seen it help another? When have you seen it abused? What have you learned from these experiences?

D. Scripture Readings

See readings for previous lesson, "Deliverance Prayer (Tradition).

E. Additional Readings

See readings for previous lesson, "Deliverance Prayer (Tradition)."

Lesson Nineteen
RELEASING THE DECEASED

INTRODUCTION

Do you know elderly people who have lived a full life and are ready to be with Jesus, and yet who seem to hang on year after year? Have you seen other elderly people die immediately after someone they loved arrived to hold their hand? We have the power to hold dying people in this life by not communicating love and forgiveness to them. And we have power to release them by loving them, forgiving them and saying the things we need to say to them. Love can release, and the lack of love can bind.

Recently we saw how love can release when we prayed with a religious sister who was interceding for a ninety-one-year-old woman who couldn't seem to die. The sister tried to become like the ninety-one-year-old woman, even letting her body take on the same posture. As she did so, she realized that the sick woman was holding on too much to a daughter, and thereby running from Jesus' loving call to eternity. So the sister prayed for the older woman to be able to let go of that daughter and to hold Jesus closer. She started praying this prayer around 9 o'clock. When the sister returned home, she received a phone call saying that the woman had died between 9:00 and 9:20 that day. Whether we lovingly pray for an elderly woman near death, or for that same woman after death, both prayers will touch that woman because love goes through space and time and will never cease being effective (1 Corinthians 13:8-13).

The prayer of release for a dying or deceased person has a great impact not only on the person meeting death but on the living as well. Often, when we pray for a person with a serious problem (e.g., depression, alcoholism, sexual deviations, etc.), we find that the problem began many years earlier when a parent, brother or other close person died. As the person works through the grieving process, a breakthrough occurs in the current problem. An unresolved death can affect us physically as well as emotionally. Research indicates that widows and widowers have ten times more physical illnesses during the year after the death of their spouse than do others in their same age group.[1] Thus, much physical and emotional illness is merely the price paid for swallowing grief and its accompanying feelings.

How can prayer help us work through the grieving process in such a way that we remain healthy? I remember when my two-year-old brother John died. My mother would reminisce about all the ways she missed John and she would cry. Those things helped. But what helped her most was to give John to Jesus in prayer, and to ask Jesus to love John in all the ways she wanted to love him. To grieve in a way that leads to healing rather than regret, we need to know that the person we miss is really loved and that Jesus is doing everything for the person that we would want to do. Knowing this begins to free us from trying to take the person back and begins to free us from buried anger and guilt over ways we may have failed to love that person. Jesus can forgive and love us, and he can forgive and love the one who has died as we entrust the person to him.

The tradition of praying for the deceased is rooted in Scripture and in the history of the Church. When my mother knelt down to pray for John, she knew that her love for him didn't end with his death, because 1 Corinthians 13:8 tells us that love never ends. John and all the deceased are part of Jesus' body just as we are (1 Corinthians 12). Through Jesus we can continue to love

1. Thomas Holmes and Richard Rahe, "The Social Readjustment Scale," *J. Psychosom, Res.*, 11 (April, 1967), 213-18.

115

everyone who is part of him. Even in the Old Testament we find Daniel praying for the deceased fathers, asking Yahweh to love and forgive them (Daniel 9:15ff). 1 Corinthians 15:29 mentions the practice of baptizing on behalf of the dead. Although we do not fully understand the meaning of this text, we do know that it was some form of prayer for the dead. In the early Church, during the first century, the Christians who were hiding in the catacombs would celebrate the Eucharist right on the tombs (many having epitaphs requesting prayer), because they wanted the prayers of the Eucharist to be for those deceased people too. Prayer for the deceased was so well known that in the third century St. Cyprian could refer to it as a practice that went all the way back to the apostles. A century later, St. Augustine's mother knew that the love between mother and child transcends death, just as my mother knew. When St. Augustine's mother died, she told her son, "All I ask is that you pray for me every time you say the Eucharist." Prayer for the deceased is a simple way we can begin to grieve and focus on Jesus' love.

We can pray for anyone who has died, especially those who most need Jesus' love. Scripture forbids seances and other forms of consultation (Deuteronomy 18:10-14), but it encourages praying for the deceased (2 Maccabees 12:46; 1 Corinthians 15:29, Daniel 9:15ff.). Praying for the deceased does not involve contacting the deceased through the use of a medium, but only loving and forgiving the deceased through Jesus. It is especially important to pray for those in our family who were difficult to love because they are more in need of Jesus' help. Perhaps there was a person in our family who was mentally ill or even committed suicide. For a long time, people who committed suicide were condemned and could not be buried in a Catholic cemetary. We cut them off from ourselves, assuming that they were beyond the realm of prayer. But the Lord does not ask us to judge or condemn people. He only asks us to love, as he loved the good thief. Although many people were condemning that thief, Jesus gave him paradise because he saw what was really in the good thief's heart. We can bring everyone to Jesus and let him love them in whatever way their hearts are open to receiving Jesus' love.

As we learn more about what drives a person to suicide, it is easier to understand that suicide is not necessarily a deliberate act of cutting oneself off from receiving Jesus' love. Perhaps those who commit suicide are like those in a burning building who feel that they have no choice but to jump as the flames come nearer to the windowsill where they stand. They jump, not because they want to die or to cut themselves off from Jesus, but because they see no other way to avoid all the flames coming at them and seemingly about to consume them. We can never know all the pressures that were in another person's life and so we have no right to condemn. Nor can we condemn ourselves if someone we love has committed suicide. I was praying with a priest recently who told me, "I feel like my father, who committed suicide when I was twelve years old, leaving me rejected and abandoned. But I also feel guilty. If I had loved him more, maybe he wouldn't have left me." Although we may have added to another's burden and need to forgive ourselves for that, our neglect or rejection alone is not enough to drive a person to suicide. It takes many hurts and pressures, usually accumulated over a long time, to force one to such a decision. Forgiving the other and forgiving ourselves releases the one who has committed suicide and releases us from reacting to it forever.

Release can happen not just when we pray for those we knew, but also when we pray for those past generations whom we may never have met. When we speak of ourselves as one bread in the Eucharist, we are speaking of the communion of saints that extends across centuries. The Jewish people had this sense of being connected to their ancestors, expressed whenever they spoke of being descended from Abraham, Isaac and Jacob. In our own country the current interest in family roots seeks to explore how the past influences us. In England we learned how much the past influences us when we met a man who had been ill with schizophrenia for twenty-one years. He imagined that there was a yellow band around his forehead, and he could hear guns going off and smell sulphur. Every year on the same day in November he would have sweating attacks. Finally this patient sought an examination from a new doctor who was reminded of pirates by the patient's symptoms. It turned out that the man's last name was the same as one of the pirate families in England, going back to 1532. There were eight sea captains in this family who had drowned and thirty-two other seamen. Unknown to this man, the most notorious pirate died in November 1595, while sweating from tropical malaria. The November date of the notorious pirate's death was the same date on which the schizophrenic patient would have his annual sweating attack. A Eucharist was held for the entire family, including all the pirate ancestors. Afterward, all the man's schizophrenic symptoms disappeared. The man's father, who had been in a mental institution for many years, was also released two weeks later. In Jesus' mystical body

(1 Corinthians 12), we are connected to people through space and time. Thus it is important to pray for our whole family tree, asking through the power of the Eucharist for the blood of Jesus to go back through all generations and cleanse whatever darkness may be there.

Often when praying for our family tree or for the deceased, it is helpful to pray for people in places that were important to them, as we do when we pray at shrines in the Holy Land or when we pray in a cemetery. Although it helps to pray lovingly anywhere for a deceased person, it seems to be especially powerful if prayers are offered in the places where the person needed more love. A British Broadcasting Company documentary film illustrated the importance of praying in such a place. This documentary concerned a straight stretch of road in England, between Charmouth and Morcombelake, where seventeen accidents had occurred in six months. Many different witnesses of these auto accidents described how they saw the car begin to swerve as the driver tried to avoid what looked like a bridal couple that seemed to pass in front of the vehicle and then seemed to vanish mysteriously. This description fit that of a bridal couple who were involved in a fatal car accident while going to their wedding. After a Eucharist was celebrated there for all those who had died on that stretch of road, the BBC reported that no more accidents occurred during the following six months nor was the bridal couple seen again.

Sometimes people report seeing ghosts, such as this bridal couple, in a certain place. Frequently the ghost appears in their home and seems to be someone they loved or wished they had loved. Whether or not ghosts are actually there, I believe that often the one who is living has a part of himself or herself that wants to relate to the "ghost" who has died, and so want to take the experience seriously. The first thing I do when people tell me that their home is haunted is to bless the house. Second, I offer some kind of prayer for the deceased person whose presence is being felt, especially a Eucharist. Finally, I try to minister to the living persons. Perhaps they sense their dead father's presence. I pray for whatever ways they still need that father in their life, and whatever ways they need to love and forgive that father so he can be released. I find that when I do these things, peace comes into the home and the sense of ghostly activity is gone. Ghosts may be as unreal as dreams, but both give messages revealing areas needing peace through healing prayer.

Much peace also comes through a kind of healing prayer that is often overlooked — prayer for stillborn, aborted and miscarried babies.

Scientists have increasing evidence that from the earliest moments of pregnancy the child in the womb is aware of what is happening and is storing up memories.[2] When such a child dies, the child is already carrying memories that may need healing. When we pray for these children we are asking Jesus to fill them with whatever love they may have missed. Perhaps they felt unloved because they were born at a bad time for the parents. It's important not only for the child but also for the family to complete the grieving process and to heal any hurts suffered by the child. We know a doctor who has worked with seventy-two anorexics. Anorexia nervosa is a disease in which the ill person (ninety-five percent are women and most of them are between the ages of twelve and twenty-five)[3] starves to death by refusing to eat. Many of these cases revealed an unresolved family death, especially a stillbirth, abortion or miscarriage. Once the baby or other deceased person was prayed for and released, the living person with anorexia was healed. Anorexia is, in many cases, the result of an unconscious wish to be incapable of conceiving children, and apparently an unresolved death, especially of a baby, can leave other members of the family fearful of the whole process of creating new life.[4] Other research indicates that anorexia can be a way of asserting one's own independence while finding one's own identity.[5] We find that in some of these situations the reason for loss of identity is an unresolved death. Working through grief can free a person to find his or her own identity rather than continue to be attached to the identity of the deceased person.

Praying for babies is important for them, important for the surviving family, and an easy thing to do. We can pray for a baby in the same way we would pray for any other deceased person. The first step is simply to grieve, to tell Jesus everything we miss about the child and to let that child be in Jesus' heart. The second step, as the child rests in Jesus' heart, is to say and do anything for the child that we missed saying and doing, e.g., holding it or telling it we forgive it for leaving. Then we leave the child with Jesus to let him say and do those loving things for us. The next step is to let Jesus fill us for all the ways we miss the child, and then to let Jesus fill the child

2. Thomas Verny, M.D., *The Secret Life of the Unborn Child* (New York: Summit, 1981).

3. *U.S. News & World Report,* 93(9), Aug. 30, 1982, pp. 47-48.

4. Ken McAll, M.D., *Healing the Family Tree* (London: Sheldon Press, 1982).

5. *U.S. News & World Report,* op. cit.

for all the ways it m
The final step is to re
to ask even that the
intercessor with Jesu
done in prayer or at t
the child through the
Whether praying for
for past generations,
loved, when we releas
life to us.

I. Group Experi

A. Common Oper

B. Video or Aud
Deceased" (30 m
We can pray for the deceased because love
and forgiveness go across space and time.

1. We have the power to hold people in this
   life or to release them to die. Love can
   release and lack of love can bind (e.g.,
   hospice in England, sister and 91-year-
   old woman).

2. When we extend the Lord's love and
   forgiveness across space and time to the
   deceased, we are affected too. Many
   emotional and physical illnesses may be
   healed when we work through the grief
   process and release a deceased person
   (e.g., Dr. Holmes' research with widows
   and widowers).

3. How do you let go of the grief when
   someone dies and move on with your
   own life? To release our grief, we need to
   know that those who have died are loved
   by Jesus and that they are part of his
   body—so that, through Jesus, we can
   continue to love them. We can ask Jesus
   to do all that we wanted to do for them
   (e.g., Matt's mother, Daniel 9, 1 Corinthians 15, practices in the early Church).

4. Whom do you pray for? Scripture forbids
   seances and consultation with the deceased, but we can pray for anyone who
   needs the Lord's help. Start with someone who was hard to love, e.g., a mentally ill person or someone who committed
   suicide. The Lord asks us to love, not to
   judge (e.g., Jesus and the good thief).

5. We cannot judge a person who committed suicide because we don't know all the
   pressures that person may have faced. In
   praying for such a person, we need with

sus to forgive ourselves too (e.g., priest
hose father committed suicide). Forgiv-
g ourselves and forgiving others
eases both of us.
ayer can reach even further than de-
sed persons whom we knew. We can
y for our whole family tree, asking
t the blood of Jesus cleanse our ances-
(e.g., British man with schizophrenia
ose ancestors were pirates).
also important to pray for a deceased
on in a place that was important to
person or the place where he or she
. Prayer in such a place helps not
to bless that place but also to release
person (e.g., road in England where
nteen people died).

8. When someone experiences the presence
   of a dead person, it may mean that there
   is something unfinished in the relationship. We can help the person by:
   a. Blessing the home.
   b. Praying for the deceased person,
      perhaps through the Eucharist.
   c. Ministering to the living person by
      asking in what ways they still need to
      love and forgive the one who has died.

9. A whole group of people that need to be
   released through prayer are babies. We
   can pray for aborted, stillborn and miscarried babies, asking that they receive
   the love they still need (e.g., studies by
   Dr. Feldmar).

10. Praying for babies who have died is also
    important for the parents and other
    family members (e.g., anorexics with a
    family history of abortion, stillbirth or
    miscarriage).

11. How do we pray for a baby?
    a. Grieve for the baby and ask Jesus to
       let that child be in his heart.
    b. Say and do for the child anything that
       we missed doing (e.g., hold the baby).
    c. Let the child say and do loving and
       forgiving things in return.
    d. Let ourselves be filled by Jesus for all
       the ways in which we miss the child.
    e. Let Jesus fill the child for any ways in
       which he or she may have missed
       being loved.
    f. Release the child to Jesus, and even
       ask that child to be a powerful inter-
       cessor for us.
    We can go through these steps in prayer
    or through the Eucharist (e.g., prayer for

Sandy and John and their miscarried baby, Diane).

Closing Prayer: to release a deceased person to Jesus and experience how he loves that person and loves us.

C. **Silent Reflection** (3 minutes). Quiet time to get in touch with what part of today's tape moved your heart most deeply.

D. **Guided Journaling** (Optional—10 minutes). See Lesson 3.

E. **Companion Sharing** (5 minutes minimum for each person to share his or her reaction to today's tape and to the past week).

   1. Share with your companion as much as you wish of what is in your heart after seeing this week's tape. Perhaps you will want to share what you have just written during the guided journaling.
   2. Share with your companion how you have experienced the Lord's presence in your life during the previous week. You may wish to share the journal response from last week that touched you the most.
   3. What are you most grateful for now and how do you need Jesus' help?

F. **Companion Prayer** (since the purpose of this prayer is healing, you may wish to pray over your companion for about 10 minutes). Lay your hands on your companion and pray as Jesus would for about 10 minutes. Let the words and silences in your prayer be those of Jesus as he is already praying in your heart. Give thanks to Jesus for what your companion is most grateful for and pray for whatever healing your companion most needs. Close your prayer by praying that your companion receive the grace of this lesson: *to grow in releasing a person who is dying or a deceased person into Jesus' hands.* Then let your companion pray over you.

G. **Group Sharing** (Optional — 15 minutes minimum). Take two minutes of silence to ask what has been most difficult and what has been most helpful in your prayer and journaling this past week. Share your reflections with the larger group. Close with a prayer thanking the Lord for the breakthroughs and for discovering the blocks where he is already bringing forth further growth.

H. **Closing Snack and Celebration** (Optional). An open-ended time to enjoy one another and to continue sharing.

II. Home Experience

A. **Daily Healing Prayer** (10 minutes). Each day choose one of the following healing or contemplation in action prayers and pray it for at least 10 minutes. These prayers are only *suggestions.* Perhaps you will find yourself drawn to pray what is in your heart using varied breathing, a symbol, a repeated word, a melody, a gesture, a drawing, or a piece of clay which you can mold. Although there are many prayers suggested, it would be best to pray only a few of them, parts of them, or to repeat from this or any other chapter the prayer that most moved your heart. Use whatever way you can best give your heart to Jesus and enter into his heart. Perhaps your prayer will be as simple as looking at a beautiful flower and taking in God's love for you. You may wish to begin your prayer by centering yourself, perhaps using the Breath Prayer (see Lesson 1). You may wish to continue with the Embrace Prayer (see Lesson 3, Prayer #2), or a similar prayer of simply resting in God's love.

   1. *Tape Prayer*
      a. As you read John 11:32-44, be with Jesus as he walks toward Lazarus and feel how much Jesus missed Lazarus. Tell Jesus about a deceased person whom you miss and how that person was special to you.
      b. In the presence of Jesus, say and do for the one you miss the things you wish you had said and done while the person was alive — any way in which your love fell short of the love that Jesus had for Lazarus.
      c. With Jesus present, receive from the person the love and forgiveness that he or she wants to give you, just as Jesus received the love that Lazarus had in his heart for him.

d. Tell Jesus what you still miss — any way in which you still want that person back.

e. In the same caring way that Jesus unwrapped Lazarus, unwrap and breathe new life into the one you miss. With Jesus, invite that person to "Come forth." See the one you miss move slowly to Jesus, until finally he or she is resting in Jesus' arms.

2. *Mother or Father's Prayer for a Deceased Baby* (Stillborn, Miscarried or Aborted)
Read Mark 10:13-16, where Jesus asks for the children to come to him.

a. *Forgiveness.* See Mary and Jesus holding the child and offering it to you. With them, hold the baby and ask forgiveness from Jesus and from the child for any way in which you failed to love the child. (Catholics who have been involved in an abortion should also make use of the sacrament of reconciliation as part of this step of receiving forgiveness.) Then take a minute to see what Jesus or the child says or does in response to you. With Jesus and the child, forgive anyone else who may have hurt the child (doctors, other family members, etc.) — anyone who, even unknowingly, didn't nourish this new life. Perhaps you or another may even experience anger at God for sending the child at the "wrong" time or for taking the child.

b. *Baptizing into Jesus' Family.* Now choose a name for the child and let Jesus wash away all hurt by baptizing the child into his family. Say with Jesus, "I baptize you (name)_____, in the name of the Father and of the Son and of the Holy Spirit." Feel the water cleansing and making all things new.

c. *Prayer.* Say a prayer for the child to receive all the love that only Jesus and Mary can give. When you really want the child to be eternally happy even more than you want him or her to be alive again, place the child in the arms of Jesus and Mary and see them do all the things that you can't do.

d. *Mass.* If you are Catholic, have a Mass said for the child and, if possible, attend it or another Mass. As you receive Communion, let Jesus' love and forgiving blood flow through you to the child and to all other deceased members of your family tree.

3. *Prayer for a Person Who Has Committed Suicide or Who Was Difficult To Love*
Read Luke 23:39-43, where Jesus promises paradise to the good thief. Stand on Calvary with Jesus and forgive the good thief.

a. Ask Jesus about pressures that were upon the person you are praying for. Ask Jesus to also show you the good that he saw in the person in the last moments, when others saw only a "condemned thief" or a suicide.

b. We are called upon only to forgive, and to leave judgment in the hands of the merciful Shepherd who seeks out every last sheep. Stay at the foot of the cross until you can see your deceased person take the place of the good thief on the cross. See yourself in the heart of Jesus on the cross, loved by the Father and extending forgiveness to the good thief. With Jesus, forgive all in this person's life until you can say Jesus' words, "This day you shall be with me in paradise." Want all that Jesus wants for this person, until you can release him or her into Jesus' hands. Know that any forgiveness you are able to give must come from God and that it is only a shadow of his mercy.

c. Ask forgiveness for any way in which you feel that you failed to give this person life, and see Jesus holding the person and breathing that life into him or her now, through your prayer. Do this until you can sense that the one you hurt is able to say "Jesus." Let the person join Jesus in looking at you with love and in giving you life too.

4. *Heart Prayer for the Deceased*
a. *Forgiving God and the Deceased and Letting Them Forgive Us.* Ask Jesus to make the deceased person you are praying for present in his heart. Tell Jesus and the person how you miss

him or her and wish you had been able to love more. Share what you wish you had said or done before the death. Share also your anger at God for the way the death occurred, the hardships caused by the death and your own feelings of being abandoned. If you are ready to forgive God, share with him your sorrow at any distance that has been between you and him since the death. Let Jesus and the deceased person share with you how they forgive you and love you. Let the deceased person share with you how he or she may need forgiveness for having hurt you. If there is anything that you need to forgive, extend this forgiveness.

b. *Receiving Love.* Ask Jesus, the Father or Mary to love you in those parts of yourself that are still lonely for the deceased person. Breathe in this love and breathe out all within you that longs for the person.

c. *Releasing the Deceased To Be Loved.* Place your hand on the heart of Jesus and pray for him to love and free the deceased in all the ways that you cannot do so. When you sense Jesus' love healing and freeing the person, take away your hand and let him or her remain even more deeply in the heart of Jesus.

5. *Praying for the Deceased at Eucharist*
   a. *Forgiveness.* At the start of Mass, forgive the deceased person and God. Ask them to forgive you too.
   b. As you offer the Mass, let Jesus stand between you and the deceased person. Allow Jesus to draw you both closer to him in his one bread, one body.
   c. As you receive Communion, allow Jesus to fill you with his love in those parts of your being where you still miss the deceased person. Then, when you are filled with Jesus' love, ask that Jesus' blood flow back through you to cleanse the deceased person and your whole family lineage of any inherited weakness or occult bondage. (Curses, seals or ancestral occult involvement should be broken by the blood of Jesus three times. Often when curses, pacts and seals are en-

acted, they are repeated three times in mockery of the Trinity. They can be broken by receiving the Eucharist and sincerely praying three times, "In the name of Jesus Christ and through the power of his precious blood, I break all curses, pacts, seals or any other occult bondage and totally give myself to my Lord Jesus Christ.") Then watch Jesus' blood flow back to bond all the deceased to himself in an eternal covenant. End by releasing the deceased person into the everlasting care of Jesus.

6. *Releasing a Person and Place Lacking Peace to Jesus*
   a. Ask Jesus what deceased person or persons may be in need of prayer in a place that seems lacking in peace. Pray for them in that place (and, if possible, have a Eucharist for them there also).
   b. Bless the place with holy water, asking that all darkness be removed and that each room be filled with Jesus' love and light. (If you find any occult books or objects, dispose of them.)
   c. Bless the people who live in the place now, and let them pray a short prayer committing their lives and their home to Jesus.

7. *Prayer for Releasing a Dying Person*
   a. Choose a person whom you need to release more deeply to Jesus before he or she dies.
   b. Use the steps of the Heart Prayer (#3) to release them. Or read John 19:25-27 and ask Mary to help you give the one you love into the Father's hands just as she helped John.

8. *Rosary for the Dying or Deceased*
   Say the rosary, with its prayer that asks Mary to pray "now and at the hour of our death." Use the glorious mysteries and at each decade pray for a different person.

CONTEMPLATION IN ACTION PRAYERS

Take a moment and ask for the grace to

release a person who is dying or a deceased person into Jesus' hands. Then go and do one of the following:

9. Spend an hour caring for someone who has been left behind by the deceased person you are praying for.
10. Visit someone who is dying or write a letter to him or her, saying what you want to say before that person dies.
11. Gather stories and photographs of the deceased members of your family so that you can love them more.
12. Spend a day celebrating in honor of the deceased person who loves you the most. Be aware of how that person is in the heart of Jesus loving you throughout the day. Take a few minutes to bask in the special love that person has for you through Jesus.

B. Daily Journal (5 minutes)

1. Share with Jesus when during this prayer or during the day your heart was deeply moved — perhaps a moment of being grateful for or of longing for healing in *releasing a person who is dying or a deceased person into Jesus' hands.*
2. Write in your journal how Jesus responds (what he seems to do or say in response to what you have told him). If you can't get in touch with Jesus' response, write what most moves you as you speak to him or what are the most loving words you want to hear.

OPTIONAL HOME EXPERIENCES

C. Personal Reflection Questions

1. In what way have you found that love and forgiveness connect you with others even when they are not physically present to you?
2. What would you want others to do for you if you were dying?
3. What have you done that helped a person to die?
4. What deceased persons need your love and forgiveness?
   a. Who were the most unloved and difficult people? Who died without a sense of being loved (e.g., suicides, etc.)?
   b. Whom in your family do you miss the most?
   c. Are there any ancestors that need prayer? (i.e., are there any problems that seem to get handed down from one ancestor to another?)
   d. If a living person experiences hearing voices, who in the family tree might be crying out for help?
   e. Have there been any stillbirths, miscarrages or abortions, i.e., children who need to be lovingly committed to God so that they can be even closer to him and to you rather than forgotten by you?
   f. Are there any houses or other places belonging to your family that are considered "disturbed"? By whom?
   g. Has anyone in the family been involved in the occult?
5. In what way do you most miss a deceased person and how do you most want to invite Jesus, Mary or the Father into that longing?
6. In what way do you need to forgive God and the deceased person and receive their forgiveness of you?
7. How effective do you think it would be to offer a Mass for a deceased person whom you haven't really forgiven and perhaps even wish were not a part of your family?

D. Scripture Readings

Exodus 20:5: Sins of the father are handed down for four generations.
Deuteronomy 18:11: We are forbidden to consult the deceased.
1 Samuel 28: Saul is in trouble for consulting the deceased Samuel.
Daniel 9:20: Daniel confesses his sins and the sins of his ancestors. Gabriel hears the prayer.
2 Maccabees 12:42-46: Judas Maccabeus prays for the deceased soldiers to be freed from their sins.
Luke 7:11-17: Jesus prays for the dead son of the widow of Naim.
1 Corinthians 13: Love bonds us together beyond death.
1 Corinthians 12:12: We are all one body, connected together.
1 Corinthians 15:29: Baptism on behalf of the dead indicates some form of prayer for the deceased.

E. Additional Readings

Healing the Dying, by Mary Jane Linn, Dennis Linn and Matthew Linn (New York: Paulist Press, 1979).

The Everlasting Now, by George Maloney (Notre Dame: Ave Maria, 1980).

The Will of God, by Leslie Weatherhead (Nashville: Abingdon, 1972). What do we mean when we say that it was "God's will" for someone to die?

A Grief Observed, by C.S. Lewis (New York: Bantam, 1976).

In Memoriam, by Henri Nouwen (Notre Dame: Ave Maria, 1980).

Lesson Twenty
BAPTISM OF THE SPIRIT

INTRODUCTION

When I first heard about the baptism of the Spirit, I (Dennis) had already been a Jesuit for ten years. I thought I was living as a good religious. Why did I need the baptism of the Spirit? I was further confused since it had a scriptural (Luke 3:16) but confusing name because the baptism of the Spirit was not a baptism at all but simply a prayer for an outpouring of the Spirit's gifts. The reason I needed to receive a deeper outpouring of the Spirit's gifts was the same reason that the apostles in John 20 needed it. Before the outpouring, the apostles were frightened and "behind locked doors" (John 20:19). After the Spirit came, these same apostles who were frightened and locked in upon themselves began like Jesus to teach and preach to the Gentiles, heal the sick, and live his poverty in community. When I wonder if I need the baptism of the Spirit, the question I ask is, "Do I have any area of my life in which I am not like Jesus?" If so, then I need the baptism of the Spirit because, in giving me the Spirit, the Father is saying to me, "I have called you through baptism to be Jesus' mystical body, through the Eucharist to take on his flesh, and through confirmation to be filled with his Spirit so that you will be led and empowered as Jesus. Now receive again the outpouring of the Spirit, so that you may be more deeply Jesus with his mind and heart and do exactly the same things that Jesus did." Until the empowering Spirit came, Jesus had many apostles — and I was like them as a Jesuit — who lived with him for a long time but were still behind locked doors. I knew Jesus but lived behind locked doors fearing to preach, teach, heal and be Jesus totally living for the Father and others (John 14:12; Galatians 2:20).

The only requirement for the outpouring of the Spirit is that I am needy and asking behind locked doors. Thus I can pray for this outpouring of the Spirit as many times as there are ways of needing to be Jesus. In Acts 2, the Spirit came upon the people and they prophesied, spoke in tongues, etc. But that was not the only time the Spirit came to them. In Acts 4, the Sadducees imprisoned Peter and John. After the Sanhedrin released them, Peter and John needed the gift of boldness in order to continue preaching. In Acts 4:29-31 they and their friends prayed for this gift, and "they were all filled with the Holy Spirit and spoke the word of God with boldness." These people, who had received an outpouring of the Spirit two chapters earlier, found themselves in a new situation in which they needed the Holy Spirit again, this time to give Jesus' boldness. Whenever an area in my life needs to be more like Jesus, I pray for an outpouring or baptism of the Spirit.[1]

For what gifts should I pray? There are several Scripture texts that list gifts of the Spirit, e.g., 1 Corinthians 12, Ephesians 4, Romans 12. But in 1 Corinthians 13 we are told that the key gift of the Spirit is love. Thus there are as many gifts as there are ways of loving, e.g., poverty, chastity, obedience, marital fidelity, motherhood, fatherhood, writing, praying, forgiving, listening and reaching out to the needy. There are as many gifts or charisms of the Spirit as there are ways of being Jesus or being Mary. To be Mary means to be so filled with the Holy Spirit that Jesus is born in us as he was in her (Luke 1:35). And being Jesus

---

1. For the view of St. Thomas on many outpourings of the Spirit cf. Francis Sullivan, "Baptism in the Spirit," *New Covenant,* June 1982, p. 27.

does not mean being a Messiah saving all but being myself, open to all the Father's love so that even in weakness I am empowered by the Spirit to love as Jesus loves.

Though the only requirement for baptism of the Spirit is that I am needy and asking to be Jesus, I (Matt) didn't understand this at first. I thought that baptism of the Spirit was something I had to earn, almost like a merit badge. So I spent an eight-day retreat preparing myself before I asked some friends to pray for me. My attitude was, "O.K., Lord, I've done everything to earn this," rather than to admit how I hungered for it. After the prayer for the baptism of the Spirit, I did feel more peaceful, but it wasn't the dramatic experience I had expected. During the next year I experienced a deeper love of Scripture and I was easier to live with, but I still felt as if something were missing, as if the baptism of the Spirit hadn't quite "taken."

Fortunately, a prayer group nearby had a special ministry of praying again for the baptism and of helping to release the gift of tongues. So I told them, "I went through this about a year ago but not much seems to have happened. I've got more peace, I love Scripture more, I love people more, but I don't think I received any special charisms." They answered, "Well, what do you really want?" That question got to me because the founder of the Jesuits, St. Ignatius, has us ask that question all through our retreats. I saw the sad truth that I didn't really want much — and I especially did not want the gift of tongues.

I told that group that I wanted the gift of prayer. I figured that if I had the gift of prayer, I would have everything, and I would not have to ask for anything specific and be disappointed. They told me that the gift of the Spirit that is given to help us pray is the gift of tongues (Romans 8:26-27). They explained that the gift of tongues helps us to express a love and gratitude for the Lord that goes beyond words. To receive this gift, I would have to want it and then speak from my heart in order to receive it. I was also told that there are two main reasons why we can't pray in tongues. The problem usually is not with God holding back the gift; but either we don't have anything deeper than words to express to God or we fear to be like an infant who uses fumbling sounds to express what is in his or her heart. To receive any gift, we need to let go of our fear and begin using our gift. For instance, a person who wants the gift of preaching will never experience it unless he gets up and begins to speak from his heart. So it is, they told me, with the gift of tongues. The first step was

to get in touch with my love for the Lord and then try to put it into words like, "Thank you, Jesus," or "Alleluia." Soon I would reach the point where words were not enough, and then I could just let rise whatever sounds best expressed my love for the Lord.

The more I listened to their explanation, the more I wanted the gift of tongues. So I asked for it. I began by thanking the Lord for all the ways he loved me. Soon I wanted to say more than "Thank you" or "Alleluia." I wanted to give Jesus everything in me, and so with a "sheee" I breathed out everything within me in thanksgiving to the Lord. I sounded like a steam engine saying "Sheee, sheee, sheee," but it was my way of telling Jesus, "All my breath and life belongs to you."

That was the beginning of the gift of tongues for me. Even though at first it sounded foolish, the Lord wanted me to be like a child and to go beyond logical words in relating to him. So during the following days I would begin my prayer with "Thank you" for all that happened that day until I would finally want to thank Jesus with that deeper thanks that said everything will all my breath in "sheee." I found also that when I couldn't pray, I could begin with these syllables, and they would remind me of the gratitude I experienced the last time and reawaken it. The gift of tongues grew every time I used it and gave thanks. The other gifts I had prayed for that night also grew the more I gave thanks and exercised them.

It is not always easy to reach out and exercise our gifts. When Jesus gives us his Spirit, he gives us the power to resist the forces that would hold us back. But we may still feel afraid at first. The first person I prayed with for healing was a Sioux grandmother, Mary, who had become my grandmother too. Her family said that she was dying, in a two week coma, and asked if I would pray with her for healing. Though I didn't mind praying a vague prayer, I feared to pray for specific healing because I might not have the right words or I might give false expectations. But because I loved Mary so much, I overcame my fears and went to visit her. Since she couldn't talk, I just took her hand and told her that I loved her and her grandchildren loved her, and that Jesus loved her even more than we could. I asked her to take Jesus' hand and to go with him wherever he took her. I spoke that way because I thought that Mary would die soon. Then I prayed in silence for perhaps thirty seconds. When I had done all I could think of for Mary, I went off to visit other patients who could talk.

When I passed by the nurses' station a while later, they told me that Mary was now out of the coma and wanted to see me. I went in and Mary said, "You were just here to see me." I said, "Yes. How did you know?" Mary answered, "I've been hearing everything. I just couldn't move or talk. When you came in and took my hand, I felt the hand of Jesus and he talked with me. He asked me, 'What do you want?' You made me so lonesome for my grandchildren that I told him I wanted to go back and be with them. He took me right back here and I woke up." Even though I was afraid and unsure of myself, I had reached out to pray for Mary because I loved her. The Spirit didn't take away my fear, but rather gave me enough love to reach out in the midst of fear and exercise the gifts of prayer and healing. I was afraid of the gift of healing prayer, but I was given the perfect love that casts out fear and brings freedom to move beyond it.

For both the gifts of healing and of tongues, I experienced the outpouring of the Spirit as very gradual and quiet. But for other people, the outpouring of the Spirit may be experienced suddenly and dramatically. For instance, for me the gift of tongues developed as I gradually overcame my fear of looking foolish and could begin searching for a sound that expressed what was in my heart. For others, as with the apostles in the upper room, the gift of tongues comes suddenly and dramatically without any effort on their part (Acts 2:4). But it does not matter whether a gift comes in a sudden and dramatic way or develops gradually and quietly as we try to use it. The sign of whether a gift is from the Lord is not how it comes but rather what the fruits of it are (Matthew 7:21-23). For example, after praying in tongues for a week or so, we might ask ourselves, "Do we feel closer to God since we have this gift? Do we act closer to others? Are we happier and more peaceful?" If the answer is "Yes" then we can be fairly certain that it is a gift from God. If, on the other hand, the gift of tongues makes us arrogant and we look down on all who don't have it, then we can strongly question whether the gift is from God.

Although we have used the gift of tongues as an example, it is not the most important gift. St. Paul tells us that he wants us to have it, but it is really the least important of the gifts (1 Corinthians 14:5). The most important gift to pray for is usually whatever gift we fear. Recently we gave a retreat to one hundred Jesuits. When we prayed for them, almost all received the gift of tongues. I believe this happened not because it is the most important gift, but because it is what they feared most and needed most. The gifts are given to make us free. Many Jesuits, like me, tend to live in their heads and to be overly rational. Thus the Jesuit priests on our retreat needed the gift of tongues to free their hearts to better feel and intuit as deeply as Jesus. When we pray for gifts, the question to ask is, "What do I need in order to be Jesus?" Whether we are like the frightened apostles locked in the upper room, or like a frightened priest locked in his head, Jesus invites us to receive the baptism of the Spirit so that we may be Jesus.

Being Jesus is not just a matter of receiving gifts but of using all we are given in a life lived totally for the Father (Matthew 7:21-23). We receive the Spirit to the degree that our hearts cry out "Abba" and to that degree we no longer live for ourselves but, like Jesus driven by the Spirit, to lay down his life itself for the Father and for others (Romans 8:15). When we know that without the Spirit such a total laying down of our life is impossible, then we do not have the Spirit, but the Spirit has us (Romans 7:14—8:13).

I. Group Experience

A. Common Opening Prayer (5 minutes)

B. Video or Audio Tape: "Baptism of the Spirit" (30 minutes)

Why do we need the baptism of the Spirit?
1. The baptism of the Spirit invites us to be like Jesus and to do the things that he did. We can be baptized in the Spirit as many times as there are ways in which we need to be more like Jesus.
2. There are as many gifts of the Spirit as there are ways of loving.
3. The only requirement for baptism of the Spirit is our hunger for it. What matters is our need, not our worthiness.
4. The gift of tongues is the gift of prayer beyond words (e.g., Matt).
5. Gifts grow as we give thanks for them and use them. The Spirit gives us the love for others that can help us overcome our fear of reaching out and using a gift (e.g., Matt and Sioux grandmother).
6. The way in which we receive a gift is not as important as the fruits of using it — what matters most is whether a gift helps us to love God and others more.
7. The gifts of the Spirit are given to make

us free, and we need them in whatever areas we are not free (e.g., Jesuits and the gift of tongues).

8. The gifts of the Spirit are an extension of the sacraments, giving us the power to live them out (e.g., Lambert and the baptism of a child).

Closing Prayer: to help us surrender to the Spirit and receive one gift that will help us to be more like Jesus.

C. **Silent Reflection** (3 minutes). Quiet time to get in touch with what part of today's tape moved your heart most deeply.

D. **Guided Journaling** (Optional — 10 minutes). See Lesson 3.

E. **Companion Sharing** (5 minutes minimum for each person to share his or her reaction to today's tape and to the past week).

1. Share with your companion as much as you wish of what is in your heart after seeing this week's tape. Perhaps you will want to share what you have just written during the guided journaling.
2. Share with your companion how you have experienced the Lord's presence in your life during the previous week. You may wish to share the journal response from last week that touched you the most.
3. What are you most grateful for now and and how do you need Jesus' help?

F. **Companion Prayer** (choose one of the following options)

Option I:
Lay your hands on your companion and pray as Jesus would for about 10 minutes. Let the words and silences in your prayer be those of Jesus as he is already praying in your heart. Give thanks to Jesus for what your companion is most grateful for and pray for whatever healing your companion most needs. Close your prayer by praying that your companion receive the grace of this lesson: *to receive the gifts of the Spirit that will allow him or her to be like Jesus.* Then let your companion pray over you.

Option II:
1. If anyone wishes to receive the baptism of the Spirit for the first time, the whole group may wish to pray over that person.
2. You may also wish to end with a common prayer asking that those who have already received the baptism of the Spirit may now receive a deepening of the gifts of the Spirit that will allow them to grow in being Jesus.

G. **Group Sharing** (Optional — 15 minutes minimum). Take two minutes of silence to ask what has been most difficult and what has been most helpful in your prayer and journaling this past week. Share your reflections with the larger group. Close with a prayer thanking the Lord for the breakthroughs and for discovering the blocks where he is already bringing forth further growth.

H. **Closing Snack and Celebration** (Optional). An open-ended time to enjoy one another and to continue sharing.

II. Home Experience

A. **Daily Healing Prayer** (10 minutes). Each day choose one of the following healing or contemplation in action prayers and pray it for at least 10 minutes. These prayers are only *suggestions.* Perhaps you will find yourself drawn to pray what is in your heart using varied breathing, a symbol, a repeated word, a melody, a gesture, a drawing, or a piece of clay which you can mold. Although there are many prayers suggested, it would be best to pray only a few of them, parts of them, or to repeat from this or any other chapter the prayer that most moved your heart. Use whatever way you can best give your heart to Jesus and enter into his heart. Perhaps your prayer will be as simple as looking at a beautiful flower and taking in God's love for you. You may wish to begin your prayer by centering yourself, perhaps using the Breath Prayer (see Lesson 1). You may wish to continue with the Embrace Prayer (see Lesson 3, Prayer #2), or a similar prayer of simply resting in God's love.

1. *Prayer for Baptism of the Spirit* (Tape Prayer)
   a. Ask the Lord to show you one area of

your life in which you feel powerless to love (e.g., with a child, your spouse, in your ministry, etc.). What one gift do you need in order to be more like Jesus and to reach out with his love?

b. Ask the Lord to help you really *want* that gift so that you can love more. As a sign of your desire, hold out your hands to the Father, heart open and ready to receive all that he wants to give you.

c. See Jesus standing before you, sent by the Father. Hear him say to you, "Receive the Holy Spirit."

d. Breathe in the Spirit, into every cell of your body, every part of you that hungers to love more. Hear Jesus say to you, "As the Father has sent me so I send you." Receive the Spirit into whatever part of you needs to be set free to go forth in love — your hands, eyes, ears, mouth, sexuality, heart, etc.

e. You may want to close by singing, "Spirit of the Living God, Fall Afresh on Me," asking that the Spirit continue to fill you.

2. *Paul's Prayer*
a. Prayerfully read Ephesians 3:14-21.
b. Join the Spirit within you in slowly praying this prayer for a person or persons whom you wish to be so filled with the Spirit that they have all the dimensions of Christ. Listen for the moments when the Spirit within you prays more intensely and follow its lead.

3. *Praying with Another: Love Prayer*
a. Prayerfully read 1 Corinthians 13.
b. With a friend, pray for each other to be like Jesus, led by the Holy Spirit. Soak up your friend's deepest gift: love.
c. As you pray for your friend, let the Father's love flow beyond words into a melody, tongues, silence.
d. Finish with a hug, giving all the love you have received.

4. *Thanks Beyond Words*
a. Read Psalm 100, which sings praise to the Lord for his care for us.
b. Thank the Lord for his care, which

has been extended to you through all those who have loved you.

c. Continue to give thanks until words can no longer express all the gratitude that is in your heart. Then let a wordless melody express your gratitude, just as a mother sings a wordless lullaby full of love for her baby.

5. *Symphony Prayer* (Psalm 150)
a. Listen to your favorite symphony until you are swept along in its melody.
b. Rather than control your reaction to the melody, let go and let the melody move you with its rich beauty.
c. Let your whole being flow with the music in its rich and non-conceptual praise of God.

6. *Dance Prayer*
a. Get in touch with what you most want to say to God (praise, thanks, deep need, etc.).
b. Without words, use dance or gestures to say this with your whole body.
c. Finish by saying "Abba" through dance and gesture (Romans 8:15).

7. *Breathing In the Breath of Jesus*
a. Read John 20:19-25.
b. Ask for the gift you most need to be sent forth as Jesus.
c. Become aware of Jesus breathing the breath of the Holy Spirit into you and saying, "Peace. As the Father has sent me, so I send you."
d. Breathe in the breath of Jesus with everything in you that longs for the breath of life, the Spirit.
e. Focus on breathing in and out to the Spirit's rhythm, as the Spirit within you prays "Abba" more deeply with each breath.

CONTEMPLATION IN ACTION PRAYERS

Take a moment and ask for the grace to receive the gifts of the Spirit that will allow you to be like Jesus. Then do one of the following:

8. *Wind Prayer*
a. Read John 3:8: "The wind blows where it will. You hear the sound it makes but you do not know where it

comes from or where it goes. So it is with everyone begotten of the Spirit."
  b. Stand in the wind or imagine yourself under a blowing tree on a windy day.
  c. Listen to the wind and ask that it reveal where the Spirit wants to possess and fill you (perhaps an area of compromise in your life or a fear that holds you back).
  d. Let the wind blow the Spirit into you as you breathe it in and say, "Lord Jesus Christ," placing all under his control. Continue this until you sense an inner wind of the Spirit moving you as Jesus.

9. *Walking as Jesus*
  a. Read Luke 4:1-13, where Jesus is led by the Spirit into the desert.
  b. Consciously relax as a sign of giving the Spirit control over you. Then go for a walk, letting each step take you deeper into surrendering to the Father and being willing to go wherever he is asking you to go as Jesus.
  c. When you really want to walk totally into the Father's will, stop and ask the Father what he wants of you.

B. Daily Journal (5 minutes)

1. Share with Jesus when during this prayer or during the day your heart was deeply moved — perhaps a moment of being grateful for or of longing for healing in *receiving the gifts of the Spirit that will allow you to be like Jesus.*
2. Write in your journal how Jesus responds (what he seems to do or say in response to what you have told him). If you can't get in touch with Jesus' response, write what most moves you as you speak to him or what are the most loving words you want to hear.

OPTIONAL HOME EXPERIENCES

C. Personal Reflection Questions
1. If Jesus were to stand before you now and ask you what you most want from him, what would you say?
2. When was the time that you were most possessed by the Holy Spirit? What was it like to be Jesus?
3. There are several lists of charisms in

Scripture, corresponding to the many ways there are to lovingly serve others (Romans 12:6-8; 1 Corinthians 12; Ephesians 4:11). In what way are you being called to serve that you feel inadequate? What do you fear that Jesus might ask you to do?
4. There are three steps that help in receiving a gift of the Spirit:
  a. To really desire and ask for it.
  b. To use it to love, even when fearful.
  c. To thank the gift-giver for its beginnings.
  If you are struggling to receive a gift, would any of the above help?
5. When have you experienced being grateful beyond words?

D. Scripture Readings

1 Corinthians 12: Gifts to build the body of Christ (also Romans 12:6-8 and Ephesians 4:7-12).
1 Corinthians 13: The greatest gift is love.
1 Corinthians 14: Order in the use of the gifts.
Mark 1:8: Jesus will baptize you in the Holy Spirit.
John 20:19-25: Receive the Holy Spirit to be sent as Jesus and to forgive sins.
Acts 4:29-31: The apostles provide a model of praying for further release of the Holy Spirit even after the Spirit has come.
Romans 8:26-27: The Spirit within intercedes in groanings beyond words.
Isaiah 11:2-3: The Spirit's gifts: wisdom, understanding, counsel, fortitude, piety, knowledge, fear of the Lord .
Galatians 5:22-33: The fruits of the Spirit: love, joy, peace, patience, kindness, goodness, faithfulness, gentleness, self-control.

E. Additional Readings

Finding New Life in the Spirit: A Guidebook for the Life in the Spirit Seminars (Notre Dame: Charismatic Renewal Services, 1972). A course preparing participants for baptism of the Spirit. See also *The Life in the Spirit Seminars Team Manual* (Ann Arbor: Word of Life, 1973).

You Will Receive Power, by Sr. Philip Marie Burle and Sr. Sharon Ann Plankenhorn (Pecos, N.M.: Dove Publications). Another model of preparation for baptism of the Spirit.

The Holy Spirit: Growth of a Biblical Tradition, by George Montague (New York: Paulist Press, 1976). A commentary on all the major Old and New Testament texts dealing with the Spirit.

The Conspiracy of God: The Holy Spirit in Men, by John Haughey (Garden City, N.Y.: Doubleday, 1973). Examines the ways in which the Holy Spirit manifests itself in individuals and in the Christian community.

NOTE: You may wish to begin next week to prepare as a group for ending the course. For **suggestions, see Appendix H, "Final Sessions."**

Lesson Twenty-One
HEALING THROUGH COMMUNITY

INTRODUCTION

What is the easiest and most common way of being healed? Most healing happens when we are loved in the midst of what needs healing. One day we went canoeing with a friend who obviously didn't know how to canoe. At the end of the day she told us that nineteen years earlier her brother had drowned and since then neither she nor anyone else in her family could go near the water. It was only her love of us that made her risk canoeing and overcame her paralyzing fear so that she could enjoy the day. It wasn't even prayer that had healed her but just being loved in the midst of what she feared.

Likewise, on the Sioux reservation we saw, again and again, teenagers trapped by alcohol, drugs and a miserable self-image suddenly become free, mature young men. What changed a teenage boy? A sixteen-year-old girl would fall in love with him, and as he looked into his girl-friend's eyes, he would see the beautiful person she saw. He wanted to be for her all she saw and all he could be.

We grow in becoming all we can be especially when we are loved by someone who is very different. Dennis and I (Matt) are very different. Dennis is an optimist who thinks he is living in the best of all possible worlds; I am more the pessimist who is afraid he might be right. At workshops Dennis sensitizes me to what the Lord is doing; I help him to focus on what the Lord still needs to do. In Jungian terms, Dennis is a perceiver who sees and likes to leave possibilities open, while I am a judger who sees the problems and likes to make things definite before there are more problems. If it weren't for Dennis, I would have us booked up for the next five years and he would

have our calendar open except for next week. We need each other's gifts if we are to make decisions — some of which should be made now.

Our wounds become gifts especially when we share what is happening in our life with at least one other person who loves us and when we receive prayer from that person for our wounds. The leader of one healthy prayer group told its members that his priority was not that they come to prayer meetings but that all in the group would have one friend who could love and pray for them while they shared all that was happening in their lives. The U.S. Census Bureau found this to be the key to healthy families too. In 1980 it found that approximately one in three marriages end in divorce. The incidence of divorce dropped to one in fifty if the couple had been married in a church and attended church regularly together. If, in addition, a couple also prayed regularly in their family, the incidence of divorce plummeted to one in eleven hundred and five. A friend of ours who is a counselor is also excited about the power of prayer to strengthen marriages. He sees many marriages healed when he teaches the husband to pray lovingly for five minutes in silence for his wife. Then the wife prays silently for five minutes for her husband, and finally both share what they experienced while loving or being loved in prayer. Such couples find that the prayer deepens what they can share with each other and puts it all in a context of love.

By now you may be saying, "That's fine if you live with someone who is easy to love. But you should see the person I have to live with." Jean Vanier in *Community and Growth* says that in his long experience with the nearly one hundred l'Arche communities, a community does not grow unless it has at least one person who is difficult to love. It takes a difficult person to call forth from others the kind of unselfish love that is given simply because others need it and not because they can return it. But every wounded person is not just needy; that person is also gifted. The mentally retarded in the l'Arche communities call others away from bantering ideas in superficial conversations and into the world where feelings are shared. The retarded don't meet another with ideas but with a hug and honest gut reactions. Wounds make us compensate and develop other gifts. When we love the wounded, we begin to find ourselves receiving their gifts and risking new ways to love.

The beauty of my relationship with Dennis is that I don't have to have every gift. Instead, I just need to keep bringing forth all the gifts Dennis has that differ from my own. Dennis believes that healing can happen quickly, and we expressed his gift in our first book, *Healing of Memories*, with its simple approach. I believe that healing is more often a process of taking one step at a time, and this became the subject of our second book, *Healing Life's Hurts*. Both ways of healing are real, and we must be ready to let the Lord choose either one. Sometimes I fear that I am forcing my way and my views upon Dennis, and then I need to ask myself some questions: How much do I pray for Dennis and ask the Lord to keep using him even more than I want the Lord to use me? How much am I grateful for everything that happens through Dennis? Am I trying to understand Dennis, even if I don't agree with him, so that he grows deeper in his unique viewpoint rather than becoming a carbon copy of me? One of me is definitely enough! Are Dennis' strengths helping me to develop the weak parts of my personality and are my strengths helping him?

That last question is also the test for whether a community is healthy or stultifying. When we visit a community or prayer group, we don't look for a great leader or healer — because if a community is focused on one person it will collapse when that person collapses. Rather, we look for leaders or healers who call others to do what they are doing so that their gift is spread throughout the community. Are more people discovering how they can lead, take the initiative and pray for healing — or are they just becoming increasingly dependent? Even the most insensitive people can be taught how to pray intercessory prayers that keep life flowing into the community and into their own wounds. And as their wounds are healed, they will have a unique gift to offer the wounded community. Their very wounds will become gifts, as with a reformed alcoholic who can reach out to other alcoholics better than anyone else can.

It is not easy to grow by sharing our lives with one friend who loves us and by reaching out to one wounded person who needs love. When we were visiting the Madonna House community, I asked what they had learned during the past forty years about who can successfully live and grow in community. I asked, "What do you look for in people who want to join this community?" One experienced priest answered right away, "We look to see if a person is aware that he is a sinner loved by Jesus Christ. If he has experienced this, he will come to us being able to be loved in his weakness and he will be able to love the rest of us who don't always measure up." We have community, and we grow to the extent that we can give and receive love in all the ways in which we are weak.

I. Group Experience

A. Common Opening Prayer (5 minutes)

B. Video or Audio Tape: "Healing through Community" (30 minutes)

Healing happens when someone loves us and walks with us through an area of our life that we fear.
1. The easiest way to be healed is to love somebody (e.g., Dennis' canoe trip, Indians on drugs, 4th grade class).
2. The test of friendship and of community is whether we are calling forth one another's gifts (e.g., Matt and Dennis, Margaret Schlientz).
3. Healing happens when we have one person with whom we can share our life (e.g., Richard Rohr's community, families who pray together).
4. In order to grow, every community needs one difficult person who will call others to love unselfishly (e.g., Jean Vanier's L'Arche houses).

Closing Prayer: to find one person who loves us and with whom we can share our life.

C. Silent Reflection (3 minutes). Quiet time to get in touch with what part of today's tape moved your heart most deeply.

D. Guided Journaling (Optional — 10 minutes). See Lesson 3.

E. **Companion Sharing** (5 minutes minimum for each person to share his or her reaction to today's tape and to the past week).

1. Share with your companion as much as you wish of what is in your heart after seeing this week's tape. Perhaps you will want to share what you have just written during the guided journaling.
2. Share with your companion how you have experienced the Lord's presence in your life during the previous week. You may wish to share the journal response from last week that touched you the most.
3. What are you most grateful for now and how do you need Jesus' help?

F. **Companion Prayer** (10 minutes). Lay your hands upon your companion and take a moment of silence to get in touch with yours and Jesus' gratitude for him or her. Then with Jesus thank the Father for the friendship between you and for all that is special in your companion.

G. **Group Sharing** (Optional — 15 minutes minimum). Take two minutes of silence to ask what has been most difficult and what has been most helpful in your prayer and journaling this past week. Share your reflections with the larger group. Close with a prayer thanking the Lord for the breakthroughs and for discovering the blocks where he is already bringing forth further growth.

H. **Closing Snack and Celebration** (Optional). An open-ended time to enjoy one another and to continue sharing.

II. Home Experience

A. **Daily Healing Prayer** (10 minutes). Each day choose one of the following healing or contemplation in action prayers and pray it for at least 10 minutes. These prayers are only *suggestions*. Perhaps you will find yourself drawn to pray what is in your heart using varied breathing, a symbol, a repeated word, a melody, a gesture, a drawing, or a piece of clay which you can mold. Although there are many prayers suggested,

it would be best to pray only a few of them, parts of them, or to repeat from this or any other chapter the prayer that most moved your heart. Use whatever way you can best give your heart to Jesus and enter into his heart. Perhaps your prayer will be as simple as looking at a beautiful flower and taking in God's love for you. You may wish to begin your prayer by centering yourself, perhaps using the Breath Prayer (see Lesson 1). You may wish to continue with the Embrace Prayer (see Lesson 3, Prayer #2), or a similar prayer of simply resting in God's love.

1. *Tape Prayer*
   a. Prayerfully read how Jesus summoned many of his apostles in two's and how he sent them out in two's: "The names of the twelve apostles are these: first Simon, now known as Peter, and his brother Andrew; James, Zebedee's son, and his brother John; Philip and Bartholomew, Thomas and Matthew the tax collector; James, son of Alphaeus, and Thaddaeus; Simon the Zealot party member and Judas Iscariot, who betrayed him" (Matthew 10:2-4). "Jesus summoned the Twelve and began to send them out two by two" (Mark 6:7).
   b. Ask Jesus to show you the person in your life who has been your best friend. With Jesus thank the Father for the ways in which you have grown through this friendship, for any ways you are different because you met him or her.
   c. With Jesus ask the Father to give your friend the life that he or she has given you.
   d. Ask Jesus to continue to place in your life one person who can call you to growth.

2. *Jesus Praying Within Your Friend*
   Repeat Prayer #1 above, but this time be attentive to Jesus within your friend praying a prayer of gratitude to the Father for you.

3. *Prayer for Receiving the Grace of This Lesson*
   Ask Jesus to give you his ability to see

the gifts in each person and to call them forth. Breathe in this part of him with every breath and breathe out all the blocks in yourself to calling forth the gifts of another. (You may wish to pray this prayer with Mary instead of Jesus.)

4. *Gifts in Nature*
Find a favorite outdoor spot, go for a walk, or sit by a window from which you can see growing things. See how each species of plant is different and special in its own way. Thank the Father for how he brings forth roses from rosebushes, tomatoes from tomato plants, pine cones from pine trees, etc. Thank him for how he is the same kind of gardener with people, bringing forth the specialness of each one. Ask him to help you be the kind of gardener of people that he is.

5. *Calling by Name* (Isaiah 43:1)
    a. Pick one person from among your family or friends and ask Jesus what gifts he or she has and how Jesus wants you to nurture these gifts.
    b. Join Jesus in calling them forth by name, repeating it until you can say it with the deep affirming love that Jesus has. "Fear not, for I have redeemed you; I have called you by name: you are mine" (Isaiah 43:1).

6. *Martha and Mary*
    a. Read Luke 10:38-42. Then pick one person whom you envy because of his or her gifts, talents, personality, etc.
    b. Imagine that person sitting at Jesus' feet and watch what Jesus loves in that person. Join Jesus in thanking the Father for the way that he has created that person.

7. *Thomas*
    a. Read John 20:24-29. Ask Jesus to reveal to you who is the Thomas in your life, the one who demands special attention.
    b. See how Jesus wants to do anything for this person, even if it means letting his wounds be probed.
    c. Listen to Jesus' prayer for this person and let yourself be drawn into the depths of his love that would even die for the person.

8. *Community at the Last Supper*
    a. Read John 17:9-26, where Jesus prays for his community.
    b. Now with Jesus look upon the members of your community and pray with Jesus to the Father for them.
    c. Ask Jesus how he smiles at the persons in your home or community. The next time you see them, give them a smile as life-giving as Jesus' smile.

9. *Offering Peter's Gifts*
    a. Read John 21, where Jesus asks Peter to use his gift of leadership to feed his sheep.
    b. Sit with Jesus until you hear him telling you how he wants you to give new life to his sheep. You may be led to see the gift he is asking you to use as if it were held in your hands, and to imagine yourself offering it to those whom he wants to feed through you.

CONTEMPLATION IN ACTION PRAYERS

Take a moment and ask for the grace to bring forth the gifts of another. Then do one of the following:

10. *Fasting Prayer*
Fast for one day for a needy person in your community.

11. *Smile*
Ask Jesus to show you how much he loves those you will meet during the day, and spend the day spreading a smile on each person you meet.

12. *Phone Prayer*
Ask Jesus to be with you as you call a friend who needs encouragement and a compassionate listener.

13. *Community Builder*
Ask Jesus to help you exercise one of these community building actions: holding your tongue, listening, maintaining silence when criticized, readiness to serve, forgiving, speaking the truth gently with love, letting another win an argument, creating joy, welcoming another, affirming another's hopes and strengths, asking for forgiveness, thank-

ing another. Act in this way throughout one day.

14. *A Friend's Healing Love*
Ask Jesus to be with you as you spend time with a friend who loves you deeply. Revel in your friend's love for you.

B. Daily Journal (5 minutes)

1. Share with Jesus when during this prayer or during the day your heart was deeply moved — perhaps a moment of being grateful for or of longing for healing in *bringing forth the gifts of another.*

2. Write in your journal how Jesus responds (what he seems to do or say in response to what you have told him). If you can't get in touch with Jesus' response, write what most moves you as you speak to him or what are the most loving words you want to hear.

OPTIONAL HOME EXPERIENCES

C. Personal Reflection Questions

1. What was the deepest experience of friendship you have experienced? Whom do you experience the deepest friendship with now? What would help this friendship to grow in openness and depth of sharing?

2. Who in your life has brought forth your gifts and inspired you to do the same for another? What was it like to be affirmed in this way?

3. For whose gifts are you most grateful? For whose gifts are you not very grateful? Why?

4. If you were to describe the ideal person with whom you would like to pray and share your life, what would he or she be like? Who comes closest to this ideal? What would help you to be more like your ideal?

5. Who is the one difficult person in your life whom the Lord most wants you to love more?

6. When have you loved others with a deep affirming love that gave them new life? What did you experience?

D. Scripture Readings

1 Corinthians 12:4-26: The need for many gifts and unity in the body of Christ.
Luke 10:38-42: The most important work is loving without envy.
Luke 15:25-32: The elder brother who cannot rejoice in the prodigal's new life.
Matthew 18:15-20: The need to be one in correction and in prayer.
Ephesians 3:14-21: Paul's prayer for the community.
Luke 10:1-20: The seventy-two are sent out in pairs.
John 11:33-36: Jesus' love for his friend, Lazarus.

E. Additional Readings

Healing Life's Hurts
Pages 15-16, "Sharing Feelings with a Friend." When we are able to share our feelings with friends and with Jesus, we can move more quickly through the five stages of forgiveness. Knowing we are accepted by another who loves us wherever we are helps us to grow.

Chapter 16, "Getting Started: Praying Alone and with Others." We can receive healing alone as we share our hurts with Jesus in prayer, but often it is helpful to pray with a friend who can mediate Jesus' love and acceptance for us and draw us out to love in return.

Community and Growth, by Jean Vanier (New York: Paulist Press, 1979).
Healing the Unaffirmed: Recognizing Deprivation Neurosis, by Conrad Baars and Anna Terruwe (New York: Alba House, 1976). How the unconditional love given in authentic friendship can heal an unaffirmed person.
Friendship in the Lord, by Paul Hinnebusch (Notre Dame: Ave Maria, 1974).
The Broken Image, by Leanne Payne (Westchester, Ill.: Cornerstone Books, 1981). How homosexuality can be healed through the power of love and prayer.

NOTE: Since next week will be the third to last session of the course, you may wish to use some time preparing for the end of the course. See **Appendix H, "Final Sessions."**

Lesson Twenty-Two
SOCIAL CHANGE THROUGH HEALING PRAYER

INTRODUCTION

The judgment spoken of in Matthew 25:31 is a time when we meet a Lord whose love is so real that we can look at our past lives with him. As we look at our lives through his eyes and in the light of his love, the moments we will regret most are not the times we missed a prayer meeting or failed to attend church, but the times we failed to love him in the hungry, the sick, the imprisoned or in a homeless stranger. In the United States we have only five percent of the world's population yet forty percent of the world's resources. How can we better use these resources to help a world where one out of two children dies before age five and where millions who do reach age five suffer permanent brain damage from malnutrition? In the face of such social injustice Jesus is asking us to both change unjust social structures and to reach out to at least one wounded person since each one is Jesus suffering.

Ways in which unjust social structures need to be changed are different every week. The first step is to be informed by joining such groups as Bread for the World, Common Cause, Amnesty International, Network, Sojourners and other groups that analyze the causes of injustice and suggest action for changing social structures.

But in addition to changing social structures, we are called to grow in compassion by committing ourselves to loving at leat one wounded person. I try to tithe my time and spend at least one-tenth reaching out to someone I want to ignore. Sometimes it is easier to me to write letters to Congress than to reach out to the obnoxious neighbor who gets drunk and destroys my basketball hoop. After that happened at my inner city home in Omaha, I found myself angry at all the transients in my neighborhood, and I remained angry until I could forgive the one who destroyed my property. Therefore, the first step for social action is to forgive those who have hurt me so that I can reach out to others like them. Daddy King, the father of Martin Luther King, shares how at age three he was hurt by white people and determined to hate them. Daddy King says that the most important moment for his civil rights work came when he was fifteen and he heard Jesus say, "Love your enemies, do good to those who hate you," and he found that he could begin to forgive and love white people. Daddy King's forgiveness touched Martin Luther King and planted the seeds to respond to violence with non-violent forgiveness that eventually brought civil rights to the blacks. One act of forgiveness or of resentment has repercussions across generations.

Having forgiven those who hurt me, I am ready to reach out to one wounded person. Such reaching out, even though it be to only one person, can begin to change whole social structures. In Mexico we visited a leper colony where one woman began to work fifteen years ago as a way of expressing her gratitude for being healed of cancer. When she began to work there, she found the lepers living in fear of being robbed or hurt by other lepers who had been rejected and hurt even by their own families. Since their greatest need was to form community and bonds of trust, she and a handful of her friends began a prayer meeting. Atttracted by the singing, the lepers came and soon learned to receive love and reach out to each other in prayer. As they laid their hands on a leper's broken body in prayer, the women began to compassionately feel the leper's painful world and Jesus' total love for each one. The women responded by bringing food, clothing and medicine. But they could not meet the needs of three hundred lepers. So they taught the lepers how to help themselves by providing garden tools, sewing machines and many hours of patient instruction. They found out that the Mexican government had ten million pesos set aside for the care of lepers throughout Mexico, but only one million actually reached the lepers. They exposed this injustice by telling their husbands, who told other husbands. Gradually the embarrassed government officials used all the allotted money to help the lepers rather than fill the pockets of politicians. Thus a social structure was changed to help lepers throughout Mexico. And how? By a handful of women, each moved by compassion to lay their hands on and pray for one leper's broken body, until, feeling the leper's pain, they were moved to do more and more.

Like these women, we don't have to be experts or perfectly healed before we start reaching out to the wounded. In fact, our wounds remain healed and are a source of compassion if we, like people in Alcoholics Anonymous, reach out to a person like ourselves. One wise A.A. counselor told me that he can spot a reformed alcoholic who is about to start drinking again. His secret? He watches for a person who is no longer compassionately using his wounds to reach out to another alcoholic. Our very wounds give us the compassion to reach out with love, and that very act heals our wounds.

The person we are most afraid to help is usually the person who can best heal us as we reach out. I (Matt) remember visiting Carl, a Jesuit priest. Carl had suffered brain damage due to a lack of oxygen during heart bypass surgery and was changed from the dynamic chancellor of a university to a person who had little motor control, could not speak, and often wasn't lucid. When I first visited him in the hospital, I was so ill at ease that I didn't even sit down and I stayed only five minutes. I was uncomfortable because he was dying the death I dreaded most — being helpless, unable to communicate or move, stricken at the height of his career, and often unable even to know the love that was given to him.

Gradually I began to see that I could not love in Carl what I could not love in myself — the person who could only be weak. As I began in prayer to let Jesus love me in my weakest moments when I couldn't help another, couldn't pray, couldn't think, couldn't say what I wanted to say, couldn't even begin to do what I wanted to do, I began to experience my weakness inviting love and not just fear. After a month of experiencing this, I could return to visit Carl again and be comfortable with him because I was comfortable with the Carl in myself.

I returned to visit Carl during my retreat when I was at the point of meditating on the passion. I could hold a crucifix in my hand and tell Jesus I was ready for anything. But the real test was to hold the hand of Carl as he was dying and with him surrender to the Father. I told Carl that I was afraid of the death he was dying and needed his help to surrender to the Father as Jesus did no matter how suffering and death might come. I took Carl's hand and he squeezed mine as we slowly said the seven last words of Jesus, forgiving all who had hurt us and expressiong trust in the Father. Carl gave me a gift — the passion of Jesus became as real as Carl's hand, and his hand was giving me the strength to take each step he had taken. Perhaps that is what Carl was waiting for because the next day he became more ill, and two weeks later he died as he took the Father's hand forever. Carl showed me how the wounded person I fear the most is usually the person who can heal me most. Now, in reaching out to the wounded, I look not just for what I can give but for what they, like Carl, are giving to me.

How do we know whether to keep reaching out to the wounded or to draw back because we are overextended? When it is the right time to reach out, even though we may feel drained when we set out, we will almost always return more alert and alive. When we are overextended, we will almost always return burned out. In overextension, we reach out to another more because we think we *should* rather than because we *want* to, and we will want some success rather than just enjoy being faithfully present and giving without being noticed. *Should's* usually drain life also by making others feel they are a burden and more broken as we half-heartedly help them. Sometimes, as in an emergency, we need to do things we don't want to do but should do. Usually in these situations at first we don't want to reach out at all. But even in these times, if we ask the Lord to help us with our resistance and to take a first step, we may find a deeper part of ourselves that does want to reach out as I did with Carl. If we can begin to choose and enjoy doing what we *really* should do (see Lesson 24), we will have more love, less anger and little burn-out. Such was my experience with Carl as I chose him and gradually grew more and more to *want* to be with him. New life comes to us not only by relaxing but by reaching out to the needy such as Carl.

Where do we start to reach out? When a group of teachers asked Mother Teresa how they could begin to change the world, she said, "Go home and smile at your husbands." We can start now by lovingly cooking a meal or washing a dish — not to get it done but because we love the person who ate from it. It isn't as important what we do as with how much love we do it. Carl couldn't do anything, but he took my hand with the love of Jesus and that has started everything.

I. Group Experience

A. **Common Opening Prayer** (5 minutes)

B. **Video or Audio Tape:** "Social Change through Healing Prayer" (30 minutes)

How can we change whole social structures by loving one wounded person?
1. When he spoke about the end of the world, Jesus didn't tell us when it would be but only that we would be judged. Jesus will ask us how we treated him in people who were in need. If the end of the world comes through violence, it will be because we have not reached out to the suffering (Matthew 5).
2. We can learn about Jesus' compassion for the poor by loving one wounded person. Social change begins in our hearts, through forgiveness (e.g., Daddy King).
3. The easiest way to change whole social structures is to reach out and feel the pain of one person (e.g., woman who reached out to Mexican lepers).
4. We can reach out in any way that we have been wounded and have received the Lord's healing love into our wound (e.g., Jean Vanier).
5. The person we most fear to love is the one who can heal us the most if we can learn to love him or her (e.g., Fr. Carl Reinert).
6. We can reach out by tithing our time as well as our money.
7. We can begin in small ways, by reaching out to those right around us and doing the same things we always do but with more love. It's the love we give that matters most (e.g., leper's gift of flowers).
Closing Prayer: asking the Lord to show us one person whom he is inviting us to reach out to.

C. **Silent Reflection** (3 minutes). Quiet time to get in touch with what part of today's tape moved your heart most deeply.

D. **Guided Journaling** (Optional — 10 minutes). See Lesson 3.

E. **Companion Sharing** (5 minutes minimum for each person to share his or her reaction to today's tape and to the past week).
1. Share with your companion as much as you wish of what is in your heart after seeing this week's tape. Perhaps you will want to share what you have just written during the guided journaling.
2. Share with your companion how you have experienced the Lord's presence in your life during the previous week. You may wish to share the journal response from last week that touched you the most.
3. What are you most grateful for now and how do you need Jesus' help?

F. **Companion Prayer** (since the purpose of this prayer is healing, you may wish to pray over your companion for about 10 minutes.) Lay your hands on your companion and pray as Jesus would for about 10 minutes. Let the words and silences in your prayer be those of Jesus as he is already praying in your heart. Give thanks to Jesus for what your companion is most grateful for and pray for whatever healing your companion most needs. Close your prayer by praying that your companion receive the grace of this lesson: *to compassionately reach out to one needy person.* Then let your companion pray over you.

G. **Group Sharing** (Optional — 15 minutes minimum). Take two minutes of silence to ask what has been most difficult and what has been most helpful in your prayer and journaling this past week. Share your reflections with the larger group. Close with a prayer thanking the Lord for the breakthroughs and for discovering the blocks where he is already bringing forth further growth.

H. **Closing Snack and Celebration** (Optional). An open-ended time to enjoy one another and to continue sharing.

II. Home Experiences

Although we suggest daily healing prayers and journaling as usual, the priority is to visit one needy person this week (if possible, with your prayer companion).

A. Daily Healing Prayer (10 minutes). Each day choose one of the following healing or contemplation in action prayers and pray it for at least 10 minutes. These prayers are only *suggestions*. Perhaps you will find yourself drawn to pray what is in your heart using varied breathing, a symbol, a repeated word, a melody, a gesture, a drawing, or a piece of clay which you can mold. Although there are many prayers suggested, it would be best to pray only a few of them, parts of them, or to repeat from this or any other chapter the prayer that most moved your heart. Use whatever way you can best give your heart to Jesus and enter into his heart. Perhaps your prayer will be as simple as looking at a beautiful flower and taking in God's love for you. You may wish to begin your prayer by centering yourself, perhaps using the Breath Prayer (see Lesson I). You may wish to continue with the Embrace Prayer (see Lesson 3, Prayer #2), or a similar prayer of simply resting in God's love.

1. *Compassion Prayer* (Tape Prayer)
   a. Prayerfully read Luke 8:40-56. Notice that, despite all the faces in the crowd pressing in on Jesus, his compassion for Jairus' daughter allows him to stop only once (for the hemorrhaging woman) while on the way to Jairus' home.
   b. Let Jesus reveal to you the faces of people you know who are suffering.
   c. Ask Jesus for his compassion. Look at the faces and stop at the one you feel the most compassion for, the one you suffer with most.
   d. With the compassion Jesus has given you, pray for this person. Let Jesus do for the person what you cannot do.
   e. Look at Jesus and ask him what he wants you to do for the person.

2. *Prayer for Receiving the Grace of This Lesson*
   Ask Jesus to give you his compassion for the poor and the needy. Breathe it in with every breath and breathe out all the blocks in yourself to reaching out to one needy person. (You may wish to pray this prayer with Mary instead of Jesus.)

3. Read the story of the good Samaritan in Luke 10:25-37. Then be Jesus and, using only gestures, do what Jesus does as he sees a needy person you know at the side of the road.

4. Read the story of the good Samaritan in Luke 10:25-37, but this time in prayer be the needy person by the side of the road and see how Jesus ministers to you. Let yourself experience your needs, the care of Jesus, your gratitude. (You may wish to do this in prayer with gestures only.)

5. Read the story of the good Samaritan. Ask Jesus to reveal to you the people who have been the good Samaritan for you when you were in need. Thank Jesus.

6. Recall with Jesus the faces of the different people that you met today (or this week). End with 5 minutes of intercessory prayer for the neediest person. (You might also wish to do this prayer by looking at the faces in your photo collection.)

CONTEMPLATION IN ACTION PRAYERS

Take a moment and ask for the grace to reach out to one needy person. Then do one of the following:

7. Prayerfully read Matthew 25:31-46 and ask to experience Jesus in those who are needy. Ask him to help you to take the first step in tithing (one-tenth, or whatever amount you wish to start with) of your time to the poor. Then find out what the needs are in your community, such as Red Cross drivers, hospital volunteers, tutors for the illiterate, helpers for a soup kitchen, Meals on Wheels, etc. Or, perhaps you may wish to use your time to love one needy person, e.g., by sharing a meal, listening to the lonely, visiting the sick, phoning a shut-in, taking an elderly person shopping, babysitting for a busy mother who needs a night out, giving away extra clothes, etc.

8. Prayerfully read the story about the widow's mite in Luke 21: 1-3. Ask Jesus for the grace of being able to do the little things in life with a great deal of love. Then create around you a caring environment by cooking, washing dishes, etc., with love.

9. Become informed about a social issue by joining a group such as Bread for the World, Center for Concern, Sojourners, etc. (See section entitled "Additional Readings" at the end of this chapter for further information about these organizations.)

B. Daily Journal (5 minutes)

1. Share with Jesus when during this prayer or during the day your heart was deeply moved — perhaps a moment of being grateful for or of longing for healing in *being able to compassionately reach out to one needy person.*
2. Write in your journal how Jesus responds (what he seems to do or say in response to what you have told him). If you can't get in touch with Jesus' response, write what most moves you as you speak to him or what are the most loving words you want to hear.

OPTIONAL HOME EXPERIENCES

C. Personal Reflection Questions

1. When have you experienced growth or healing as you reach out to another?
2. What suffering in your life has given you compassion to be with another who is suffering?
3. What are the signs in your life that occur when you are overextended and need to reach out less?
4. Whom do you wish someone else would help? Why?
5. What keeps you from doing more for the needy? What helps you to reach out? What do you need to pray for so that you can reach out as Jesus wants you to?
6. When have you experienced seeing someone reach out to another in a way that made you want to do the same?
7. In what situation in your life do you most experience Mother Teresa's words, "I am called not to be successful but to be faithful"?
8. In what ways do you need to be better informed so that you can fight the causes of social evils?

9. What one needy person is the Lord especially inviting you to love?

D. Scripture Readings

Isaiah 58:6-11: Love for the poor is the fast that heals wounds.
Luke 4:18-19: Jesus proclaims his identity as being the one who is sent to the poor and the captive.
Matthew 25:31-46: The last judgment is based upon how we treated Jesus in the needy.
Luke 10:25-37: The parable of the good Samaritan.
Luke 19:1-10: The justice of Zacchaeus.
Luke 16:19-31: The rich man and Lazarus.

E. Additional Readings

Bread for the World has a monthly newsletter which is a valuable resource for pending legislation and analyses of issues as they relate to hunger. Address: 207 E. 16th Ave., New York, N.Y. 10003.

Center for Concern is a group of theologically based economists and other social scientists who publish a monthly newsletter (*Center Focus*) that examines global issues from a Christian perspective. Address: 3700 13th St., N.E., Washington, D.C. 20017.

Sojourners is a community of people whose monthly magazine critiques current issues from nuclear weapons to world hunger, all in the light of a biblical perspective. Address: 1309 L. St. N.W., Washington, D.C. 20005.

Something Beautiful for God, by Malcolm Muggeridge (New York: Ballantine, 1973). Story of Mother Teresa.

Healing Life's Hurts, Chapter 11, "Fifth Stage: Acceptance" (especially pages 171-73, which speak of how inner healing leads to social action).

Note: Since next week will be the next to last session of the course, you may wish to spend some time preparing for the end of the course. See Appendix H, "Final Sessions."

Lesson Twenty-Three
FINDING GOD'S WILL

INTRODUCTION

How do we know if we are listening to God or to ourselves? Whether we are making big decisions such as a change of job or ordinary decisions such as how to pray for a person, we need the gift of ears to help us listen.

How did Jesus help Peter listen to the challenge to serve by feeding his "lambs"? (John 21:5). Jesus knew that Peter would have difficulty listening, for Peter had just denied the Lord and was wallowing in the fear that he couldn't serve. But Jesus also knew that the more Peter loved him, the more Peter would listen. So when Jesus challenged Peter in John 21, he did it in the setting Peter could most experience love — a miraculous catch of fish on the Sea of Galilee. That was the most loving setting for Peter because it was the same setting where Peter first heard Jesus' challenge to serve and where Peter felt so loved that he responded with his deepest "Yes" (Luke 5:1-12). In John 21, Jesus even uses Peter's old name, *Simon* Peter," the name Peter went by when he felt so loved and had responded with his deepest "Yes." By bringing Peter back to his moment of greatest love, Peter was once again able to leave his nets and fears behind and once more give a "Yes" as he heard Jesus' challenge to "feed my lambs." If, like Peter, we wish to hear the Lord, we can get in touch with our deepest "Yes" given when we knew God's love and were ready to hear any request.

While I (Matt) was teaching on the Sioux reservation, I had an experience like Peter's which taught me how to hear the Lord. I was trying to choose between two things I didn't want — staying on the reservation to teach or leaving the reservation to do prayer workshops. I didn't want to stay and teach because half my students had quit my religion class when they were given a choice between taking religion or taking physical education. The other half, whose parents insisted they take religion, wanted to quit religion when they heard the physical education students bouncing basketballs in the gym next to our classroom. But I also feared giving healing prayer workshops because I have no special gift for miracles or hearing the Lord via the word of knowledge or visions. In healing prayer I was not comfortable depending on the Lord to act. I feared that until he acted people would be in total chaos, having nervous breakdowns and climbing walls. Although I researched and wrote down all the reasons for staying and for leaving, my fears would not let me freely choose one or the other.

The Lord had his own plan for making me free to choose. One night I was driving along next to a cliff when a drunken driver began weaving down the hill toward me. To avoid him, I turned too far off the road and started for the cliff's edge. Fortunately, my back bumper hooked on one lonely guard post that swung the car around and back up on the highway but facing the wrong way. Amazed that I could move, I stepped out on the highway. I moved my arms in gratitude for life given again after I had felt certain that I would end up either dead or paralzyed. I was grateful for everything; even the $500 dent was beautiful because it had saved my life. I was so grateful to the Lord for having saved my life that I just wanted to offer him my life and to serve him in whatever way he desired.

To my surprise I found that I could now gratefully choose anything the Lord wanted because I was so aware of how even to breathe was

God's gift to me. The next day I was even eager to teach, and I told the Lord that I would teach forever if that was what he wanted. I was no longer looking for results, only the chance to serve and return his gift of life. Also, I no longer feared healing prayer workshops but knew that the Lord had a reason for keeping me alive, and if it were to give workshops, he would again protect me. I was so much in touch with his love that I finally voiced a deep "Yes, I will do whatever you wish" that was deeper than any of my fears. Perfect love does cast out fear and gives freedom to hear and find God's will.

How, then, did I go about hearing and finding God's will in deciding whether to teach or to give workshops? Since both were good choices, it was not immediately evident which to choose, but since I had researched the consequences of each, I was ready to do the actual choosing. In my prayer I returned to the moment of my deep "Yes" upon that highway and felt how my life belonged to God. Then I stood on that highway matching both possibilities against my deepest "Yes." My deepest "Yes" resonated most with surrending to retreat work, making me even more dependent on God than teaching did. This choice of retreat work was confirmed as I later prayed over Scripture passages and as I consulted with those who loved the Lord and really knew me, including my superior. He scared me by asking me to go into retreat work with Dennis full-time for ten to fifteen years. All my fears surfaced again and I had to return in prayer to stand on the highway and find that his suggestion matched my deepest "Yes" better than did the part-time work I had wanted. By consulting prayer, Scripture, and those who love the Lord most and know me, I can always test whether I am hearing God's will.

The final test for heaing God's will is whether living it out brings life to me and to others. Is this choice the way I can best give and receive love? If it isn't, I must go back over the whole process and find out where I heard my will, especially in my fears or dreams, rather than God's will. God confirms his will with the gift of life even in the midst of conflict. Some days I experience conflict when I am rewriting something for the tenth time and it still isn't right, or when I suddenly feel as discouraged as the broken person speaking to me. But even on these days of deep conflict, deeper peace comes from a deeper "Yes" that says, "Yes, Lord, even if this conflict doesn't change, I will keep trying as long as it is your will." This same deep "Yes" and peace Jesus had, in the midst of conflict causing him to sweat blood, as he surren-dered to his Father in Gethsemani. The conflict doesn't disappear but there is strength to do the Father's will and this brings life to all. The test is not whether I feel the high of my original "Yes" but whether I feel its depth and surrender, thereby making me ready to do anything that will help me to give or receive God's life more deeply. God's will often means the cross, but it always means giving and receiving more of his life and love.

Perhaps, by now, listening to God's will sounds very complex, but it is as simple as listening to a baby cry at night. Who is the first to hear the baby cry? Usually the person who loves the baby most sleeps less soundly so as to be alert to any way the baby might be in trouble. The parent who loves the baby most also will be the least likely to turn over in a warm bed and let the baby cry itself to sleep. Love not only strains to hear the needs of the one loved but overcomes all obstacles in responding to the needs. Listening to God is as simple and as profound as a mother listening to her baby.

I. Group Experience

A. Common Opening Prayer (5 minutes)

B. Video or Audio Tape: "Finding God's Will" (30 minutes)

How do we know what God is calling us to?
1. If we want to hear the Lord speak to us about our present situation, we can start by getting in touch with the time when we said our deepest "yes" (e.g., Jesus and Peter).
2. Our deepest "yes" helps us to face our fears and hurts, so that we can choose without being controlled by them (e.g., Matt's decision to leave the reservation).
3. What we hear the Lord saying to us needs to be confirmed: in our own prayer, by Scripture, by others with good judgment who love the Lord and who love us, and in the real experience of living out our decision.
4. Sometimes we go through all the right steps of trying to hear the Lord, and we're still not sure or we make the wrong decision. What matters most is not that we hear everything perfectly, but that we take the next loving step. When we're not sure, the thing to do is whatever would be most loving (e.g., mother who thought her son was dying).

5. When the Lord is really speaking to us, it leads us to give and receive more love. *Closing Prayer:* saying "yes" as Mary did.

C. **Silent Reflection** (3 minutes). Quiet time to get in touch with what part of today's tape moved your heart most deeply.

D. **Guided Journaling** (Optional — 10 minutes). See Lesson 3.

E. **Companion Sharing** (5 minutes minimum for each person to share his or her reaction to today's tape and to the past week).

1. Share with your companion as much as you wish of what is in your heart after seeing this week's tape. Perhaps you will want to share what you have just written during the guided journaling.
2. Share with your companion how you have experienced the Lord's presence in your life during the previous week. You may wish to share the journal response from last week that touched you the most.
3. What are you most grateful for now and how do you need Jesus' help?

F. **Companion Prayer** (since the purpose of this prayer is healing, you may wish to pray over your companion for about 10 minutes). Lay your hands on your companion and pray as Jesus would for about 10 minutes. Let the words and silences in your prayer be those of Jesus as he is already praying in your heart. Give thanks to Jesus for what your companion is most grateful for and pray for whatever healing your companion most needs. Close your prayer by praying that your companion receive the grace of this lesson: *to find God's will.* Then let your companion pray over you.

G. **Group Sharing** (Optional — 15 minutes minimum). Take two minutes of silence to ask what has been most difficult and what has been most helpful in your prayer and journaling this past week. Share your reflections with the larger group. Close with a prayer thanking the Lord for the break-throughs and for discovering the blocks where he is already bringing forth further growth.

H. **Closing Snack and Celebration** (Optional). An open-ended time to enjoy one another and to continue sharing.

II. Home Experience

A. **Daily Healing Prayer** (10 minutes). Each day choose one of the following healing or contemplation in action prayers and pray it for at least 10 minutes. These prayers are only *suggestions.* Perhaps you will find yourself drawn to pray what is in your heart using varied breathing, a symbol, a repeated word, a melody, a gesture, a drawing, or a piece of clay which you can mold. Although there are many prayers suggested, it would be best to pray only a few of them, parts of them, or to repeat from this or any other chapter the prayer that most moved your heart. Use whatever way you can best give your heart to Jesus and enter into his heart. Perhaps your prayer will be as simple as looking at a beautiful flower and taking in God's love for you. You may wish to begin your prayer by centering yourself, perhaps using the Breath Prayer (see Lesson 1). You may wish to continue with the Embrace Prayer (see Lesson 3, Prayer #2), or a similar prayer of simply resting in God's love.

1. *Mary's "Yes"* (Tape Prayer)
   a. Prayerfully read Luke 1:34-38: "Mary said to the angel, 'How can this be since I do not know man?' The angel answered her: 'The Holy Spirit will come upon you and the power of the Most High will overshadow you; hence the holy offspring to be born will be called Son of God.' . . . Mary said: 'I am the servant of the Lord. Let it be done to me according to your will.' "
   b. Position your entire body as Mary's was when she said, "Let it be done to me according to your will." Let your breathing, your hands, the way you sit or stand be just like Mary as she says her deep "Yes." Repeat her words, "Let it be done to me," until they resound in your heart as deeply as Mary's "Yes."
   c. Then take a deep breath and ask the Father to bring to mind one moment

in your own life when you said a deep "Yes" to him. Perhaps it was after a near death experience, or when you hit rock bottom and had nowhere else to turn, or when you experienced his unconditional love and forgiveness.

    d. Enjoy that moment with the Father and give him thanks as you once again rest in his love that enabled you to say that "Yes."

2. *Do You Love Me?*

    a. Prayerfully read John 21.

    b. Jesus used the seashore where he had first found Peter, a miraculous catch of fish after catching nothing, and Peter's old name, "Simon," to remind Peter of the time when he loved Jesus so much that he left everything on the shore to follow Jesus. Let Jesus help you recall the times when he empowered you to be loving. What scene stands out in your mind?

    c. Reexperience that scene with Jesus and hear him say your name and ask, "Do you love me?" Look into his eyes, see that he would do anything for you, and hear him continue to repeat this question until you can no longer withhold your answer. Respond to him.

    d. Then hear Jesus say, "Feed my sheep." Share your response with him.

3. *"Yes" Centering Prayer*

    a. Relax your body and sit upright. Then, bask for a few minutes as he says, "I love you (*your name*)."

    b. When you sense his love, breathe it all in with the word, "Father," and surrender all as you breathe out, "Yes." Continue to take in more love with each inhalation and to give a deeper commitment and "Yes" with each exhalation.

    c. After a few minutes, close by saying the Lord's Prayer slowly, phrase by phrase.

4. *Magnificat "Yes"*

    a. After Mary conceived Jesus, she expressed her "Yes" with the Magnificat (Luke 1:46-55). Spend a few minutes simply praising God with your own Magnificat, or take Mary's Magnificat and pray it line by line to express your "Yes" in a prayer of thanksgiving and praise.

5. *Writing Prayer*

    a. Write Jesus' question, "Do you love me?" Then write Peter's answer and continue it as you think Peter might have as he continued to talk with Jesus.

    b. Then write Jesus' reply and continue it with what Jesus puts in your heart for Peter. During another time of prayer, you might wish to substitute yourself for Peter.

6. *Gratitude for Decisions*

    a. Recall a good decision you have made. Thank Jesus for everything that helped you to make that decision.

    b. Another time you might wish to recall a bad decision you have made. Ask Jesus what you can learn from that experience, and give thanks.

7. *Pros and Cons*

    a. Get in touch with the time that you said a deep "Yes" to Jesus.

    b. With Jesus, consider prayerfully a decision that you must make in the present. Write down the reasons against the decision and the reasons in favor of it.

    c. Recall again your deep "Yes," and ask what decision in the present would be most consistent with it.

8. *Surrendering All*

    a. Make a list of the people and things that you love most. Put the list on your heart and tell Jesus how much you love each one—so much that you want what is best for everyone and everything that you love.

    b. Hold the list out to Jesus and surrender each into his will and care, to do with whatever he wishes. Where there is a struggle, see how Jesus loves that person or thing and ask to trust him.

    c. Thank Jesus for all that you have been able to surrender and for the freedom this gives you to hear his will at any cost.

9. *Sealed Orders*
   a. Imagine that you are with the Father, as he is about to send you forth to be born into this world. Hear him tell you the kind of person he has made you to be and the special purpose that he has for your life.
   b. See the person that you are meant to be in your mind—how you look, how you carry yourself, what you are doing, whom you are with, etc.
   c. Consider a choice or decision that you must make in the present.
   d. As you stay in touch with the person within you that you were created to be, ask yourself which choice or decision is most consistent with your deepest self.

CONTEMPLATION IN ACTION PRAYERS

Take a moment and ask for the grace to find God's will. Then do one of the following:

10. *"Yes" to the Present Moment*
   Live the day choosing each event with Mary's "Yes," just as she put her whole heart into caring for Elizabeth's house. For example, wash dishes not just because they are dirty but as a way of saying "Yes" to the Father's will in the present moment.

11. *Listening with Thanks*
   During the day, stop to listen to every sound. Thank God for all that you hear as he speaks to you through his creation. You might want to treat yourself to listening to your favorite music.

B. Daily Journal (5 minutes)

1. Share with Jesus one of the decisions that you made during the day. What part of it was a "Yes" that the Lord would have chosen with you and what part was a compromise based upon more superficial wishes and desires?

2. Write in your journal how Jesus responds (what he seems to do or say in response to what you have told him). If you can't get in touch with Jesus' response, write what most moves you as you speak to him, or what are the most loving words you want him to say to you.

OPTIONAL HOME EXPERIENCES

C. Personal Reflection Questions

1. What helps you listen to your best friend? To God?
2. What moments in your life made you want to surrender and say a deep "Yes," giving everything to God? When did you say your deepest "Yes"? What would help you to surrender at the same depth now? Why do you want to or not want to do this?
3. The moment of your deepest surrender is an experience of readiness to hear anything that God might ask of you, rather than just your more superficial thoughts and desires. Recall how you felt at a moment of deep surrender, because that openness is a measuring stick against which to measure the openness you have now. Now, think of a decision that you are trying to make. If you had had to make the same decision at the time when you were experiencing your deepest surrender and "Yes" to God's will, how would you look at the decision? If you wanted only the best way of surrendering all to God, what would you do?
4. When did you feel most free? Was it when you could do whatever you wanted, or when you wanted to do anything that God asked of you? Is freedom having an infinite number of choices, or is it putting your whole self behind God's choice? What are the signs of real freedom?
5. Jesus was free enough from all of his fears and needs that he could even freely choose death on a cross. When in your life have you freely chosen the cross and found that it brought you deeper freedom?
6. God's will is for us to love him with our whole heart, and to love our neighbor as ourself (Matthew 22:37-38). With this in mind, what is Jesus asking you to give more time to? Less time to?

D. Scripture Readings

John 21: Simon, do you love me?
Luke 1:26-55: Mary's "Yes."
Luke 9:57-62: Leaving everything to follow God's will.

145

Luke 10:25-28: The criterion is love of God and love of neighbor as oneself.

1 Thessalonians 5:16: Rejoice always, never cease praying, render constant thanks; such is God's will for you in Christ Jesus.

E. Additional Readings

The Art of Christian Listening, by Tom Hart (New York: Paulist Press, 1980).

He Leadeth Me, by Walter Ciszek (New York: Doubleday, 1973). Finding God's will, even during twenty years of imprisonment.

Letters by a Modern Mystic, by Frank Laubach (New York: Frank Laubach, 1955). Learning to surrender to God at every moment.

Note: Since next week is the final session of the course, you may wish to use your time according to the suggestions given in Appendix G, "Gratitude Session," and Appendix H, "Final Sessions." You may wish to have an additional meeting after next week, and use the entire meeting as a Gratitude Session.

Lesson Twenty-Four
HEALING BY CHOOSING

INTRODUCTION

Our whole person thrives when we choose what life presents. Who have the fewest number of colds? Studies show that persons on their honeymoon seldom have colds because their immunity is raised as they say "Yes" to all of life. Likewise the day with the greatest number of heart attacks is not Friday but Monday when we are not looking forward to choosing for the rest of the week. Choosing events and people in life can bring health; refusing to choose them can bring dis-ease.

Recently a friend, Anna, shared with me how choosing her father brought health after years of depression. She knew that her depression started years ago when her father kept the family in poverty by drinking away the paycheck. She also knew that her depression stemmed from an inability to forgive her now deceased father. Yet she found herself unable to understand how her father could do such a thing, and thus she was unable to forgive him. Finally, she saw that her depression and inability to change herself were exactly what her father experienced, and were exactly what drove him to drink and to hurt his family against his will. Once she felt his world, she could forgive him and once again choose him as the father chosen for her by God.

The lifting of Anna's depression, when she chose her father, would have been no surprise to Francis of Assisi who believed that such a choice brought perfect joy. One day while walking in a biting snowstorm, Francis asked his freezing companion, Brother Leo, what was perfect joy. Before Brother Leo could tell him that it was a warm fire and hot Franciscan soup, Francis started to answer his own question. "Brother Leo, if all the Minor Brothers gave the finest examples of holiness and virtue, and healed cripples and could make the blind see, drive out devils, and even bring the dead back to life, write down that this is not perfect joy. . . . Even if we knew the secrets of the future and of hearts, write down that this is not perfect joy. . . . Even if we should preach so well as to convert all the infidels, write down that this is not perfect joy." Finally, Brother Leo, irritated at having to write down in the blizzard all the wrong answers, yelled, "For the sake of God, Francis, tell me now what is perfect joy!"

Then Francis cried out with great joy, like an organ pouring forth music from all its stops: "When we arrive at the Portiuncula in a little while, wet to the skin by the snow and freezing with cold, plastered with mud and tortured by a gnawing hunger, and then, when we knock at the door and the Brother Porter asks: 'Who are you?' and we answer: 'Two of your Brothers,' and he says: 'You are lying. You are two tramps who go around deceiving the people and robbing the poor! Get out of here!', and he leaves us standing outside in the cold and the snow until late at night, and we humbly and meekly realize how well he knows us, and we knock again, and he angrily strikes us down and beats us with a club, and we endure it all willingly, without complaining and lamenting, out of love for our Lord Jesus Christ — O Little Brother Lamb, note that is perfect joy! For above all the gifts of the Holy Spirit which Christ gives to his friends is the grace of conquering oneself and of

147

suffering pain, injustice, and mistreatment willingly, for love of Christ!"[1]

For Francis the desire to be treated like Jesus and to give in return the love of Christ was not the desire of a masochist who loved pain. Because Francis loved a Person, and not pain, choosing to be treated like Jesus brought perfect joy. And because choosing to return love even to an enemy required of Jesus and of Francis a deeper, more unselfish love; such love brought a deeper, more perfect joy. Thus Francis believed that a hurt could not destroy but could only bring perfect joy to the person who with Jesus chose to love in the midst of the hurt.

To choose to go through hurts with Jesus could be masochistic unless we, like Jesus, also tried to change the evil which could be changed. We are to choose only what God has chosen. In his agony Jesus was not a masochist but he asked the Father to change all that could be changed while at the same time asking his Father to help him choose the things that could not be changed. "Father, it it is possible, take this cup from me; yet not my will but yours be done" (Luke 22:42). Praying such a prayer with Jesus might help someone like Anna to choose what cannot be changed, such as her deceased alcoholic father. But another praying such a prayer with Jesus might be helped to reach out and struggle with an alcoholic whose alcoholism is not to be chosen but rather changed. In both cases to be treated like Jesus and to love in return means to choose to love the alcoholic whether he changes or not. Like Jesus, we are to hate the sin by praying and working for a change, while at the same time we are to choose to love the sinner.

But perhaps the biggest challenge in choosing will not come from choosing the person who has or who will hurt us most, but rather in choosing the present moment. Recently we met a priest who in working for human rights has been threatened with prison. When we asked how he was preparing himself for the inevitable imprisonment, he said, "I choose every hour of my life. When I go to lunch or to work, I choose the people with whom I am eating or working. When I pray, I choose to pray." In choosing the present moment strength is built up within this priest to choose an uncertain future.

What does it mean to me to choose the present moment? First of all, for me (Matt) it means choosing those things about me that cannot be changed — my height, IQ, an aging body, and a congenital bone disorder. It means choosing to be five feet three inches tall rather than an imposing six feet that would help to convince everyone that all I say is true. Can I choose being short and having to rely on Jesus rather than my height to convince another?

But in addition to choosing things about me that can't be changed, choosing the present moment means choosing these moments when I say, "I wish this were different" or "I wish this were over." Can I choose the cold shower, the dirty dishes left by the insensitive, the food served at a meal, the dismal weather, the interrupting phone call, or whatever I wish were not present? Does each of these events drain life from me as I try to play God and design the day without any friction? Can I find reasons for choosing each of these moments such as choosing to listen to a boring person because he needs love and I need to grow in my capacity to love without return? Can I choose the times I can't write, or can't pray, or do I just grow depressed and more unable to write or pray? Often I find that I can't write or pray because I really don't want to; I would rather be doing something else. If I can find out why I really want to pray or write, I usually can. Choosing the present replaces burn-out with energy to burn.

But sometimes I will choose the present and find that I am still burned out. Can I then choose to feel my present feelings that I don't want and hear what they want? Can I feel a tired body asking for rest, a sluggish mind needing mental or physical exercise, impulsive sexual drives with fantasies revealing my buried desires, fears flickering like ghostly shadows where I feel overextended, or edgy anger revealing conflict and need for change? When I choose to hear my feelings rather than fear them, I choose to hear their message asking for more life when I have been choosing death.

Each moment we, like the priest working for human rights, are confronted with the choice: "Choose life or death" (Deuteronomy 30:19). Death and burn-out come from wishing that what I was doing were over; life and health come from recognizing that what I wish were over can be chosen to bring perfect joy.

I. Group Experience

A. Common Opening Prayer (5 minutes)

---

1. Felix Timmermans, *The Perfect Joy of St. Francis* (N.Y.: Doubleday, 1955), p. 130.

B. Video or Audio Tape: "Healing by Choosing" (30 minutes)

Changing with the Father what can be changed, and choosing with him those situations which cannot be changed at this time.

1. We have the greatest resistance to disease at those times when we are saying "Yes" to life (e.g., honeymooners).
2. Some things in our life should be changed, but some things cannot be changed. Health and wholeness come when, with the Father, we change what can be changed and choose with him those things which at this time do not change (e.g., woman with alcoholic father, Matt's bones, cold showers).
3. Choosing something in our life includes getting in touch with why we want it.
4. We can find out what we need to choose by asking what we wish were over with. If we can choose the little things, we grow in freedom to choose the bigger things that the Lord may call us to (e.g., Jesuit in Korean jail, Dennis cleaning the yard).
5. The freedom to be treated as Jesus was and still respond with love is the greatest gift of the Holy Spirit (e.g., St. Francis and perfect joy).

Closing Prayer: to choose the things that the Father has chosen for us.

C. Silent Reflection (3 minutes). Quiet time to get in touch with what part of today's tape moved your heart most deeply.

D. Guided Journaling (Optional — 10 minutes). See Lesson 3.

E. Companion Sharing (5 minutes minimum for each person to share his or her reaction to today's tape and to the past week).

1. Share with your companion as much as you wish of what is in your heart after seeing this week's tape. Perhaps you will want to share what you have just written during the guided journaling.
2. Share with your companion how you have experienced the Lord's presence in your life during the previous week. You may wish to share the journal response from last week that touched you the most.
3. What are you most grateful for now and how do you need Jesus' help?

F. Companion Prayer (since the purpose of this prayer is healing, you may wish to pray over your companion for about 10 minutes). Lay your hands on your companion and pray as Jesus would for about 10 minutes. Let the words and silences in your prayer be those of Jesus as he is already praying in your heart. Give thanks to Jesus for what your companion is most grateful for and pray for whatever healing your companion most needs. Close your prayer by praying that your companion receive the grace of this lesson: *to change what he or she is called to change and to choose what cannot be changed.* Then let your companion pray over you.

G. Group Sharing (Optional — 15 minutes minimum). Take two minutes of silence to ask what has been most difficult and what has been most helpful in your prayer and journaling this past week. Share your reflections with the larger group. Close with a prayer thanking the Lord for the breakthroughs and for discovering the blocks where he is already bringing forth further growth.

H. Closing Snack and Celebration (Optional). An open-ended time to enjoy one another and to continue sharing.

II. Home Experience

A. Daily Healing Prayer (10 minutes). Each day choose one of the following healing or contemplation in action prayers and pray it for at least 10 minutes. These prayers are only *suggestions*. Perhaps you will find yourself drawn to pray what is in your heart using varied breathing, a symbol, a repeated word, a melody, a gesture, a drawing, or a piece of clay which you can mold. Although there are many prayers suggested, it would be best to pray only a few of them, parts of them, or to repeat from this or any other chapter the prayer that most moved your heart. Use whatever way you can best give your heart to Jesus and enter into his heart. Perhaps your prayer will be as simple as looking at a beautiful flower and taking in God's love for you. You may wish to begin your prayer by centering yourself, perhaps using the Breath Prayer (see Lesson 1). You may wish to continue with the Embrace Prayer (see Lesson 3, Prayer #2), or a similar prayer of simply resting in God's love.

1. *Healing by Choosing Your Agony* (Tape Prayer)
   a. Think of a situation in your life that isn't changing and that is hard for you to choose. Tell the Father all the things that you would like changed. Then prayerfully read Luke 22:39-46 and identify with Jesus in his agony.
   b. Look at your agonizing situation and, with Jesus, pray, "Father, if it is possible let this pass from me. Yet not my will but your will be done." As you move your lips, pray Jesus' words until you can pray them with the same intensity and feeling that he did.
   c. Ask Jesus that you be gifted by your agonizing situation just as his agonizing situation gifted him. As Jesus' agony gave him compassion to reach out to the soldier with the severed ear, the women who were weeping, the good thief and others in their agony, let Jesus show you the people you can compassionately reach out to because of your agonizing situation.
   d. Jesus' agony also gifted him with a neediness that allowed him to receive help and come closer to Simon carrying his cross or John who was entrusted to care for Mary. Let Jesus show you the people he has sent you to help you with your struggle.
   e. Finally, Jesus' agony brought him face to face with the Father. He could angrily pray, "My God, my God, why have you forsaken me?" And, with total trust, he could say, "Into your hands I commend my spirit." Thank the Father for any way that your struggle has brought you face to face with him.

2. *Prayer for Receiving the Grace of This Lesson*

Ask Jesus to give you his ability to choose the Father's will for him. Breathe it in with every breath you take and breathe out any blocks in yourself to surrendering to the Father. (You may wish to pray this prayer with Mary instead of Jesus.)

3. *Dream Prayer*
   Recall a recent dream. Recall any dark or frightening images, e.g., a wild animal, a distorted face, etc. Often such images represent parts of ourselves or aspects of our lives that need more love and acceptance. Put the image into the loving hands of Jesus, asking him to work in your inner spirit providing whatever love and healing that part of you needs. Watch Jesus as he loves and transforms that part of you, freeing you from fear of it.

4. Ask Jesus to help you choose to love a difficult person, even if that person does not respond. Then get in touch with all the things that you find difficult to choose in this person. Take a glass and a pitcher of water, and one by one pour into the glass each thing you find difficult to choose. When you have poured into the glass everything that you find difficult in the person, hold it up to the light and ask that choosing this person become life-giving to you.

5. With Jesus, choose yourself — your age, size, IQ, and each part of your body.

6. Say the morning offering slowly, consciously choosing with Jesus as you say each word all that will come in the day. Or, make up your own morning offering to choose the day.

7. *Choosing Your Day*
   a. Read Jeremiah 1:4-10. Hear the tender way that God speaks your name. Then say your name until you can say it with just as much care as God says it.
   b. As the Father speaks your name, breathe in all that comes from him and breathe out your whole self with the word, "Father." Breathe out the ways you feel "too young," inade-

quate or too inexperienced to face the day. Breathe in all that you need from the Father.

8. Slowly say Charles de Foucauld's translation of the Lord's Prayer, the "Prayer of Abandonment." Say it three times. The first time, hear Jesus saying it to you. The second time, say it as Jesus to the Father. The third time, say it with Jesus to the Father.

PRAYER OF ABANDONMENT

Father, I abandon myself into your hands;
do with me what you will.
Whatever you may do, I thank you:
I am ready for all, I accept all.
Let only your will be done in me
and in all your creatures —
I wish no more than this, O Lord.
Into your hands I commend my soul:
I offer it to you
with all the love of my heart,
for I love you Lord,
and so need to give myself,
to surrender myself into your hands,
without reserve,
and with boundless confidence.
For you are my Father.

9. *Healing the Future*
   a. Read Luke 22:39-46, the agony in the garden.
   b. Ask Jesus to help you create in your imagination the scene of what you most fear or want to be able to face in the future.
   c. Face the fear or hurt until you feel it in your body. Share how you feel with Jesus.
   d. Ask Jesus to help you absorb how he would respond to the same situation —his thoughts and feelings.
      1. What does Jesus want done to prevent what he fears ("Remove this cup . . .")?
      2. How does Jesus promise that growth will come if it is the Father's will for you to go through what you most fear to face?
         (a) How would Jesus go through it? What would he say, do, see, etc.?

In our imagination, react like Jesus.
      (b) After doing this, what is still difficult for you to face? How does Jesus find a gift in this fear?
   e. Live out Jesus' reaction by taking one step to face this fear (e.g., take a step closer to the feared cliff; if you fear death, make out a will; etc.).
   f. Thank Jesus for whatever has happened during the prayer and rest in his strength.

CONTEMPLATION IN ACTION PRAYERS

Take a moment and ask for the grace to change what you are called to change and to choose what cannot be changed. Then do one of the following:

10. Ask Jesus for the grace of living in the present moment. Then spend a day being grateful for everything that you notice— the weather, leftover food, a cold shower, the person who squeezed the toothpaste tube in the middle, etc.

11. Ask Jesus for the grace of choosing to change what he is calling you to change. As a symbol of that desire, choose to change one thing that can be changed to represent how you want to choose life. It can be as simple as oiling a squeaky door, straightening a crooked picture, or doing spring housecleaning that is always put off.

12. Ask Jesus for the grace of choosing a task that you want to ignore. Then do that undesired task, and do it for the love of the Lord and others. It might be writing a letter, scrubbing a floor, or listening to a non-stop talker.

13. Ask the Lord for the grace of choosing your feelings. Then recall the feeling you least liked experiencing during the day (e.g., tired, fearful, lonely). Thank the Lord for that feeling and the problem that it was trying to alert you to. Ask Jesus what to do next about the causes for your feeling.

B. Daily Journal (5 minutes)
   1. Share with Jesus when during this prayer or during the day your heart was deeply moved — perhaps a moment of being grateful for or of longing for

healing in *changing what you are called to change and choosing what cannot be changed.*

2. Write in your journal how Jesus responds (what he seems to do or say in response to what you have told him). If you can't get in touch with Jesus' response, write what most moves you as you speak to him or what are the most loving words you want to hear.

OPTIONAL HOME EXPERIENCES

C. Personal Reflection Questions

1. How do you know whether to work and pray for a thing to be changed or to choose it as it is? When are you to do both?
2. Often we have to go through a struggle (sometimes involving the five stages of forgiveness) before we can honestly choose a situation. What is difficult for you to choose now? What is the next step or stage?
3. In what areas of your life is God asking you to choose yourself just the way you are?
4. When have you experienced that choosing something gave you more energy and life?
5. What in your present circumstances drains life from you to the point that you might be wishing it could be avoided: Are there any dimensions of this that you need to choose?
6. Jesus chose Jerusalem and the cross. What is your Jerusalem and cross? How do you know it is really your cross rather than someone else's, and how do you know that you are meant to carry it rather than try to change it? If it is really your Jerusalem and cross, how does Jesus want to walk with you toward it?

D. Scripture Readings

Luke 22:39-46: The agony of choosing what God has chosen.
John 15:16: You did not choose me but I chose you.

1 John 4:19: The power to love because God first loved us.
1 Corinthians 1:27: God chose the foolish to shame the wise.
Ephesians 1:4: God chose us in Jesus before the foundation of the world.
Romans 8:28-39: For those who love God, all things work together for good and nothing will be able to separate us from the love of Christ.
1 Thessalonians 5:16: God's will is that we rejoice always.

E. Additional Readings

Healing Life's Hurts, Pages 171-173, "Acceptance Can Be Healthy." Whatever our situation, we have the freedom to choose whether to hate or to offer the forgiveness of acceptance. When we accept the suffering we cannot change and forgive, we are free to grow from our situation and even to relieve the suffering around us.
Chapter 14, "Healing the Future." Jesus wants us to give him our fears of the future so that he can first show us how to prevent the evil — and then how we can grow from what must be faced. When we have given Jesus our fears of the future, we are free to "give thanks in all circumstances" (1 Thessalonians 5:18).

Chapter 15, "Healing the Future Through Dreams." Healing a dream is a safe way to heal the subconscious, because we dream what is struggling to become conscious and healed. We can come to terms with many things we are afraid to face by inviting Jesus into our dreams.

Note: You may wish to have an additional meeting, during which you express your gratitude for all that the Lord has done for you during these last weeks (unless you have already used some of your time this week to share your gratitude). See Appendix G, "Gratitude Session."

Appendix A
JOURNALING: WRITING A LOVE LETTER

For years I went to journaling workshops and was sold on the value of journaling to help focus my inner life. But I seldom journaled. When the time for journaling came at the end of the day, I found myself too tired for an exercise that seemed like school homework. Even when I tried to write, little came and I kept reworking its awkward expression. But I also found myself a month or so later wishing I had recorded an insight or moving experience rather than letting it slip away without drawing life from it. I was amazed at how others could talk about what their experiences taught them while I had a hard time even vaguely remembering mine. I only *had experiences* while others were reflecting and *becoming experienced*.

On the other hand, I found I enjoyed writing letters to friends and I would talk about what was happening in my life and what it meant to me. The more I loved a person, the more I had to share myself and not just *what* was happening but *how I felt* about it. What I could not do in journaling, I was doing in my letters and finding it not work but fun. For example, I could never journal on what my religious vows meant to me but I wrote four pages to a friend who asked me why I wanted to take final vows. My letter was filled with misspellings and half thoughts because it was written late at night with my heart more than with my head—and that's why it was so special. After that letter I found new growth in myself: deeper gratitude for and commitment to my Jesuit call, a desire to serve the poor and not just those who are appreciative, a deeper trust in allowing God to work through my poverty, a desire to grow in a celibate love that treats all as my family, and an openness to receive love that made me more grateful for what was given in each moment. I seemed to grow more from writing that one letter than from any other single thing I did that year. I was journaling beause I loved a friend so much that I wanted to share my heart, and I focused only on sharing my heart and not on how I spelled or expressed myself.

So I began journaling primarily through my letters, especially Christmas letters sharing the whole year. I could never write my annual Christmas letter until I took time to recall the love of the friend I was writing to, and then I would begin to remember things I wanted to share. I would just recall a good time together, then think about what I most wanted to share — and soon I'd find my pen racing. As I finished the letter, I could even guess how my friend would answer me because I knew he would say the most loving thing in his heart too. The more I loved another, the more I could also guess at his loving response to me.

Suddenly I found I could do this in prayer with Jesus. I would just relax in his presence and recall a time when I experienced his love — often whatever I was most grateful for that day. Then I would start to write a word of thanks and what I wanted to share with him. It didn't even have to be in sentences because Jesus understands just a word — but sentences did help me to clarify what I really wanted to share. I usually told him what I was feeling and what I most wanted. Then I would write my name, followed by what I thought Jesus would say — just as I could guess what my friend would write because he loves me.

But is it Jesus or only my imagination replying to me? Any words that help me know more that I am loved are really the voice of Jesus. If I can write a love letter to Jesus it is only because I have heard his voice in the letter he has already written to me. "Love then consists in this, not that we have loved God but that he has first loved us" (1 John 4:10). Journaling is simply writing a love letter to Jesus and listening to the love letter he wrote first.

The more my letter is a love letter, the more I will hear anything Jesus says because love makes the heart strain to hear all. Who is the first to hear a baby cry at night? Usually whoever is most concerned about the baby will be sleeping the lightest and will be less likely to turn over for more sleep. A loving mother will hear the baby's cry and also know immediately whether the baby is hungry, wet, tired, afraid, cold or in some danger. Love opens the heart's ears to hear what others ignore and to make sense of what is nonsense to others. The more our love for Jesus is as deep as a mother's love for her baby, the more we will hear the voice of Jesus and understand it.

So, when I question whether it is really Jesus or only my own imagination replying to me, I can ask myself: Do I know more that I am loved and do I have a love for Jesus as deep as a mother's love for her child? The more I can give and receive love with Jesus and others, the more I have heard his voice.

Following are instructions that may help you to journal by writing a love letter to Jesus and receiving the one he writes back to you. But journaling will happen not so much by discovering the best technique as by discovering the best Friend.

Instructions:
1. Share with Jesus by writing in your journal when during this prayer or during the past day you experienced the most struggle or growth.
2. Write in your journal how Jesus responds (what he seems to do or say in response to what you have told him). If you can't get in touch with how Jesus responds, write what most moves you as you speak to him, or what you most *want* him to say to you.

Examples:

Step 1: Sharing with Jesus
a. Focus on Jesus. Relax in his presence — look at a cross or just imagine relaxing with him by a stream or favorite place until you feel quieted and secure.
b. With Jesus, look at the day and pray to find the moments of gratitude and of longing for healing.
   Gratitude:
   The times you are most grateful for, e.g., catch-

ing life from a friend, working with care rather than just to get something done, what you did as Jesus rather than alone (e.g., I listened to John as Jesus would but my angry response was me alone), moments of faith or hope, any moment of giving or receiving love with God or another, etc.
Desire for Healing:
The times you are not so grateful for, e.g., times of doubt, temptation, gloom, confusion, selfishness, anxiety, running away by working or withdrawing, not listening, failing to choose the present moment with Jesus, any moment of failing to give or receive love with God or another, etc.

Step 2: Writing Jesus' Response
a. Focus on Jesus. See the look on his face, hear his words, see the way his hand rests on your shoulder. Get in touch with how he sees all, and ask, "Is his view the same as or different from my view?"
b. When you know how Jesus loves you, then write his response to you.

For today, I wrote the following:
Matt, I was happiest today when you listened to John's monologue about his harsh boss and tried to receive my love for John and affirm him through your respect. You looked at him and loved him just as I did with the rich young man. But you let some of his anger remain in you and you were restless during your prayer. Maybe you could have just shared with me how you struggle to love a person like John and how you don't like anger in him or in yourself. Let me love you and forgive you the way you are rather than just the way you want to be. Come to me with your burden and I will refresh you.

Journaling Examples from the Movie "Simple Ways To Pray"

In our movie "Simple Ways To Pray," seven people each took five minutes to go through the same two steps of sharing with Jesus and then being attentive to Jesus' response. Following are three examples from this lesson of what a person shared with Jesus and then what his or her journal entry might be.

Example 1: A journal entry recording what Jesus says.

(After sharing with Jesus four things about his job and family situation that he wished would change, Chuck wrote down what he thought Jesus was saying to him.)

"I know the hurts you feel. Men have hurt me too. Trust in me and have faith and I will help you."

Thus, one way to journal is to write down in a few sentences, as Chuck did, just what you sense Jesus wants to say to you.

Example 2: A journal entry recording what Jesus does.

(After sharing with Jesus what she wished she could have said or done for her son Scott before he died, Tommy watches her in her spirit and describes what Jesus does.)

"Jesus is sitting on the bed with Scott. He has his hand on Scott's head. Then he puts his arm around Scott's shoulder."

Thus, a second way to journal would be to write in a few sentences what Jesus wants to do for you or another.

Example 3: A journal entry recording what moves you the most as you speak to Jesus, or what you most want him to say or do.

(After silently sharing with Jesus how sorry she is that on the day she wanted to run away from her father he had a heart attack and died, Gale begins to cry and writes the following.)

"I want to know that he (my father) loves me. Most of all, I want him to know how much I love him. I never told him that, Lord."

The third way to journal is to write in a few sentences what moved you the most, i.e., what you most wanted or experienced most intensely.

Additional Suggestions for Journaling

If you don't have a sense of what Jesus is saying to you, perhaps one of the following will help.
1. Look at a picture of Jesus looking at you. Look at him with love until you sense what he wants to say, just as a mother's love knows what the wordless face of her baby is saying.
2. Ask Jesus when he felt like you or when he met someone like you. Today are you more bold than Peter or doubting Thomas, Martha or Mary, the prodigal son or the elder brother, the Pharisee or the publican, or . . .?
3. With Jesus' love in your heart, what would you tell your friend if he or she wrote what you have written in your journal? Write this response to your friend.
4. Try reading your journal entry aloud, listening to it with love and understanding. Then write your response.
5. Simply write what you most want Jesus to say to you, and then underline the parts that would come from a God who is perfect love and truth.

Appendix B
WHEN NOTHING WORKS IN PRAYER

Have you ever felt that you've tried everything to help you pray and nothing works? During my thirty-day retreat I kept searching for the right place, posture, time for prayer, or special exercise that would make my prayer alive again. Usually if I simplify my prayer so I think less and love more, I can pray again. But this time not even a simple word or image between *Genesis* and *Revelations* moved my heart. Then I thought I was the problem, so I searched to uncover the sin in my life or the change God might be asking so I could pray again. I shared with God all my hidden fear, anger and guilt over not being able to pray but there seemed to be no God listening and certainly no solution. My spiritual director told me that it was purification to teach me how to love God more unselfishly without return and to receive God into my poverty. But I wanted not to be purified but to pray again. I felt like a hypocrite, teaching others to pray and then not being able to pray myself during the most important retreat in my life.

During that retreat the only time I could vaguely sense God's presence was when I was watering the garden. I could feel my care for the thirsty tomatoes and know that God too cared for me even if I couldn't feel it or respond any better than a barren tomato plant. So while others shared with the retreat director their latest technicolor ecstasy, all I had to share was how I felt like a tomato. Like my tomatoes I let my Gardener love me not because I was earning his care with great tomatoes but because I was a thirsty plant who needed him to live. I told God I wanted to pray his way even more than my way and just breathed his care and strength into my weakness. I was finally taking his healing, forgiving love into the self I most wanted to change.

That was the beginning of the change. My prayer didn't change overnight, but the very struggle became a way to love God and others. My struggle to pray awakened my hunger for God and a deeper surrender to his power when mine could do nothing. In my struggle I slowly accepted the fact that God's love didn't have to be earned but only needed to be invited by my weakness and failure. I became a bit more able to work with less thought of return, to take new risks and to bounce back after failure because it was O.K. to be a thirsty, barren, but loved tomato plant. Little by little I gave up and let God be God. I accepted a bit more gratefully whatever came from his hand — the outcome of my dry prayer, the cold rainy day, a truth I found hard to hear, the unwanted interruption, the person or task present to me at the moment.

I didn't recognize this gradual change until visiting Carl, a priest who after heart surgery was left paralyzed, unable to speak and confused. Carl wanted to die, yet feared death. When I had visited him before my retreat, I stayed only three minutes and nervously paced around as I talked about his flowers. I could not stay in his room because he was dying the very death I feared — paralyzed, confused, unable to speak and seemingly abandoned by a God who wasn't helping him to get better or to die.

Some weeks later the thirty-day retreat began, and when nothing worked in my prayer I experienced feeling paralyzed, confused, unable to speak a heartfelt prayer, and seemingly abandoned by God. Like the paralyzed priest, I struggled to be in control but finally had to simply let God love me in my poverty when I could do nothing for him. I was letting his healing love touch the deepest part of me that feared not just losing him in prayer but losing him at death if it was as terrifying as Carl's. In the middle of my retreat I again visited Carl. This time I found a peace within me that allowed me to visit him for an hour because God's love for me in my poverty was deeper than my fear of Carl's death. Together we went through the seven last words by which Jesus surrendered to a death much like Carl's and we both surrendered with Jesus to whatever life or death the Father might have for us. The next day Carl became more ill and within three weeks he was in the hands of the Father to whom he had entrusted his spirit. Death is simply letting God have total control. We prepare for it every time we let God love us in any struggle, including the struggle to pray or to live.

So if even the struggle to pray can be a time of deep growth, how do you measure growth in prayer? Growth in prayer does not mean that prayer gets easier but that it gets deeper until we become faithful to spending time with Jesus even when we don't feel like it. Growth in prayer like growth in a friendship is not measured in terms of positive feelings or insights that ebb and flow, but rather in terms of commitment to others and to God. For example, even when feeling grouchy and tired from a long day at the office, a dedicated husband may choose to kiss his wife because his love for her is deeper than surface feelings. His kiss says, "I love you and live for you at a deeper level than anything else happening in me. I wish I could be more for you but I love you even if I don't feel more or have anything brilliant to say to you. I also know that you love me even if I am too tired to feel it." So too our prayer is not measured by the surface images, insights, voices, or self-satisfying experiences that leave us feeling good but rather by the degree to which we lovingly live for God and others more deeply than anything else happening in us. More important than what happens in prayer is the faithfulness and love that causes us to surrender ourselves through the very struggle to pray. Often it is only through times of struggle in life and in prayer that God can break open the selfishness and need to be in control that prevent us from living more deeply for God and others without looking for return. So when nothing works, it is probably because God is working.

Note: For an excellent treatment of why God purifies our prayer through struggle and how to walk through it, cf. *When the Well Runs Dry*, by Thomas H. Green, S.J. (Notre Dame: Ave Maria, 1979). When having difficulty with prayer, it is also wise to seek a spiritual director to help discern what is happening in your life and prayer.

Appendix C
SCRIPTURE PRAYER HELPS

The following steps are only a guide and should be set aside when you find your own way to meet Jesus in the Scriptures.

1. *Passage.*
   Choose a Scripture passage you want to pray rather than have to pray. Begin by asking, "What do I want?" Maybe you are tired and want to rest with Jesus on the lakeshore (John 21), or maybe you are fearful and need courage to walk on water (Matthew 14:22-33). Maybe you need to forgive a stinging remark with Jesus on the cross (Luke 23:34). If you have no strong desires, you might return to the passage you read most recently that spoke to your heart. Ask Jesus in your own words for what you want.

2. *Read.*
   Treat the passage as you would a personal letter from the person who loves you the most. Read the passage in a reverent whisper, so that each word is spoken directly to you with the power that made Levi leave everything for the sake of just two words, "Follow me." Read the passage three times: once for understanding with your mind, once to love Jesus, and once to be loved by Jesus.

3. *Focus on Jesus.*
   Close your eyes and take a few minutes to quiet your body in a relaxed yet erect listening posture. Then begin to breathe in and out the word "Jesus," building up a hunger for him as you hunger for breath. When you breathe out, give Jesus yourself and all your tensions, while hearing him say your name in the way he alone loves you and calls you. How you continue to

say "Jesus" changes because with each breath you can open a deeper part of yourself to Jesus and give him a deeper part of your life. If you get distracted simply return to saying, "Jesus." Continue to do this until you sense how Jesus is looking at you and loves you.

4. *Enter the Scene.*
   Enter whatever part of the scene in the passage moved you the most. Once you are with Jesus, you might use your senses to get more fully into the scene. You might walk with Jesus down the dusty Emmaus road, adapting your gait to his and listening as he reveals how he sees what is discouraging you. You might smell the dust and the perfumed lilies of the field, feel the warm sunlight and uneven stones under your feet, hear the birds chirp to punctuate your steps, and search Jesus' face to guess what he is going to say. It's easy to guess because Jesus (love itself) always says only the most loving possible words. When you get in touch with what you most need to hear, you are hearing Jesus calling you to deeper faith, hope, love, surrender and openness.

5. *Pause.*
   Once you are with Jesus, enjoy him as you would your best friend. Revel in loving and being loved, in surrendering all, and in knowing his mind, and heart so well that you can guess his reactions. What does he do or say that surprises you, challenges you or strengthens you? How does he respond to your needs? What does he want? If you feel lost, return to the passage and then to Jesus again. Don't worry about having the "right" images or about how you are praying. Even St. Teresa of Avila was never

able to clearly visualize Jesus. So simply rest with Jesus, surrendering all and taking him into your heart.

6. *Thanks.*
End by sharing your heart and giving thanks for all that has happened. Open yourself to be grateful even for the difficult, distraction-filled, dry times that deepen your love and make you want to give even when there is little response. These times can make you aware of how much your prayer and entire life depend on Jesus rather than on your own efforts. Ask Jesus to reveal any way in which you may be able to improve your prayer and ask him for a hunger for the Giver and not just for the gift.

Appendix D
TASKS OF THE GROUP LEADER

If a group intends to go through the course together, a leader should be chosen who can either delegate or be responsible for the following tasks:

I. Before the Meeting

Listen to the first four sessions long before the first meeting. If there are any defects in the tape, do not hesitate to return the tape and ask for a replacement. Repeat this process with each additional tape.

II. During the Meeting

a. Initiate the Common Opening Prayer and songs.
b. Do the timing for: Silent Reflection, Companion Sharing, Companion Prayer.
c. Lead any optional experiences (Guided Journaling, Group Sharing).
d. Tell the group what material will be covered during the next meeting, especially if you are going to use an optional lesson (e.g., Simple Ways To Pray [Follow-Up]," "Footwashing Service") or a variation in format (see Appendices E, F, G, H, and I).

e. Enlist volunteers to help with the closing snack and celebration. (You might want to use this time to celebrate birthdays and anniversaries of group members.)

The group leader is also entrusted with a pastoral concern for the participants. Almost all the dynamic of healing will happen as the leader encourages the group to listen empathetically, love, and pray rather than give advice. However, if some participants need help beyond what they are receiving with their companion(s), it is helpful to have other persons available who can listen and provide this extra help. In other cases, the role of the group leader may be to find someone else who can help.

The most important part of pastoral concern is to pray intercessory prayer daily, if possible, asking that each participant meet Jesus through his/her prayer and through the process of sharing with a companion.

The group leader should feel free to vary any part of the program to fit the needs of the group. Perhaps the suggestions in Appendices E, F, G, H, and I will offer variety and meet group needs.

Appendix E
SUGGESTED VARIATIONS IN FORMAT

1. Occasionally have two pairs of companions join together for richer sharing and companion prayer in a group of four (or six, if companions are in threes).
2. After eight sessions, meet the next week for a Eucharist and a prayer time during which participants have a chance to share with the whole group whatever they are most grateful for during the previous eight weeks. (See Gratitude Session, Appendix G.) Perhaps conclude the evening with a party or celebration.
3. After watching or listening to a tape, take ten or more minutes for participants to share their reactions with the whole group.
4. At another session, have those who wish to do so share their journal entries with the whole group. You might ask the question, "What in the past week (month, etc.) from your journal gives you the most life?"
5. After a taped teaching, choose a personal reflection question from that lesson. Allow five minutes for quiet reflection, and then have the whole group share their responses together.
6. Do a common project together as a group. For example, after the "Social Change Through Healing Prayer" session, use the next meeting time to work in a soup kitchen, write letters to Congress, visit a nursing home, etc., and then reflect together on this real life experience. Another topic might be addressed by seeing a certain movie together.
7. Make a retreat together. Do the next series of teachings over a weekend, with time for discussion and interaction. Or give a retreat to others using the Suggested Retreat Schedule (Appendix I).

Appendix F
PRAYER COURSE ADAPTATIONS FOR COUPLES

The first few groups who took this course included several married couples. In one case, the course was part of a program specifically for couples. For me, one of the greatest joys of working with this course has been watching the effect it has on marriages. I've seen couples deepen their communication with one another, learn how to pray together and share their relationship with God—and most of all become truly friends in the Lord.

Below is a suggested format which married couples might wish to use in making these exercises together. The difference from the usual format is in the emphasis placed upon the relationship between the couple. The grace prayed for in each exercise is asked not only for each individual but also for the relationship itself. Thus, a couple praying for the grace of receiving love in Lesson 3 would ask specifically to be able to receive love from each other. Or, a couple praying for the grace to forgive as Jesus does in Lesson 6 would ask specifically to be able to forgive each other. Not only married couples but others in committed relationships might want to use the format suggested below, e.g., family members, members of a religious community, ministry teams, etc.

I. Group Experience

  A. **Common Opening Prayer** (as usual).

  B. **Video or Audio Tape** (as usual).

  C. **Silent Reflection** (as usual).

  D. **Guided Journaling** (optional—as usual).

  E. **Couple Sharing** (couples meet as companions, using the same questions suggested for Companion Sharing).

  F. **Couple Prayer** (after praying for each other, for each one's needs and for the grace of the lesson, the couple prays together for that grace to be given specifically in their relationship with one another).

Option: After praying as a couple, two or three couples may wish to join together in a group. Each couple might pray for each other couple, thanking God for their marriage and asking him for all the growth in love between them that they wish for in their own marriage. The intercession of the Holy Family might be asked that each couple might experience the kind of love that Mary and St. Joseph had for each other.

  G. **Group Sharing** (optional—couples might wish to use some of this time to share how the experience of the course is affecting their relationship).

  H. **Closing Snack and Celebration** (optional—as usual).

II. Home Experiences

  A. **Daily Healing Prayer** (each person has an individual prayer time of at least ten minutes. The prayers in each lesson that ask for healing and growth in relationships might focus upon the marriage relationship).

B. Daily Journal (as usual).

C. Couple Prayer (ten minutes each day, perhaps using the following suggestions).
1. As you pray together, thank Jesus for all the things you are grateful for in each other.
2. Ask your spouse what he or she most needs from Jesus today. Ask Jesus for whatever way your spouse most needs his help.
3. Ask Jesus to help you grow closer to one another each day, and ask him that you continue to receive the grace of this lesson: *(grace of that week's lesson)*— especially in your relationship with each other.

You may also wish to use this time to pray any of the preceding daily healing prayers together. You may wish to pray together at the Eucharist for a deeper release of the grace of the sacrament of marriage in your lives.

OPTIONAL HOME EXPERIENCES

D. Personal Reflection Questions (spouses may wish to reflect on these questions individually or to share them as a couple).

E. Scripture Readings (as usual).

F. Additional Readings (as usual).

Appendix G
GRATITUDE SESSION

Every eight sessions or so, you may wish to spend one session giving thanks for the growth that has taken place during the previous weeks.

I. Group Experience

A. Opening Song and Prayer

B. Description of the Session. The leader of the group might take a few minutes to describe the plans for this session.

C. Scripture Reading (use one of the following, or another appropriate passage).

Matthew 5:14-16 You are the light of the world. (Perhaps read it in a darkened room and have each person light a candle later, during the sharing time.)

Mark 6:34-44 Parable of the loaves multiplied through the disciples' hands. (Perhaps give each person a piece of bread and let each one get in touch with how the Lord has given him or her gifts to share with others during the past weeks. As each shares about this growth during the sharing time, let all also share the bread.)

Matthew 13:4-12 or 13:31-32: Parables of the seed. (Perhaps give each person a seed and let all get in touch with what the Lord has given them to plant. Then let each one plant it during the sharing time, perhaps in a pot of soil.)

Matthew 25:14-30: Parable of the silver pieces. (Perhaps give each person a blank check on which to write what he

or she has been given and is returning to the Lord.)

Luke 21:1-4: Widow's mite. (Perhaps give each person a penny and let each get in touch with how, although the gifts we can give may not seem like much, the Lord looks only at the generosity behind them)

D. Sharing

1. *Option I.*
   a. Divide into groups of four to six, including your companion(s).
   b. Silence. Take a few minutes to let the Scripture passage sink in. Let each person ask: What gift of growth (symbolized by the light, bread, seed, silver piece or mite) has Jesus given during the past _____ weeks to me and to each person in my group, so that we can give thanks and bless the growth? Since we are all Christ's body and share all of his gifts, let us ask Jesus to reveal all our gifts and help us to be as excited about another's gift as we are about our own gift.
   c. Let any one person begin by mentioning another in the group and describing how he or she has seen Jesus in that person and how the person has helped him or her to grow. Thank Jesus for these things. Let each of the others in the small group do the same to affirm and give thanks for this person.
   d. After all in the group have described

and given thanks for how they see Jesus in the person, let that person respond by describing and thanking the Lord for his or her own growth and for how the group has nurtured this growth.

  e. End by having the whole group pray over this person to bless these gifts and growth. (This is the time to light the candle, share the bread, plant the seed, and give the check or penny to the Lord.)

  f. Repeat steps c, d and e with each person in the group.

2. *Option II.*

  a. The entire group remains together.

  b. Silence. Take a few minutes to let the Scripture passage sink in. Let each person ask: What gift or growth (symbolized by the light, bread, seed, silver piece or mite) has Jesus given during the past _____ weeks to me and to each person in my group, so that we can give thanks and bless the growth? Since we are all Christ's body and share all of his gifts, let us ask Jesus to reveal all our gifts and help us to be as excited about another's gift as we are about our own gift.

  c. Those who wish to might share their moment of greatest growth during the preceding weeks.

  d. After all who wish to do so have shared their moment of greatest growth, the rest of the group might want to pray over those persons to bless the gifts and growth they have described. (This is the time to light the candle, share the bread, plant the seed, and give the check or penny to the Lord.)

E. The session might conclude with five minutes of silence, with all present holding hands in a circle and letting Jesus' love pass from one to another.

Appendix H
FINAL SESSIONS

4th to Final Session

During this session, announce that during most of the week the regular homework of daily prayer and journaling should be done as usual, but on one or two days each person should use the time to pray over and write his or her response to the following questions:

Do I want to continue this experience in some way after the course is finished? If so, how?

For example you may find that you might want to:

a. Stop because of other commitments.
b. Split up and start the course for others, perhaps at several different days and times.
c. Have periodic gatherings, e.g., a future retreat, project or liturgy.
d. Use the same course format and continue with other tapes by Dennis & Matthew Linn. If you are interested in learning to pray with others, you may wish to use *Praying for Healing Seminar: Learning to Pray With Another*, by Dennis & Matthew Linn and Sheila Fabricant. This course consists of 12 30-minute teachings available on audio or videotape, and has an accompanying guidebook. If you are interested in ministry to the dying, you may wish to use *Dying to Live: Spiritual Care for the Dying and Their Families*, by Bill & Jean Carr and Dennis & Matthew Linn. This is a series of 8 30-minute taped teachings available on audio or videotape, based on the book *Healing the Dying*, by Mary Jane Linn, Dennis Linn and Matthew Linn (Paulist Press, 1979).
e. Use the same course format and continue with tapes by other speakers, e.g., *Jim Wheeler, S.J., School for Spiritual Growth and Inner Healing, 3019 Truman N.E., Albuquerque, N.M., 87110*. Also, *ALU, 504 Antioch Ln., Ballwin, Mo. 63011*, has tapes on prayer and healing by many speakers.
f. Other suggestions???

3rd to Final Session

Group Experience: Take extra time to have those who are interested in continuing in some way share their suggestions and list them on a blackboard for all to copy. Perhaps there is one thing that the majority would like to do and the group can take the first steps to implement this. More likely, there will be several different desires, and those with the same desire might form a small group and discuss how they want to implement their desire. For example, those who want to start new groups for others using the same tapes might plan on how they want to work together to share tapes and equipment if they want to start more than one new group. Others might want a weekly Scripture teaching with time to share how they prayed over that Scripture teaching and how it called them to live during the week. See if there are common desires and let implementation groups be formed around them.

2nd to Final Session

Small Implementation Groups: Let those who are desiring to continue in some way after the course meet in their small implementation groups and spend ten minutes working out details and sharing information they have gathered since the last meeting (e.g., availability of tapes and equipment, etc.). Then let the entire group meet together so that each of the implementation groups can share their plans for the future. Perhaps others will wish to join them or support them in some way.

Final Session

Use the format for the Gratitude Session (see Appendix G). After this session the small implementation groups may wish to meet for further; planning.

Appendix I
SUGGESTED RETREAT SCHEDULE

Friday Evening

- Overview of Weekend
- Opening Prayer and Songs
- "Healing Through Gratitude"
    Taped Teaching
    Prayer Experience—to get in touch with being loved (use prayer experience on tape or from "Healing Prayer" section of workbook).
    Sharing in Twos of Prayer Experience
- Closing Songs of Praise and Gratitude
- Optional: You may wish to end the evening by listening to "Healing through Beatitudes."

Saturday

- Opening Prayer and Songs—songs with actions to help wake up.
- "Simple Ways To Pray"
- "Simple Ways To Pray—Follow-Up"
- Coffee Break
- Instructions on Prayer Exercises and Journaling
- Quiet Time—to do a prayer exercise and the journaling question for "Simple Ways To Pray."
- Sharing in Twos
- Optional Variation: Use "Healing Through Beatitudes" instead of "Simple Ways To Pray." Use the exercise from "Beatitudes" on "Your Testimony" (#7) and share about it in twos.
- Begin "Forgive and Re-Member"

Lunch

- "Healing One Memory Prayer"
- "Healing by Discovering Our Sin"
- Quiet Time—to do a prayer exercise and journal question.
- Sharing with Partners—share for ten minutes regarding tape, journal question and healing prayer exercise.

Dinner

- Optional: "Healing by Accepting God's Forgiveness"
- Footwashing
    Show or listen to tape.
    Representative couples wash feet.
    Everyone is encouraged to wash feet and receive prayer for inner healing.
- Party to celebrate forgiveness and new life.

Sunday

- "Physical Healing (Tradition)"
- Physical Healing (Practice)"
- Prayer—for those who are sick.
- Other options for Sunday:
    "Social Change Through Healing Prayer"
    "Healing Through Community"
    "Healing by Choosing"
- Closing Mass or Worship—include time for public sharing in answer to the question, "How have I experienced God's healing love this weekend?"

Appendix J
BLESSING OF OIL (FOR USE BY LAITY)

Our help is in the name of the Lord,
R. Who made heaven and earth.

EXORCISM

God's creature, oil, I cast out the demon from you
by God the Father almighty†
who made heaven and earth and sea and
all that they contain. Let the adversary's
power, the devil's legions, and all Satan's
attacks and machinations be dispelled
and driven afar from this creature, oil.
Let it bring health in body and mind to all who use
it, in the name of God † the Father almighty, and
of our Lord Jesus Christ † his Son, and of the Holy
Spirit † the Advocate, as well as in the love of the
same Jesus Christ our Lord, who is coming to
judge both the living and the dead and the world
by fire.
R. Amen.
Lord, heed my prayer.
R. And let my cry be heard by you.
The Lord be with you.
R. And also with you.

Let us pray.
Lord God almighty,
before whom the hosts of angels stand in awe and
whose heavenly service we acknowledge, may it
please you to regard favorably and to bless and
hallow this creature, oil, which by your power has
been pressed from the juice of olives. You have
ordained it for anointing the sick, so that, when
they are made well, they may give thanks to you,
the living and true God. Grant, we pray, that those
who use this oil, which we are blessing † in your
name, may be delivered from all suffering, all
infirmity, and all wiles of the enemy. Let it be a
means of averting any kind of adversity from man,
made in your image and redeemed by the precious
blood of your Son, so that he may never again
suffer the sting of the ancient serpent, through
Christ our Lord.
R. Amen.

(The oil is sprinkled with holy water.)

Note: Taken from *The Roman Ritual*, trans. by
Philip Weller (Milwaukee: Bruce, 1964), p. 573.
When blessed by a priest, the oil is a sacramental
much like holy water, to be used by the laity with
any prayer they desire. This oil should not be confused with oil blessed by a different formula for
conferring the sacrament of anointing the sick
and used only by a priest. For more on the lay use
of oil blessed with the above prayers, cf. "A Lay
Person Can Anoint Licitly with Blessed Oil,"
Homiletic & Pastoral Review, January 1982, pp.
67-68.

Appendix K
WHERE TO ORDER FILMS AND TAPES

FILMS

The following 16mm. films by Frs. Dennis and Matthew Linn, S.J. may be rented or purchased from Mass Media Ministries, 2116 North Charles Street, Baltimore, Md. 21218; (301) 727-3270.

"The Power of Forgiveness" (30 minutes, color)
"Simple Ways To Pray" (30 minutes, color)
"New Life Through Forgiveness" (with Dr. Bulent Tunakan, 20 minutes, color)
"The Power of Intercessory Prayer" (20 minutes, color)

VIDEOTAPES

The videotapes for this course may be purchased individually, in sets of four programs each, and in the entire series of twenty-four programs. Order from: Paulist Press, 545 Island Road, Ramsey, N.J. 07446, (201) 825-7300.

For information regarding rental of videotapes, contact Paulist Press or Prayer Course Video Rentals c/o Merton House Charismatic Resource Center, 4453 McPherson, St. Louis, Mo. 63108; (314) 533-8423.

AUDIO TAPES

The audio tapes for this course may be purchased from Paulist Press, 545 Island Road, Ramsey, N.J. 07446, (201)825-7300.

ADDITIONAL PROGRAMS

Praying for Healing Seminar: Learning to Pray with Another, by Dennis & Matthew Linn and Sheila Fabricant. Series of twelve 30-minte teachings available on audio or videotape, with accompanying guidebook. This seminar could serve as a follow-up to the present *Prayer Course*. Topics include healing power of scripture prayer, steps of praying with another, grieving and prayer for the deceased.

Dying to Live: Spiritual Care for the Dying & Their Families, by Bill & Jean Carr and Dennis & Matthew Linn. Series of eight 30-minute teachings available on audio or videotape, accompanied by the book *Healing the Dying*, by Mary Jane Linn, Dennis Linn & Matthew Linn. How to be with a dying person—and how to live more fully—by praying through the seven last words of Jesus.

Both of the above programs may be purchased from Paulist Press, 545 Island Rd., Ramsey, N.J. 07446, (201)825-7300. Videotapes in ½"VHS format may be borrowed on a donation basis from Video Rentals, 4453 McPherson, St. Louis, MO 63108, (314) 533-8423.

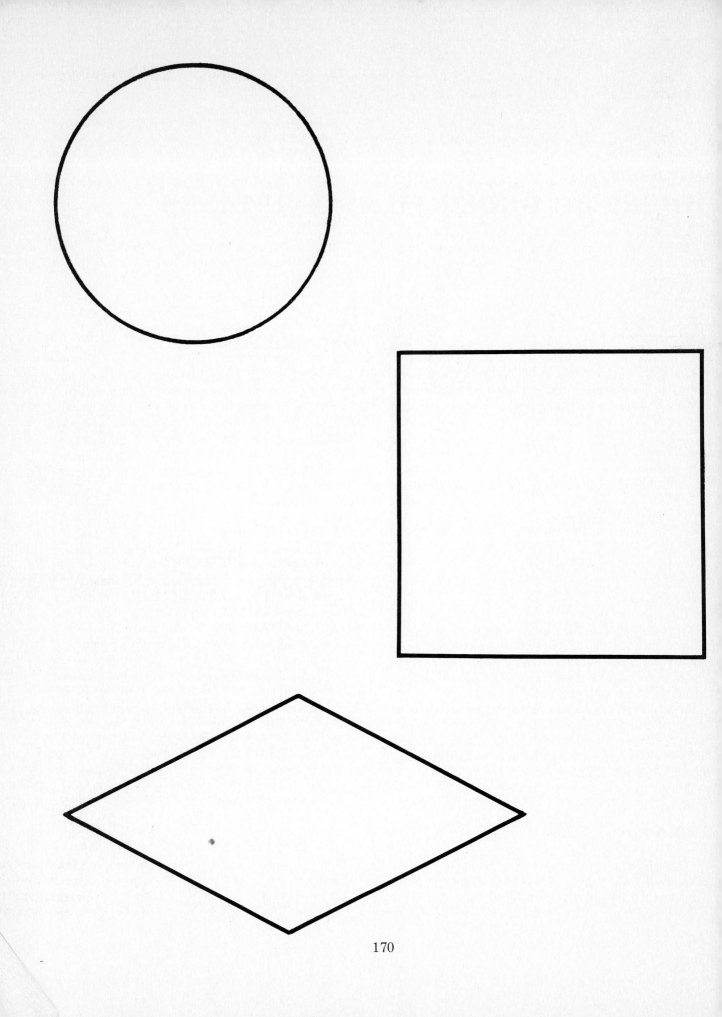

170